Educational Philosophy for 21st Century Teachers

Thomas Stehlik

Educational Philosophy for 21st Century Teachers

palgrave
macmillan

Thomas Stehlik
School of Education
University of South Australia
Magill, SA, Australia

ISBN 978-3-319-75968-5   ISBN 978-3-319-75969-2   (eBook)
https://doi.org/10.1007/978-3-319-75969-2

Library of Congress Control Number: 2018935412

Cover illustration: © Andrea Kamal, Getty Images

Printed on acid-free paper

This Palgrave Macmillan imprint is published by the registered company Springer International Publishing AG part of Springer Nature.
The registered company address is: Gewerbestrasse 11, 6330 Cham, Switzerland

Acknowledgements

My thanks and acknowledgements to: Christobel for the many conversations, ideas, and suggestions that have contributed to shaping the book; my three beautiful daughters for educating their dad; Ballinglen Arts Foundation in Ballycastle Ireland for their warmth and generosity in providing an inspiring space where parts of this book were written; colleagues in Australia, Finland, Ireland, Canada, and Sweden for conversations, conviviality, support, references, and interest in the global education project; Pasi Sahlberg for reference to his features of the Global Education Reform Movement; and the University of South Australia for granting me study leave and time away from teaching in order to complete this book.

A Note to the Reader

This book refers to many sources and references that provide a historical perspective to the narrative, and even though the content is still relevant to a discussion of educational philosophy, in some cases the language is outdated. Some quotes therefore include gender exclusive language which I would normally avoid using. However, I have chosen to present such quotes verbatim, and in those cases I ask the reader to suspend judgement of the medium and focus on the message.

Contents

1 Introduction: What Is Education for?   1
    1.1   'I Hated School…'   3
    1.2   Why This Book?   6
    1.3   Part I: The History of Philosophy and the Purpose of Education   7
    1.4   Part II: Schooling Versus Education   7
    1.5   Part III: The Kingdom of Childhood   9
    1.6   Part IV: 'I Always Wanted to Be a Teacher'   10
    1.7   Part V: Case Studies of Educational Philosophies   11
    1.8   Part VI: The Future of Education   12
    References   13

Part I   The History of Philosophy and the Purpose of Education   15

2 The Importance of Philosophy   17
    2.1   A Brief History Lesson   17
    2.2   Ancient Philosophy   18
    2.3   Branches of Philosophy   19
    2.4   Plato and the First Academy   20

2.5   Medieval Philosophy   22
2.6   Modern Philosophy   24
2.7   Types of Knowledge   29
2.8   The Evolution of Philosophy and Knowledge   31
2.9   The Importance of Philosophy to Education   34
References   36

3   The Purpose of Education   39
3.1   Definitions, Meanings, and Models   39
3.2   Practical and Contemplative Activity   42
3.3   Reciprocity   45
3.4   Forms of Education   48
3.5   Educational Philosophy   54
References   55

Part II   Schooling Versus Education   57

4   School: History, Meaning, Context, and Construct   59
4.1   Definitions, Distinctions, Developments   59
4.2   Which School or College Did You Go to?   63
4.3   Evolution and Revolution   68
4.4   Differentiation and Dual Systems   75
References   81

5   School: Rhetoric, Reality, and Revisionism   83
5.1   Schools as Places and Spaces   83
5.2   The Massification and Marketisation of Education   86
5.3   The Global Education Reform Movement   90
5.4   Responses to GERM   94
5.5   It Takes a Whole Village to Raise a Child   97
References   102

Part III   The Kingdom of Childhood   105

6   Development over the Life Span   107
   6.1   The Kingdom of Childhood   107
   6.2   Nature or Nurture?   116
   6.3   Play Is a Child's Work   121
   References   126

7   The Twenty-First-Century Child   129
   7.1   From Infancy to Adolescence and Beyond   130
   7.2   The Millennial Child   133
   7.3   The Quantified Self   138
   7.4   Nature Versus Technology   144
   7.5   The Millennial Parent   148
   References   155

Part IV   'I Always Wanted to Be a Teacher'   159

8   Teaching the Teachers   161
   8.1   'I Always Wanted to Be a Teacher…'   162
   8.2   History of Teacher Education   165
   8.3   Content Knowledge Versus Pedagogical Knowledge   168
   8.4   The Philosophy of Teaching   173
   8.5   Who Teaches the Teachers?   177
   References   179

9   The Role of the Teacher   181
   9.1   Teaching as Art and Science   182
   9.2   You Are Not Alone   185
   9.3   Who Owns the Curriculum?   189
   9.4   Curriculum Responses   193
   References   198

Part V   Case Studies of Educational Philosophies   201

10   International Comparisons and Case Studies   203
   10.1 Finland: Equality Begins at the Blackboard   203
   10.2 The Worldwide Waldorf School Movement:
         Education Towards Freedom   214
   10.3 Green School Bali   224
   10.4 Conclusion to This Chapter   229
   References   230

11   Thinking Outside the Classroom   233
   11.1 Deschooling   235
   11.2 Not-school   237
   11.3 Doing School Differently   241
   11.4 Youthworx   242
   11.5 Unschooling, Homeschooling   244
   11.6 Gap Year   247
   References   254

Part VI   The Future of Education   257

12   Predicting Unknown Futures   259
   12.1 Twenty-First-Century Skills: What Are They?   259
   12.2 The Classroom of the Future   265
   References   269

13   A Holistic View of Education   271
   13.1 'Can't Buy Me Love'   271
   13.2 Mother Nature's Child   276
   13.3 The Future Is What We Make It   279
   References   282

References   285

Index   301

List of Figures

Fig. 2.1   Joining the dots—turning information into knowledge   35
Fig. 4.1   Sorting by age and gender began even as the children entered
            school in 1898. (Greenwich, London, England)   64
Fig. 4.2   Separate entrances for students and everyone else…but given
            the placement of the apostrophe, did St Patrick's have only one
            student?! (Ballycastle, County Mayo, Republic of Ireland)   65
Fig. 4.3   Post-compulsory education: specialisation of schools, Amos
            sports college   81
Fig. 6.1   The threefold development of life over seven-year cycles   112
Fig. 6.2   The kindergarten at Willunga Waldorf School—a safe, nur-
            turing, and enriching environment   125
Fig. 7.1   Homo Zappiens vs Homo Sapiens   138
Fig. 10.1   The forest as a teaching resource: trainee teachers on excur-
            sion, Eastern Finland   207
Fig. 11.1   Nine dots puzzle solution   235

1

Introduction: What Is Education for?

I have never let my schooling interfere with my education.
Mark Twain

This book is about education in the twenty-first century, how it has developed, and what it means for teachers, parents, schoolchildren, and educational policy makers in post-modern western societies through an educational philosophy lens. It is intended as a manual for twenty-first-century educators, and by the term *teacher*, I am being inclusive of all adults who are involved in bringing up children in our societies. In this regard I am firmly influenced by the notion that as a parent, *you are your child's first teacher* (Baldwin 1989), and by the well-worn but resonant saying: *It takes a village to raise a child*.

Like Mark Twain I also make a clear distinction between *schooling* and *education*. It will be important as you read this book to arrive at a shared understanding of these terms—as well as terms like *training, teaching, learning, curriculum, assessment*, and so on—to unpack their meaning, their etymology, their use, and abuse in different contexts such as everyday parlance, academic language, policy jargon, and bureaucracy-speak.

© The Author(s) 2018
T. Stehlik, *Educational Philosophy for 21st Century Teachers*,
https://doi.org/10.1007/978-3-319-75969-2_1

The intention of the book is to stand back and take a big picture view of education and its attendant terminology, assumptions, myths, and influences. It is offered as a long meditation on a discipline that has been an occupation and interest for my entire life and career—as a student, teacher, parent, teacher educator, and educational researcher. The more I have pursued this interest, the more I realise that education is everywhere, affecting and influencing us in many forms, from the overt experience of formal institutions like schools, to the subtle effects of lived experience of the world and the influences of people and things that we interact with on a daily basis.

In a crowded and busy modern world, we often do not have the time to stand back and contemplate big questions of meaning as we become bogged down in the minutiae of detail and the demands of daily life. My experience of working in university teacher education in Australia for over 25 years has also reinforced the view that, as emerging professionals, beginning teachers have less opportunity to discuss and consider fundamental questions such as *What is education for?* and *What is my role and purpose as a teacher?* Teacher education courses have become crowded with regulatory requirements and mandatory subjects in behaviour management, assessment policy, and curriculum content, leaving little room for reflection and discourse.

In 1978 I completed a one-year Graduate Diploma in Education at the University of Adelaide to qualify as a secondary English and humanities teacher. In addition to the subject area courses, there were four core courses in this program that covered the history, sociology, psychology, and philosophy of education. Since then, theory has gradually given way to practice. At the University of South Australia where I became a lecturer in education, subjects related to the philosophy of education gradually disappeared from the Bachelor of Education (BEd) around 2010. Despite the BEd being a four-year program—the minimum required length for a teaching qualification in Australia—such subjects became the casualty of a policy shift towards pragmatism and regulation, which saw them sidelined and eventually crowded out. It is intended therefore that this book will be seen as a resource for those beginning teachers—as well as anyone else with an interest in education past, present, and future—to engage with and reflect on those philosophies (and philosophers) which have underpinned and influenced the very educational institutions, teaching methodologies, curriculum frameworks, and learning environments that we have inherited today.

1.1 'I Hated School…'

In a first world country like Australia, almost everyone has been to school at least up to a certain year level, so everyone has an opinion of school based on their own experiences. For many people these experiences have been challenging and uninspiring at best or extremely negative and distressing at worst. Australians also have a culture of criticism concerning the profession of teaching, compared to countries like Finland where teaching is seen as a noble profession and teachers are highly regarded as 'candles of the people' lighting the way to knowledge (see Chap. 10). In Australia even the politicians get in on the act of disparaging teachers, with erstwhile Federal Minister of Education Christopher Pyne engaging in teacher bashing in the media and even in parliament (Pyne 2014).

Pyne was using 'teacher quality' as a measure of school performance, looking for reasons why Australian schoolchildren were not performing so well in international academic assessment programs such as the Program for International Student Assessment (PISA). And yes, while research has shown that the role of the teacher in a traditional classroom is important for successful outcomes, this is often based on the *relationships* established with students as much as on a teacher's content knowledge, and is clearly only one part of a much bigger picture in which other significant factors come into play, such as adequate funding and resourcing of public schools (Stehlik 2011). The fact that the proportion of Australian schoolchildren now attending a non-government school is over one-third and growing demonstrates that parents are voting with their feet and choosing private independent schooling—if they can afford it (see Chap. 5). Pyne himself attended a Catholic school and so his view of education would have been influenced—and skewed—by that experience.

As part of my academic research work, I had the experience of leading a research project working with young people who were disengaged from school and undertaking alternative learning programs outside the mainstream curriculum (a growing trend—see Chap. 11). I was working with a colleague who was an experienced research assistant, highly educated with a PhD, and to all intents and purposes an intelligent and well-adjusted woman. Yet when she accompanied me to a primary school in the southern suburbs of Adelaide to interview the principal, I noticed she was becoming increasingly agitated. Waiting outside the principal's office, she looked terrified and I asked her what the matter was. She said she had not been in a primary school since she was a student herself, over 30 years ago, and this was bringing back bad memories of her experiences as a young girl. She had suffered under a male teacher who had been abusive, violent, and manipulative and who regularly sent her to the headmaster for punishment for minor infringements of his sadistic discipline (Note: in those days the principal was invariably male). I reassured her that things were different now, teachers were not like that (I hoped!), corporal punishment was banned years ago, and the principal we were about to interview turned out to be a charming professional woman who put us both at ease.

But I was disturbed by this event, as it recalled bad memories of my own schooling during the 1960s and early 1970s: suffering bullying from cruel, sadistic, or cold teachers—as well as bullying from other kids—and being punished by severe headmasters who seemed to relish in giving 'cuts' to the hands or back of the legs with a cane. Why did these people get into teaching if they disliked children so much that they could physically and mentally abuse them? And yet I also had some warm, wonderful, and inspiring teachers who were positive role models and managed to get me interested and inspired in subjects that I loved—English, geography, and history. On balance, and despite some of these Dickensian characters, I did reasonably well at school and even came 'top of the class' in the upper primary years. And this seems to have been the experience of many of us—despite a random series of mixed experiences and unpredictable situations that as children we have little or no control over, most people have 'survived school' and managed to come out reasonably unscathed, even having learned something.

However, there are also many victims of the schooling system: young people who leave school early, are disengaged or discouraged, act out and get into trouble, experience bullying and social exclusion, have low literacy and numeracy and reduced career opportunities, and no interest in further education. I often think that we do our children a dis-service by sending them to an institution for the best years of their lives, sitting in classrooms of rows of desks, in a large group of kids of the same age, who are all expected to achieve in all subjects at the same pace and level. Compare this, say, with growing up in a tribal or village society where children of various age groups can interact and learn by looking out for, and being looked after by, each other. As a parent I know that children need boundaries but they also need the freedom to be a child and be able to experience what Rudolf Steiner called the 'Kingdom of Childhood' (see Chaps. 6 and 7).

But I am concerned at the cumulative effect of these negative experiences of school, especially as it is apparent that many parents who have a low regard for the education system are projecting this onto their children—whether intentionally or subliminally—and it becomes an inter-generational issue, leading to the type of 'teacher bashing' mentioned already. Like my colleague, it seems that many adults are under the mistaken apprehension that not much has changed since their own school days, and the teachers and classrooms that they experienced are the same ones they are sending their children to today. I therefore advocate for a more positive discourse around education in our society today, and in the hope that being more informed will lead to being more enlightened, I offer this book.

Finally, it is not surprising that the effect of spending so many of our formative years at school results in aspects of school life entering our dream life. I still clearly remember a dream that I had as boy of about ten or 11 years old, in which I was at school but only dressed in a pyjama top… I was in the asphalt quadrangle surrounded by other boys and girls, doing some sort of PE while desperately trying to cross my legs and cover up my lower nakedness. I think this is probably a very common sort of Freudian dream, being naked or not properly dressed in public, but the fact that I can visualise the dream 50 years later suggests to me how very *exposed* I felt at school—not only different with a funny European surname, odd sandwiches made with rye bread instead of square white bread, and white legs instead of a bronzed Aussie tan, but somehow removed from what was actually going on. Even as a school student I think that subconsciously I was already asking the question: *What is education for?*

The incursion into the dream world escalates when one becomes a teacher, reflecting the deep emotional investment involved in the profession. I spent ten years in various high schools teaching English and other humanities subjects, eventually escaping to the world of adult education and university teaching, where behaviour management and classroom control are not such pressing issues. But those years of standing in front of out-of-control classes and rebellious or bored adolescents resulted in recurring dreams which I can still have to this day, 25 years later. The dream (or nightmare really) usually takes the form of me not being prepared for the class, or having misplaced important paperwork, often standing in front of the class with no trousers on, and helplessly watching things deteriorate around me. Other colleagues have told me very similar stories of such experiences invading their sub-conscious dream life, even long after retiring from teaching. The feeling of not being in control is a fundamental and deep human fear, and it is also not surprising that public speaking has long been identified as the number one fear, even ahead of fear of flying or fear of heights.

1.2   Why This Book?

Reflecting back on my years as a teacher and my struggles with teenagers in classrooms, I see now that neither they nor I really wanted to be there. For me it was a job, not a career or a calling, and while I loved literature, drama, and poetry, I was lucky if I could inspire one student in a class of 30 adolescents to feel the same, severely distracted as they were by hormones and puberty and not at all interested in dead poets or classical literature (although Shakespeare's *Romeo and Juliet*, for example, is a perfect piece of literature for this age and a story that they can relate to). For the students, much of the curriculum did not have enough meaning or relevance to their immediate lives. So our task as teachers, parents, educators, and generational role models is to somehow offer a glimpse of culture, beauty, humanity, and creativity in the midst of the dross and daily grind required by curriculum writers, education bureaucrats, and faceless policy wonks responsible for the 'system' we have. But how did we get to this situation? Who decided all of this in the first place? On what do we base our educational decision-making? What is the rationale for 'schooling' as opposed to education? This is what I aim to tease out in the following chapters of the book, set out in six sections.

1.3   Part I: The History of Philosophy and the Purpose of Education

Chapter 2 takes us back to classical Greece and the origins of the concept of *philosophy*, a term that combines the Greek words for love and wisdom and so literally means the *love of wisdom*. From the influential work of Aristotle, Plato, and Socrates, a brief history through time includes consideration of some of the major movers and shakers in philosophical and educational thought from ancient through to modern times. At the same time, the chapter introduces and unpacks key terms and concepts related to education that we have inherited and use daily but often take for granted.

Chapter 3 enters into a discussion of the purpose of education in modern societies, given the systems of thought that we have inherited. Is the purpose of education to develop the individual or for the benefit of society, or both? Notions of reciprocity are examined, for example, individual uniqueness balanced with the common good and reproduction of society balanced with developing character. Should school-based learning be oriented towards a vocation or for lifelong learning? How do we develop and value human and cultural capital?

The key question for this section is: *What have we learned from history?*

1.4   Part II: Schooling Versus Education

Part II then moves from the past to the present and the future, looking at the schools we have today, how they have developed, how they are developing, and how they might evolve in the future in terms of structure, function, process, and product.

Chapter 4 examines the history, meaning, context, and construct of schooling. It includes a discussion of definitions, origins, and early examples and investigates the extent to which schools function as social sorting and socialisation agencies as well as knowledge factories. Schools are analysed in terms of their establishment, development, and purpose with case study examples of experimental schools attempting to break the 'factory model' of universal mass education that resulted from the Industrial Revolution. As students, parents, teachers, and citizens, what are our expectations and hopes for schools compared with our experiences and realities? What are the similarities and differences between government and independent schools? How can we classify and make sense of the varying philosophical and educational rationales on which they are based? The notion of 'school choice' is a recent development but is there really a choice? Why are some schools free while others charge high fees? Is there a correlation between funding and student outcomes?

Chapter 5 compares the rhetoric of school with the reality of what children experience, then queries how, why, when, and where we educate our children, and how school choice should be an informed decision but has become a hotly debated issue in a commodified educational marketplace. The massification and marketisation of education are examined in the light of such trends as the Global Education Reform Movement (GERM), accountability standards for teachers, and a curriculum focused on narrowly defined vocational outcomes. The Age of Enlightenment introduced the reductionist idea of categorising everything from clouds to humans, and we still think of education as being categorised into separate subject areas according to a taxonomy of knowledge developed in the mid-eighteenth century. Responses to these trends are examined, including the alternative view that 'It takes a whole village to raise a child'. How do we understand and work within these opposing positions in the twenty-first century?

The key question for this section is: *How have we applied what we have learned from history?*

1.5   Part III: The Kingdom of Childhood

The third section considers what the Kingdom of Childhood looks like in the twenty-first century, in the light of technological, social, economic, and global developments. Some things have stayed much the same over the years, others have changed drastically. This section also addresses those who are charged with the care, support, and upbringing of our children—parents, guardians, and families.

Chapter 6 provides an overview of development over the life span, with reference to key educational theorists whose work has influenced contemporary thinking and practice around human physical, mental, emotional, and spiritual development, including the early work of Friedrich Froebel who recognised that *play is a child's work*, to the work of Jean Piaget and Rudolf Steiner in child development and human development. The debate about the influence of nature vs nurture in child development is examined with reference to the literature on 'wild children'.

Chapter 7 introduces the notion of the 'twenty-first-century child', in the light of contemporary and often challenging and complex contexts in which children are now growing up. Educators and other professionals (psychologists, social workers, and youth workers) note an alarming increase in diagnosed disorders among children and young people such as attention deficit hyperactivity disorder (ADHD), autism, depression, and anxiety. Children and young people are now labelled as 'digital natives', tangled up inextricably in the world wide web, with toddlers, tweens, and teens seen as consumers of education as well as consumers of goods and products. As a result, education has also become a commodity. Reactions and responses to these modernist trends driven by information technologies and the media include various 'back to nature' initiatives such as the Forest School movement in the United Kingdom and Europe and bush kindergartens in Australia. At the same time, children are increasingly becoming exposed to real societal dangers in the form of sexual, physical, and emotional abuse. The chapter also addresses those who are charged with the care, support, and upbringing of our children—parents, guardians, and families. *Parenting as a vocation* is introduced and discussed, in the light of the various roles that parents have in educating their children and managing their own learning about parenting. The child-parent relationship and the child-parent-teacher relationship are examined in relation to the roles and responsibilities of all the actors in this model. For example, what are the assumptions and expectations from the different perspectives of these actors around a concept like 'homework'?

The key question for this section is: *How should children and adults learn?*

1.6   Part IV: 'I Always Wanted to Be a Teacher'

Part IV is for and about teachers and the teaching profession—an examination of the reasons why some are called to the job as if to a vocation while others just fall into the role and how consideration of educational philosophy is important in maintaining and developing not only an understanding but a love of the profession.

Chapter 8 is about 'teaching the teachers', a critical aspect of the whole education system, but an aspect in which I claim educational philosophy has taken a back seat to educational pragmatics. Pre-service teacher education is regularly under the media spotlight in terms of concerns about teacher quality, lowering standards, and ideological biases. A brief history over time shows that 'teacher training' in teachers colleges has gradually been replaced by 'teacher education' in universities, where educational theory is meant to inform educational practice and vice versa. The perennial question of whether teachers are sufficiently prepared to meet the challenges of the profession on graduation is still debated and remains largely unanswered. At the same time, in-service teacher education and ongoing professional development of teachers should be given just as much attention. With a move towards continual reflective practice and professional learning communities among beginning as well as experienced teachers, a consideration of personal and professional educational philosophies becomes paramount.

Chapter 9 introduces the role of the teacher in the bigger picture of education as one of the helping professions similar to the professions of psychology, social work, and primary health care. As such, teachers need to see themselves as part of a cluster of professional roles providing an integrated and holistic contribution to education that goes beyond the classroom and school to the wider community. Educating and nurturing children and future citizens is a huge responsibility and can put unreal expectations on teachers to do it all alone, and sharing this important task in a joined-up approach can reduce stress and burnout. In fact, as explored in other chapters and one of the underpinning messages of this book, teaching is not an activity exclusively limited to those who are labelled as 'teachers'. Comparative views of the profession from local and global perspectives show that in countries like Finland, teaching is a 'favourite occupation', yet in Australia, anywhere from 30% to 50% of teachers leave the profession within the first five years. Some examples of enlivening teaching as an art as well as a science are given via creative and imaginative ways of thinking about pedagogy and curriculum as well as content.

The key question for this section is: *What is my role and purpose as a teacher?*

1.7   Part V: Case Studies of Educational Philosophies

This section of the book compares education systems in a number of different countries, cultures, and settings. The intent is to provide case study examples of the ways in which culture, climate, language, ethnicity, geography, space, and place do make a difference.

Chapter 10 offers some international comparisons and case studies:

Equality begins at the blackboard: *Finland*
Education towards freedom: *The Worldwide Waldorf School movement*
Education for social and environmental sustainability: *Green School Bali*

Chapter 11 explores alternative learning programs that operate outside of school, applying adult learning methodologies, often employing the creative arts as a point of interest for young people otherwise disengaged from the standard curriculum, and mostly delivered not by schoolteachers but by community educators, parents, and many others. They are a form of education now characterised as part of the 'Not-school' movement, which includes all out-of-school educational experiences such as homeschooling, which itself is part of an emerging trend of 'unschooling'. School leaving age and school retention are all issues related to how long we expect young people to remain in institutionalised learning situations, while pathways to further education and/or careers are no longer simply linear, and gap years are becoming the norm.

The key question for this section is: *What is education for?*

1.8   Part VI: The Future of Education

This final section concludes the book by attempting to make some predictions about unknown futures and the trends, opportunities, challenges, and threats that can be imagined given the discussion and argument developed in the previous chapters. If we accept the proposition that we are now in a knowledge society (or knowledge economy) in which certain twenty-first-century skills will be required and that thinking globally while acting locally is not just rhetoric but reality, what would the schools of tomorrow look like? Would we even have schools? Chapter 12 looks at the notion of 'twenty-first-century skills', otherwise known as 'soft skills' such as communication, collaboration, cooperation, and creativity, compared with 'hard skills' such as literacy, numeracy, and content knowledge. What will the classroom of the future look like in delivering these contrasting aspects of the curriculum, given the contemporary demands of the 'fourth industrial revolution'? Can creativity and imagination be taught? How do we turn information into knowledge in a world of information overload? What is the process of the 'getting of wisdom?'

Chapter 13 addresses a number of questions for consideration in terms of learning from the past, informing the present, and planning for the future in education. What should a curriculum look like? Given the notions of the crowded curriculum as well as the hidden curriculum, what are our priorities in preparing children and young people for life in the twenty-first century? What can be characterised as 'Nice to know' vs 'Need to know'? For example, would adolescent secondary students gain more from learning about developing successful relationships than how to master calculus? Parenting is a skill that seems to be an assumed one—but why is that skill not taught? How do we measure successful learning outcomes? How can national curricula be delivered consistently but with allowances for local differences? 'Success for all' is a catchcry among education policy makers, but how achievable and realistic is it? Is empowering learners and learning how to learn more important than acquiring content knowledge? The chapter and the book conclude with the proposition that a holistic view of education—inclusive of but going beyond schooling—is needed in a world where knowledge is becoming increasingly fragmented, digitised, and disposable. Putting our children's happiness and wellbeing at the centre of the education project I suggest would be a good place to start.

The key question for this section is: *What can we learn from experience to shape educational futures?*

References

Baldwin, R. (1989). *You are your child's first teacher*. Berkeley: Celestial Arts.

Pyne, C. (2014, April 17). Australians to have their say on teacher education. *Media Release*, Thursday. https://ministers.education.gov.au/pyne/australians-have-their-say-teacher-education. Accessed 23 Mar 2018.

Stehlik, T. (2011). Relationships, participation and support: Necessary components for inclusive learning environments and (re)engaging learners. Chapter 7, In T. Stehlik & J. Patterson (Eds.), *Changing the paradigm: Education as the key to a socially inclusive future*. Brisbane: Post Pressed.

Part I

The History of Philosophy and the Purpose of Education

2

The Importance of Philosophy

This chapter takes us back to classical Greece and the origins of the concept of *philosophy*, a term that combines the Greek words for love and wisdom and so literally means the *love of wisdom*. From the influential work of Aristotle, Plato, and Socrates, a brief history through time includes consideration of some of the major movers and shakers in philosophical and educational thought from ancient through to modern times. At the same time, the chapter introduces and unpacks key terms and concepts related to education that we have inherited and use daily but often take for granted.

2.1 A Brief History Lesson

Philosophy is about everything: how we know what we know, how we define our place in the universe, what we believe and how we judge truth, beauty, and justice. Ethics, in particular is about the good life and how we learn to be happy. (Frohnmayer 2016)

In considering the history of philosophy, I am here taking a particularly European/Western perspective as this has been the main influence

© The Author(s) 2018
T. Stehlik, *Educational Philosophy for 21st Century Teachers*,
https://doi.org/10.1007/978-3-319-75969-2_2

on the development of modern western education. For the purposes of this book, Middle Eastern, East Asian, and Indian philosophy are not included.

From this perspective, there have been three major periods of western philosophical thought:

Ancient: Greco-Roman (circa seventh century BC to fifth century AD)
Medieval: Christian-European (circa fifth century to sixteenth century AD)
Modern: From around 1600 to today

2.2   Ancient Philosophy

Any consideration of the importance of philosophy in the twenty-first-century western world has to begin with classical Greece, since the term itself is derived from the Ancient Greek language, combining the word for love, *philos*, with the word for wisdom, *sophia*—literally means the *love of wisdom*. The term *wisdom* is itself one that will be unpacked and explored in the following chapters, since it is an important concept in understanding the stages of development of a human being. Pythagoras (570–495 BC) has been credited with coining the term *philosophy*, and whether that is true or not it reinforces the fact that, while we might remember Pythagoras for his mathematical theorem, philosophy in Ancient Greece encompassed 'any body of knowledge' including disciplines such as mathematics which we would now consider one of the sciences.

The Hellenic culture that emerged in ancient Greece between 700 and 400 BC saw an unprecedented development in concepts of civilisation and applied thought that have endured to this day, and influenced many of our current systems of thought, governance, and education. Their achievements in creating a rational, scientific attitude to the universe were equally balanced with a blossoming in art, drama, and literature and a concern for truth, beauty, and moral values. However, their own way of looking at the world on a day-to-day basis was very different to ours.

The Hellenic view of nature was centred in their religion—nature was living and companionable, and all living things including plants and animals contained a spirit. Humankind was not seen as the centre of the universe but as part of a bigger cosmic progression. In contrast to our experiences of Christianity and a contemplative approach to spirituality, Ancient Greek religion was extroverted, not introverted. Their religious beliefs were outward-looking, not introspective. In fact, in Ancient Greek there is no language equivalent for words like *person, personality, individual, the self, self-consciousness, ego,* or I, with daily life and society being more communal and community-minded. The political ideal for Athens was therefore based on a true concept of *democracy*—a word and an ideal that we have also inherited from Ancient Greece.

The Greek Gods were considered on a higher plane than mortals, but more like elder brothers and sisters than the father/creator image of the Christian God. They were not creators of the world but also products of the world with their own evolution, their own problems and foibles, and thus were not perfect or above reproach. The epithet *as above, so below* represents this notion.

In this world view then, it is not surprising that the Greeks had a clearly defined philosophy of living. They found the world extraordinarily interesting and developed a sense of wonder about it and a desire to know how it works. In the opening sentence of his *Metaphysics*, Aristotle boldly states that 'all men naturally desire to know'. In a book on the importance of philosophy to the past, present, and future of education, this is an idea—and perhaps an assumption—that we will explore.

2.3   Branches of Philosophy

For the Greeks, *Natural Philosophy* was the study of the physical and natural world. It included astronomy, medicine, and physics.

Moral Philosophy included ethics—the study of goodness, right and wrong, justice, virtue, and beauty—from which we gain the word *ethos*, which can mean both 'custom' and 'character'.

Metaphysical Philosophy involved the study of existence, and included the concept of *logos*, or logic. Meta-physick literally means 'what comes after physics'.

From these we have inherited what we now refer to as the natural sciences (e.g. physics, mathematics, chemistry, biology) and the social sciences (e.g. psychology, sociology, economics, education). It is interesting to note also that the Greek word *logos* means 'knowledge of'…so that, for example, the word *psychology* means 'knowledge of the psyche'…and in Ancient Greek *the psyche* referred more to what we would now understand as *the soul*.

2.4   Plato and the First Academy

Plato (428–348 BC) is without doubt the most significant figure from the Ancient Greek world in considering the development of modern education. In fact, it has been claimed that "the European philosophical tradition…consists of a series of footnotes to Plato" (Whitehead, cited in Livingstone 1959: 111). Himself a student of the equally influential philosopher Socrates (470–399 BC), Plato is credited with establishing the first *academy*, a place for learning that was the template for what we would consider today as formal educational institutions such as schools and universities.

Plato embodied the ideal of philosophy encompassing 'all bodies of knowledge', natural, moral, and metaphysical. For example, from him we have inherited such diverse things as the notion of *platonic love* in human relationships, as well as the mathematical formulae for *platonic solids*—three dimensional geometric shapes such as cones, spheres, and cubes. The well-known parable of 'Plato's Cave' demonstrates his thinking around the distinction between reality and perception, which in effect was an early form of constructivism—the theory that the real world is not absolute but is mediated and constructed by our individual perceptions of it, which are in turn determined by culture, socialisation, and upbringing.

[Plato's Cave: In Book VII of *The Republic* Plato outlines the 'Allegory of the cave' as follows:

Ordinary people are imprisoned in a shadow-world cave, only able to look at the wall. A fire behind them casts shadows of actors moving between them and the fire. Unaware of the true reality hidden from them, the prisoners believe that the shadows represent reality. When a prisoner is released from the cave, he initially suffers from the sun's blinding brightness, yet as his eyes adjust he begins to see the truth. If he were to return underground to enlighten his former fellow prisoners, they would not believe him, for they couldn't even imagine a world beyond the shadows dominating their existence, for that is all they have ever known.]

Plato made aesthetic sensibility the basis of his ideal education system, believing that "all grace of movement and harmony of living – the moral disposition of the soul itself – are determined by aesthetic feeling: by the recognition of rhythm and harmony" (REF Fuller?). This fundamental value is significant to education and will be re-visited in subsequent chapters.

Plato wrote extensively about education for young children and was an early adopter of the principle of freedom: "Avoid compulsion and let your children's lessons take the form of play. This will also help you to see what they are naturally fitted for" (Republic VII: 536). The importance of play for young children was 're-discovered' in the nineteenth century by educators like Friedrich Froebel who is credited with establishing the first kindergarten, with play-based learning now being a central theoretical plank of early childhood education.

However, Plato's Academy did not provide universal education for all sections of Hellenic society—in fact, it was extremely exclusive, open only to males and to those from certain families. This practice of education being exclusive to certain sections of society, in particular males, has been carried through the centuries and is still with us today in various forms. Furthermore, Plato's Academy was not based on any formal program of study organised into separate subjects as we would know today. Plato's idea of learning was based around conversation and discussion on a range of topics, based on the *Socratic Method*—a method that uses *questioning* as the basis of discourse through reason and logic, or *dialectics*. The Socratic Method—also referred to as Socratic questioning—recognises that the *process* adopted in a learning situation is just as important as the content under consideration, and is still a valid *pedagogy*.

[Pedagogy: from the Greek 'to lead a child'. Modern definition: 'the art and science of teaching and learning']

Aristotle (384–322 BC) was one of Plato's students at the Academy and carried on the Platonic tradition of seeing education as a process—combining a study of the natural world with the development of moral character, through dialogic communities incorporating the dialectic method. His approach to scientific method was founded on *empiricism*, the view that we can only arrive at truth and factual knowledge through direct sensory experience. This is the basis of all modern science that relies on methodical observation, experimentation, testing, and proving of hypotheses to arrive at logical conclusions. From Aristotle we have inherited the methodology of *action research*, defined as "systematic inquiry by practitioners about their own practices" (Zeichner 1993: 200). Aristotelian Action Research maintains that the process of bridging the gap between theory and practice can occur through the action-reflection cycle—recognising that practically oriented, deliberative activity is important, but that reflecting on and theorising about that activity will enhance the learning process. This is particularly important today in the notion of the *reflective practitioner* and the 'Teacher as Researcher movement', which will be discussed further in Part IV.

Aristotle however was also a key figure in developing the branch of Metaphysical Philosophy that influenced philosophical thinking into the medieval period, which became dominated by the church and theology. While the rise and spread of the Roman Empire saw classical Greek philosophical thinking followed and maintained, with many extant examples of references to figures like Plato and Aristotle in Roman art and literature, the vast empire eventually collapsed around the fifth century AD, when much of this intellectual tradition became lost to the western world. The period in history which followed is therefore referred to as the Dark Ages, when formal academic learning almost disappeared from secular life and was only to be found in monasteries, with Latin becoming the medium for written thought, while knowledge of Ancient Greek was almost completely lost.

2.5   Medieval Philosophy

It is very interesting to note that the rise of the Islamic world from about the eighth century AD was responsible for maintaining and developing some of the ancient philosophical traditions that were otherwise lost to the west, in addition to introducing many of the scientific and intellectual foundations that we take for granted today. For example, up until that time, the numbering system was based on Roman numerals, and the Romans did not have the concept of zero. The modern numbering system that we use today was introduced by Persian and Arabic mathematicians, who also gave us words like *algebra* (al-jabr, in Arabic literally means 'bone setting').

Meanwhile, the domination of the Christian church and clergy in the so-called Dark Ages saw secular knowledge being replaced by sacred knowledge in Europe, with monasteries becoming centres of learning, and knowledge of Ancient Greek only being kept alive in remote places such as Ireland.

An enduring image and concept from Christian theology that is relevant to our discussion is the *Tree of Knowledge*. While earlier references to this go back to Babylonian times, the version outlined in Genesis, the first chapter of the Bible, provides the foundation not only for the notion of 'original sin', but of our modern concept of knowledge. In that story, the Tree of Knowledge bears the forbidden fruit that Adam and Eve eat despite being warned not to. Prior to that, humans did not have a concept of good and evil; everything in the Garden of Eden was good. After the 'Fall of Man', humanity became exposed to knowledge of everything that was available, both good and bad, including things that were sinful, as represented by Adam and Eve 'losing their innocence' and covering their naked bodies. Gaining knowledge therefore implies a duality of balancing knowledge of the good with knowledge of the bad, requiring the need for new social codes based on strict morality—greatly influencing education.

The aesthetic sensibilities that were so much a part of the Platonic tradition therefore were overridden by Christian morality into the Middle Ages (fifth to fifteenth centuries), with only the logical intellectualism of the Aristotelian tradition remaining from the world of classical philosophical thought. The key outcome from this period was the development of the philosophy of religion, with major figures including Thomas Aquinas and Augustine, the former a bishop and the latter a monk.

Augustine (354–430 AD), later to become canonised as St Augustine, was a key figure in the latter part of the Roman Empire. His contribution to education included recognising the importance of critical thinking skills, an idea that was taken up with vigour by philosophers in the modern period.

Thomas Aquinas (1225–1274 AD) was an Italian cleric who introduced specific ideas about teaching, learning, and pedagogy which have greatly influenced modern education. For example, he believed that teaching in 'classes' was better than giving individual tuition, as it encouraged competition, emulation, group discussion, and debate.

However, probably the most significant development in education during the medieval period was the establishment of universities during the Carolingian Empire (800–888), so named after the emperor Charlemagne (742–814 AD), during whose reign most of Western Europe was again united under one dynasty 300 years after the decline of the first Roman Empire. Charlemagne established by decree schools in abbeys across his extensive dominions, which became known as the *Scholastic* tradition, from the word scholastics, which literally meant 'schoolmen'. From these centres of learning, modern universities gradually evolved, providing a 'universal education' initially for clerics, eventually becoming open to the secular world.

> In the field of education and learning the Carolingian age saw the establishment of a common basis for European scholarship…If medieval Europe possessed a common fund of ideas, it was largely due to the work of Carolingian scholars. (Strayer 1955: 52)

2.6   Modern Philosophy

The Renaissance period (1355–1650) saw a return to classical Greco-Roman thought and revival of aesthetic activity and Platonism, which can be seen today represented in classical art and architecture from the period, as well the emergence of the idea of *Humanism*. Although still based on a rationalist and logical structure of learning, Humanism departed significantly from the medieval pre-occupation with the afterlife by being more concerned with the here-and-now and the development of human self-realisation, reinforced by the recognition that the Greeks and

Romans had built up magnificent civilisations based on their native talents rather than superstition or faith (Fuller 1955).

The Renaissance was followed by a period from the early 1700s known as the Enlightenment, which saw scientific methods and reductionist approaches to knowledge gaining traction in what was actually a reaction against the monarchy and the church, as well as building on advances in technology and scientific discovery. Enlightenment thinking sparked radical movements that eventually led to social upheavals such as the French revolution in Europe and the American War of Independence, and would ultimately result in the modern notions of economic rationalism, free markets, and the universal rights of the individual.

Enlightenment thinking can be credited with the promulgation and *secularisation* of knowledge that was previously held and controlled by the church and the clergy, and was seen at the time as crucial for social and individual emancipation and education of the masses. A great example of this is the publication of *Encyclopaedia*, with the first English *Cyclopedia* published in 1728, followed by the more comprehensive French encyclopaedia edited by Denis Diderot from 1751 to 1772 and the first major reference book to feature a large number of separate contributors. Diderot famously claimed that he wanted to 'change the way people think' by making available 'all the world's knowledge' to the public and future generations. While earlier Greek publications such as *Geographica* by Strabo from around 75 BC had mapped knowledge of the ancient known world, by the 1700s the discovery of 'new worlds' had greatly expanded the possible horizons of knowledge and consciousness. Furthermore, the invention of the printing press in 1440 by Johannes Gutenberg had since made it possible to promulgate written information more widely to those who were literate and could afford access to books, leading to the establishment of some the world's great libraries.

One of the foremost of the Enlightenment thinkers was the English philosopher John Locke (1632–1704). His influence on education included the notion that a child is born with no pre-determined ideas, that their mind is different from an adult's and is effectively a blank slate, or *tabula rasa*. Locke's concept of the 'noble savage'—that the native people of places like the recently discovered New World deserved recognition as sentient human beings with souls—greatly influenced the democratic independence movement in America. Locke also developed a theory of mind that has evolved into modern ideas about identity and the self, based on the value of introspection (Gibson 1917). In this, he was in turn influenced by the French philosopher Rene Descartes (1596–1650) who is credited with the saying 'I think, therefore I am'—an aphorism which puts self-consciousness and self-awareness at the centre of any intellectual or sensory process. In addition to his theories of dualism—the separation of mind and body, in which each can be in control of the other—Descartes invented key mathematical principles and symbols that are still fundamental to mathematics today: Cartesian coordinates to map a point in space as represented on x and y axes, and superscript to represent a number multiplied by itself (squared or cubed for example), to name only two.

However, the most influential person from this period who is credited with being the 'father of modern education' was Comenius (Jan Amos Komensky 1592–1670), a Czech educator who was an early champion of universal education. In his book *Didactica Magna* (1633), Comenius outlined an educational sequence and structure that would lay the foundations for our modern education systems: kindergarten, elementary school, secondary school, college, and university, with society being responsible for the education of all its children until the age of 18. He was an early advocate of providing education 'according to the nature of the child' which evolved into a strong movement in late eighteenth- and nineteenth-century European educational thought. For Comenius:

> ...the child was seen as a non-distorted image of God and was not to be abused by brutality or force, but be subject to a Christian upbringing and education. For its time [this] was a very positive view of the child as a gift from God, yet in need of discipline and education. (Dahlin 2006: 11)

Comenius was not only a theorist but also a pragmatist, introducing a number of innovative and practical educational resources and methods. He believed that a child should learn to read in their mother tongue, and so published pictorial textbooks for children, written in their own language rather than in Latin. His *Orbis Pictus* published in 1658 is a type of encyclopaedia of general knowledge and one of the first picture books produced expressly for children, subsequently published in many different languages (Pikkarainen 2012).

Many people will have heard of Jean-Jacques Rousseau, the Swiss philosopher who in 1762 published his controversial book *Emile, or On Education*. In this work, Rousseau took the idea of education 'according to the nature of the child' to its extreme, returning to the Platonic principle of freedom and going further to advise that "you should give your scholar no verbal lessons; he should be taught by experience alone" (Rousseau 1921: 56). Emile was presented as an idealised child whose education was mapped out by Rousseau in his treatise as a series of specific and very didactic instructions to his tutor. Even though unrealistic for universal public education—Emile was to receive one-to-one tuition in a pleasant country house and be allowed free play whenever he liked—Rousseau's theories which included a strong aversion to treating children as passive recipients of factual information gained strong traction and have been further championed by twentieth-century educationalists like John Dewey and Paolo Freire (see below). In addition his view that the child should be regarded as a child and not a small adult was revolutionary, but has eventually become acknowledged and is discussed in detail in Part III, 'The Kingdom of Childhood'. Rousseau's influence on educational theory and practice has been considered 'tremendous', in that he is also credited "with giving a new theme to children's books: the appreciation of the wonders of nature" (Patterson 1971: 8).

Meanwhile, another Swiss philosopher, Johan Pestalozzi (1746–1827), also believed that every aspect of a child's life contributed to the formation of their character, personality, and reason, which is encapsulated in his declaration of 'learning by head, heart and hands'. This idea of a child-centred approach to learning and of educating 'the whole person' led directly to the work of Friedrich Froebel (1782–1852) who has already been mentioned as the founder of the kindergarten movement and a promoter of learning through play and games.

'Head, heart, and hands' and 'educating the whole child' are also some of the foundational principles behind the educational philosophy of Rudolf Steiner (1861–1925), who founded the worldwide Waldorf School movement in 1919, based on his theories of child development which were outlined in his extensive writings and lectures. Steiner

Education and the Waldorf School approach will be discussed in some detail in Chap. 10, but it is sufficient to note here that Steiner was not only building on the earlier work of German philosophers Friedrich Schiller and Johann von Goethe but returning to the Platonic ideal of aesthetic sensibility—'the recognition of rhythm and harmony'.

Before moving on, it is apparent that up until now all the historical figures mentioned have been men. You may be asking, were there no women philosophers? The answer is 'yes', but as in many other fields, the contribution of women throughout history has not received the same attention, respect, and coverage as men. One who is definitely worthy of mention is Mary Wollstonecraft (1759–1797), an English writer and philosopher who was a follower of Rousseau but also an early feminist and champion of equality of opportunity for women, writing about the education of girls who had largely been ignored in the story of *Emile*. Unfortunately Wollstonecraft died young (in childbirth) and is mostly remembered now as the mother of Mary Shelley, the author of *Frankenstein*. However, contemporary feminists have recognised her important contribution to literature—including children's literature—and her perceptive views on educational equity, as shown in this quote:

> Women are not naturally inferior to men – they appear to be only because they lack education. (Wollstonecraft 1792)

The Italian physician and educator Maria Montessori (1870–1952) also contributed to the growth of freedom in education through her pioneering work in establishing the Montessori Method and the associated worldwide movement in early and elementary schooling, based on the view of the child being allowed to explore the natural world and learn through a stimulating environment. Even more interesting was the fact that, as an example of a woman who rose above nineteenth-century prejudices to become a celebrated physician, academic, and educator, Montessori single-handedly created worldwide interest in the importance of educating young children in a more holistic, humane, and loving way through her charisma and force of personality. Her lecture tours of Europe, India, and America throughout the early part of the twentieth century backed by her innovative use of film and the keen interest of the media in her "youthful feminine charm" combined with her "professional accomplishments and intellectual ability" did much to support the establishment of many schools based on her methods (Kramer 1976: 53). This was an early example of the way in which the 'cult of personality' could influence and direct public opinion in a particular field through the growing power of the media, which can be seen today in the way in which many people base their information and opinions on what they receive through the popular media, by definition *mediated* information.

Another important contributor to the development of our contemporary understanding of early childhood education was the English activist, social reformer, and educator Margaret McMillan (1860–1931), who was motivated by the work of Froebel to establish nursery schools in England for poor and deprived children suffering from the urban squalor resulting from the industrial conditions in Victorian and Edwardian London. Her pioneering of a play-centred approach in a natural setting for infants has only recently become established practice in early childhood learning and has provided the foundation for current trends such as the Forest School movement (see Chaps. 6 and 7).

2.7   Types of Knowledge

Returning to the educational world view of the Ancient Greeks, it is important to note their understanding that knowledge was not absolute, but relative to varying applied situations and contexts. We can identify at least four different types of knowledge from ancient philosophy, but this list is not exhaustive and neither are the types completely separate or in any particular order, as they can overlap and interact. However, it is useful to know these terms and to be able to identify these knowledge types, and their application in an educational sense will be immediately obvious:

Episteme—This is scientific knowledge that is based on enquiry, research, and evidence, as exemplified in laws and principles that have been proven and accepted as fact, for example, Newton's first law or mathematical theorems. From this, we understand the word *epistemology* to mean the theory of knowledge.

Techné—This is craft or art knowledge—practical skill-based knowledge used in the process of creating and making products. From this we have the word *technology*, which is understood to be applied science or in fact episteme applied to practical applications.

Praxis—This is knowledge based in social practice and implies some form of action. In fact, *acting* or being in the world requires praxis knowledge and acknowledges the *agency* of the individual.

Phronesis—This is an interesting and subtle form of *professional knowledge* that is more a kind of virtue-infused wisdom based on experience, rather than abstract scientific or values-free technical knowledge.

Wisdom then is an important word to unpack and understand, and it is not surprising that the Greek philosopher Heraclitus came up with a definition as far back as the sixth century BC:

To see things accurately, and not rely on prejudices and preconceptions.

We associate wisdom now with the later stages of human development. For example, we would not think that a child possessed wisdom; we assume that wisdom comes with age and experience. However, we would also hope that a young child, in their formative and early years, would not have already developed 'prejudices and preconceptions' but would be open to all new information and experiences with a sense of unbiased inquiry. So why would they not possess wisdom? Perhaps they do… but perhaps we also need to ask whether young children can 'see things accurately', and in fact need to acknowledge that for very young children, their world view is very limited and information is not only sensory but is mediated and often interpreted (through their own prejudices and preconceptions) by the adults who surround and are responsible for them and to a certain extent by other children—siblings, relatives, friends, schoolmates. A word that is often used in conjunction with the getting of wisdom is *insight*—which perhaps is a more accurate term for the kind of internalised and occult knowledge that may be gained with age and experience.

[Occult = secret, or hidden]

Child development will be discussed more comprehensively in Part III, but for now it is sufficient to ponder on the various forms of knowledge as presented above, and to think about how they are associated with different ages and stages of development, and whether the concept of wisdom is something that comes to people only when they attain adulthood (like wisdom teeth). Suffice to say that the Socratic Method, introduced above, is based on the assumption that discourse or dialectic conversation requires putting aside one's prejudices and preconceptions to arrive at an accurate understanding of any topic by listening only to the rational line of argument based on logic and evidence, rather than on bias or emotion. In this regard, wisdom can transcend as well as encompass all of the types of knowledge discussed. *Phronesis* is not values-free and can result in a biased and narrow-minded view. Wisdom can be informed by, as well as be a result of, *praxis*. *Episteme* can involve purely contemplative theoretical activity which has no practical application. The effects of *techné* without a moral compass informed by *wisdom* can be disturbing in the creation of art, and deadly as a result of the products of technology.

2.8   The Evolution of Philosophy and Knowledge

Throughout the twentieth century, educational philosophy can be seen to be an interesting but selective accumulation of most of the theory and practice that evolved over the preceding two and a half centuries of western philosophical thought. Newton's image of 'standing on the shoulders of giants' in order to see more clearly by building on the work of those who have gone before is apt.

For example, the American educationalist John Dewey (1859–1952) built on the work of Rousseau by also emphasising the importance of experience with his well-known idea of 'learning by doing'. Dewey and his student George Herbert Mead (1863–1931) spearheaded *pragmatism* in philosophical thought, "often seen as the first original philosophical 'school' to originate from North America" (Biesta 2012: 247). Pragmatism suggests among other things that consciousness is not separated from action and interaction, but is an integral part of both—a nod to the idea of *praxis*. Dewey also established an early form of 'free school' in Chicago in the late 1890s—the *Laboratory Schools* (see Chap. 4). Writing in the 1920s, the American adult educator Eduard Lindeman (1885–1953) believed that education in the future would be defined 'by situations, not subjects', echoing the Platonic ideal of freedom. The Brazilian Paolo Freire (1921–1997) was a community educator and activist who had strong and influential views on child education, also decrying the 'jug and mug' approach of filling 'empty vessels' with facts. His metaphor however was the 'banking concept' of education, where "students are the depositories and the teacher is the depositor" (Freire 1996: 233).

Contemporary educationalists such as Daisy Christodoulou point out how pervasive these educational theories have become in the modern classroom and curriculum, giving examples from the United Kingdom where the teaching of factual knowledge has almost disappeared in favour of students learning through self-directed inquiry-based projects. She suggests that this is throwing the baby out with the bathwater and that committing facts to long-term memory is actually critical to developing problem-solving and critical thinking skills (Christodoulou 2014).

The English educationalist Herbert Read, writing about the problem of education in the aftermath of World War II, set out an elegant appeal for returning to the Platonic ideal of aesthetic sensibility being the basis of an ideal modern education system in his fascinating text—*Education through art* (1948). Subsequent chapters will expand upon this and include more of the views of late twentieth-century and contemporary educational commentators and philosophers on the 'problem of education' in modern times.

However, larger shifts in thinking that occurred throughout the twentieth century are also important to consider in bringing our historical overview of educational philosophy up to date. These include the influential work of American Thomas Kuhn (1922–1996) whose book *The Structure of Scientific Revolutions* introduced the idea of *paradigm shifts* in thinking and knowledge—that throughout history we have witnessed points in time where a revolution occurred that challenged accepted knowledge, and a new paradigm (world view, or framework of understanding) emerged. Examples from history include the universal view that the world was flat until proven otherwise through scientific exploration and discovery, the belief that the earth was the centre of the universe until proven otherwise by Galileo and others, and so on. During the last century, we have witnessed paradigm shifts in scientific thinking, with Newtonian physics being extended by Einstein's theory of relativity, and even supplanted by quantum physics.

There have also been paradigm shifts in general thinking across a range of disciplines from the rational/mechanistic/dualist view inherited from Aristotle to more organic/biological/integral ways of seeing the world. These include the work of James Lovelock (1989) whose Gaia theory suggests that the planet as a whole is a self-regulating and holistic entity, and the emergence of Chaos Theory (Gleick 1987), leading to the concepts of complex adaptive systems and self-regulating organisations. At the same time, Aristotelian binary logic has led directly to the development of computer language ('bits' = binary digits) and enabled a revolution in information technology, mass media, communication, and entertainment, through personal devices linked by the world wide web.

So while we can say that a majority of individuals in the modern western world now have unprecedented access to information and knowledge, as a collective civilisation we have advanced certain forms of knowledge at the expense of others. Knowledge has become more and more specialised, as reinforced by increasingly narrow education pathways, so that someone could be an 'expert' in a very obscure subject area but have very limited general knowledge. For example, the average person is no longer brought up with the types of basic survival knowledge and skills that existed in agricultural and subsistence societies prior to the industrial revolution, reliant as they are on power, water, food, and basic necessities coming from somewhere else at the turn of a switch or tap or a visit to the supermarket. Teaching these 'disappearing skills' is now being offered in 'Repair cafés', for example, in Edinburgh where people can learn among other things the apparently lost art of darning (Moore 2017). Many children growing up in cities and urban environments often do not even know that milk comes from cows—they have only experienced it coming out of a carton. As we will see in subsequent chapters, 'back to nature' movements in education have also been part of a shift in thinking, as a reaction against this industrial/intellectual/rational model of schooling that we seem to have inherited.

2.9   The Importance of Philosophy to Education

Education as we know it today in all its various forms could be considered to have evolved and developed over the course of history from the thinking, writing, actions, and influence of the philosophers introduced and discussed in this chapter. Educational institutions structure their programs around subject categories in the natural and social sciences that originated in Ancient Greece. Teachers use forms of *pedagogy* such as Socratic questioning in the classroom on a daily basis and engage in Aristotelian practitioner action research—whether they are aware of it or not. The word pedagogy itself is derived from the Greek and literally means *to lead a child*. It is now used widely to refer to the wide range of theories and practices applied in teaching and learning situations, and has been defined as "the art or science of teaching" (dictionary.com).

Many educational programs are still based on the Renaissance idea of providing a general liberal education that crosses disciplines and integrates the sciences with the arts, combining practical knowledge with aesthetic sensibility. Religious schools are still closely linked to theological traditions as well as offering a modern curriculum. Individuals use Encyclopaedia and/or their modern equivalent—the Internet—to access information and knowledge.

Yet it is important to distinguish between information and knowledge. As the illustration quite simply suggests, *information* can be a random series of unconnected facts, figures, or opinions; *knowledge* requires understanding, effort, and agency in 'joining the dots' and looking for patterns, sequences, and structures that make sense and give meaning (Fig. 2.1).

However, as we have seen, knowledge is not absolute or free from values, morals, or contexts and raises the question of whether all knowledge

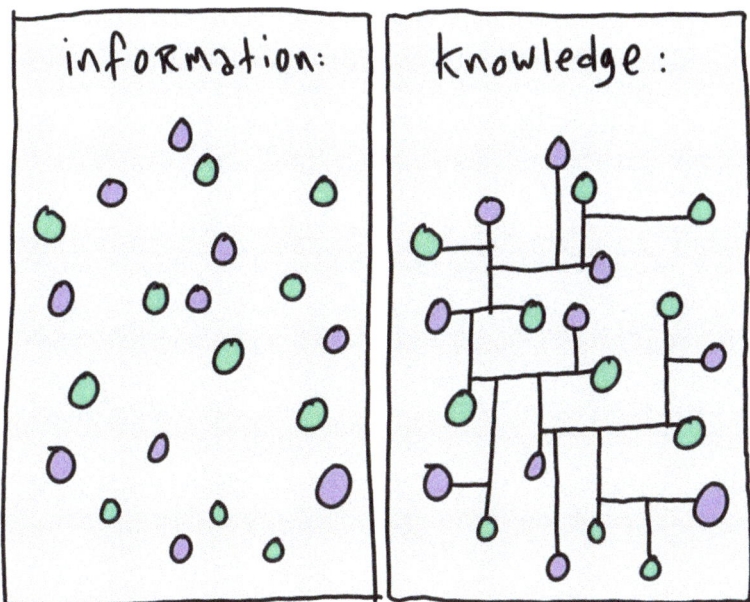

Fig. 2.1 Joining the dots—turning information into knowledge

should be freely available to all citizens in a democratic ideal, whether there are some things that we *need to know* while other things are just *nice to know*, and in fact given the almost infinite possibilities available in the information age, how do we make decisions about what forms of knowledge are important for society to reproduce and pass on to subsequent generations? This becomes the dilemma in determining what we teach, how we teach it, when we teach it, and ultimately, why?

A further set of questions arises in discussing the historical development of philosophy, education, and knowledge over the period of western civilisation that has been the focus of this chapter. That is: To what extent is knowledge cumulative over time? As a civilisation, have we become more collectively wise as a result of what we have learned from history? The more educated we become, should not the general level of wisdom in the world increase? If so, why do we still have wars, hunger, disadvantage, and inequality? Of course, it is apparent that education is not universally available for every world citizen in the same way, and for many not at all. In addition there are many forms of knowledge that have been lost over time which actually may have contributed to our better survival as a species—practical, spiritual, and collective knowledge. The modern era seems to be dominated by technical knowledge which in many forms is destructive; but at the same time, we are experiencing an unprecedented wave of *global consciousness* driven by the information age and the very same technology. Some contemporary commentators believe however that as part of the evolutionary process, human consciousness is evolving, and that civilisation as we know it could be experiencing a shift from the mechanistic/industrial model to a more integral/collective/spiritual awareness (Dahlin 2006; Zajonc 2016).

The second chapter in Part I will then continue to address these questions in the light of what we have inherited and learned from educational philosophy through history up to the present time and begin to explore and unpack the function and purpose of education, then and now.

References

Biesta, G. (2012). George Herbert Mead: Formation through communication. In P. Siljander, A. Kivela, & A. Sutinen (Eds.), *Theories of Bildung and growth: Connections and controversies between continental educational thinking and American pragmatism* (pp. 247–260). Rotterdam: Sense Publishers.

Christodoulou, D. (2014). *Seven myths about education*. Oxfordshire/New York: Routledge.

Dahlin, B. (2006). *Education, history and be(com)ing human: Two essays in philosophy and education*. Karlstad: Karlstad University.

Freire, P. (1996). *Pedagogy of the oppressed*. London: Penguin.

Frohnmayer, J. (2016). *Socrates the rower: How rowing informs philosophy*. Champaign: Common Ground Publishing.

Fuller, B. A. G. (1955). *A history of philosophy* (3rd ed.). New York: Holt, Rinehart and Winston.

Gibson, J. (1917). *Locke's theory of knowledge and its historical relations*. London: Cambridge University Press.

Gleick, J. (1987). *Chaos: Making a new science*. New York: Viking Books.

Kramer, R. (1976). *Maria Montessori: A biography*. Oxford: Basil Blackwell.

Livingstone, R. (1959). *The rainbow bridge and other essays on education*. London: Pall Mall Press.

Lovelock, J. (1989). *The ages of Gaia*. Oxford: Oxford University Press.

Moore, S. (2017, April 13). Shop till you drop belongs to a long-gone decade of boom. *The Guardian*, p. 5.

Patterson, S. (1971). *Rousseau's Emile and early children's literature*. Metuchen: The Scarecrow Press.

Pikkarainen, E. (2012). Signs of reality: The idea of General Bildung by JA Comenius. In P. Siljander, A. Kivela, & A. Sutinen (Eds.), *Theories of Bildung and growth: Connections and controversies between continental educational thinking and American pragmatism* (pp. 19–29). Rotterdam: Sense Publishers.

Read, H. (1948). *Education through art*. London: Faber and Faber.

Rousseau, J. J. (1921). *Emile, or on education* (trans: Foxley, B.). London: Dent.

Strayer, J. (1955). *Western Europe in the Middle Ages: A short history*. New York: Appleton-Century-Crofts Inc.

Wollstonecraft, M. (1792). *Vindication of the rights of woman*. London: J. Johnson.

Zajonc, A. (2016). Contemplation in education. In K. A. Schonert-Reichl & R. W. Roeser (Eds.), *The handbook of mindfulness in education*. New York: Springer.

Zeichner, K. M. (1993). Action research: Personal renewal and social construction. *Eduational Action Research, 1*, 199–219.

3

The Purpose of Education

This chapter discusses the purpose of education in modern societies, given the systems of thought that we have inherited, and addresses the question of the extent to which the purpose of education is to develop the individual as well as to benefit society. Notions of reciprocity are examined—for example, individual uniqueness balanced with the common good and reproduction of society balanced with developing character. Should school-based learning be oriented towards a vocation or for lifelong learning? How do we develop and value human and cultural capital?

3.1 Definitions, Meanings, and Models

'Education' is a word loaded with meaning, and with different meanings. The word itself comes from the Latin *educationem,* meaning 'a rearing, training'.

© The Author(s) 2018
T. Stehlik, *Educational Philosophy for 21st Century Teachers,*
https://doi.org/10.1007/978-3-319-75969-2_3

Definitions of education from the *Online Dictionary* include:

1. the *act or process* of imparting or acquiring general knowledge, developing the powers of reasoning and judgement, and generally of preparing oneself or others intellectually for mature life
2. the *act or process* of imparting or acquiring particular knowledge or skills, as for a profession
3. a degree, level, or kind of schooling: for example, a university education
4. the *result* produced by instruction, training, or study: to show one's education

The first two definitions refer to the word education in its verb form, as an *act or process* that can be experienced; the others imply the noun form, of education as a 'thing' that an individual can possess or show, for example, by a diploma or certificate, by a title or position.

These definitions are also rather limited in terms of the holistic and universal view of education taken in this book and easily demonstrated with practical examples. For example, 'preparing oneself or others intellectually for mature life' is a purely academic view of education and is not inclusive of the possibility of preparing oneself physically, emotionally, or spiritually. Given the quote at the head of this chapter, Plato believed that 'spiritual ignorance' was a fatal flaw in education at both the individual and societal levels, which, as will be discussed later in the chapter, should be considered as reciprocal parts of a larger whole. We have also seen *emotional intelligence* emerge in the last few decades as a framework for identifying and even measuring human emotions, attitudes, and behaviours. If we can measure IQ (intelligence quotient), the argument is that we can also measure the emotional quotient, or EQ (Goleman 1995). Finally, physical development is critical for young children as manifest in physical education, sport, movement, and also the manual arts, which have long been part of school curricula.

Holistic education by definition includes the whole child or person, and attending to the 'head, hands, and heart' is reflected in the pedagogical approach of attending to respectively *knowledge*, *skills*, and *attitude* in all subject areas. In psychology, this trilogy is referred to as the *cognitive*, *psychomotor, and affective* domains. While the second definition above includes 'knowledge *or* skills', this cancels out the notion of needing to combine both knowledge *and* skill, and leaves out the affective domain altogether. One could think of many professions where the affective domain would be as crucial as the other two in daily work-life situations, for example—nursing, social work, and teaching, to name a few.

A well-known and pervasive model popularised in the 1950s by American psychologist Benjamin Bloom (1913–1999) actually separates the *act or process* of learning into these three domains and attempts to map a sequential taxonomy of knowledge, skills, and attitudes, starting at basic levels and building cumulatively to mastery level in each domain. *Bloom's Taxonomy* (Bloom et al. 1956) has received criticism over the years as being too instrumental and simplistic, but as with any model, it is worth considering as a representation of what might actually be happening in the act or process of learning, especially in considering education as a lifelong process, where an individual at any age may find themselves on a 'lower rung' of one or more of the domains in Bloom's ladder when confronted with new learning situations. In the realm of skills, the classic example is learning to drive a car—a complicated series of manual skills that become second nature after practice, but at first puts one in the situation of novice at the level of basic fundamental movement. We even describe someone who is a novice in a given situation or context as 'being on L plates'. In the affective domain, human interactions and relationships are constantly requiring adjustments in attitude and understanding. Becoming a parent is a significant example of this and will in fact be explored in more depth in Chap. 7.

'Imparting or acquiring general knowledge' is reflected in what is generally referred to as a *liberal education,* providing a sound basis in a range of subject areas that will be useful for life, or as a foundation for further specialised study, as distinct from a *vocational education* which is aimed at a specific trade or occupation. At this point we need to interrogate the word *training*, which is one of the initial Latin meanings of education, but nowadays has different connotations. We apply the word in a wide spectrum of contexts: for example, from training for athletics or sport, training animals such as horses, right down to toilet training. But is training the same as education? If not, how is it different? We often associate training with skill-based activity, not 'intellectual preparation'. Unfortunately, this has produced a two-tiered system of education where those pursuing a vocational path are often seen as less academic than those pursuing a general or professional path.

Even though I believe training should be seen as a *sub-set of education* in the holistic and inclusive view of education this book is promoting, as we shall see in the next chapter, school systems and educational institutional structures have often developed along dual lines, serving to promote and maintain this distinction between the practical and the academic. 'Developing the powers of reason and judgement', as suggested above in the first definition of education, could equally apply to learning a practical trade as to gaining a liberal education, which we assume involves learning about the society one has been born into, and becoming socialised into the morals and values of that society. This brings us back to two philosophical questions: (1) the difference between applied learning and learning for its own sake and (2) reciprocity between the individual and society.

3.2   Practical and Contemplative Activity

Practical activity is undertaken for a purpose or goal. For the benefit of society, it is therefore described as *self-centred* and focused on bettering ourselves, for example, through technology and the applied sciences by creating and improving products, services, and quality of life. The question asked is 'What good is it?'. If an activity cannot be shown to have practical application and contribute towards the survival and development of the species, is it worth pursuing? Is it rather an indulgence and a waste of time to pursue at all?

Compare this with contemplative activity which is an end in itself, may serve no apparent practical purpose, and is purely a result of curiosity and inquisitiveness. Instead of being self-centred, it is *self-transcending*. It may come from a desire to explain things, to look for patterns and meaning. The questions asked are 'Why is it?' and 'What is it?'. This is exemplified by the *pure sciences* (such as mathematics or logic) as distinct from the *applied sciences* (such as engineering or medical science). Or in the social sciences, examples include theorising about very obscure questions such as 'whether Jesus was gay', which was the actual topic of an Australian PhD thesis. Many would consider this kind of study to have no practical use whatsoever, but it is still a form of education, with the potential to *inform* or at least get other people thinking, debating, and probably arguing about the topic…and if so it would be a perfect example of the Socratic Method, developing the powers of reasoning and judgement.

According to classical philosophy, education needs to serve both purposes—practical and contemplative. The act or process of discourse, critical thinking, and contemplation are seen as educative even if they produce no perceived outcomes. Moral values and building character should be seen as equally important to society as learning a craft or a skill. Compare this with our education systems now which are based on learning objectives, achievement, testing, and outcomes—all focused on pre-determined goals. Contemporary commentators like Ken Robinson believe that 'schools kill creativity' through this approach, and that creativity leads to discovering things for the sake of interest only with no immediate usefulness (Robinson 2006). If we take the view that we need to understand the world in order to better it, then contemplative activity can equally lead to applied and practical outcomes. Albert Einstein is a great example of this process.

Equally, if we are always just 'eyeing the prize', or focussing on outcomes, achievements, or goals, then all human activity would consist of concentrating entirely on the ends without considering the means. In reality, for example, in working life, the practical and the contemplative should be intertwined. 'Job satisfaction' is a concept that is inclusive of doing things for some motive or practical outcome required by the job, as well as enjoying the process of the work as an end in itself. In an educational setting, the equivalent would be focussing on academic outcomes as well as recognising that the education process itself is part of the bigger picture. The job satisfaction argument loses its attraction however, the more mundane and labour-intensive a job is—for example, working on a production line, factory work, repetitive unskilled labouring—where there is not much to contemplate about the process of repeating the same act day in, day out. For this reason, early industrialists tried to interest factory workers in 'bettering themselves' through offering evening classes in liberal studies subjects—not at all related to their trade or vocation.

A classic example of this occurred in Germany after World War I when the industrialist Emil Molt, the founder of the Waldorf-Astoria cigarette factory in Stuttgart, organised free afternoon lessons in foreign languages, painting, history, and geography as an introduction to the broader questions of life and learning, generously counted as paid work time. Molt was trying to put into practice the recognition of contemplative activity in economic life, not just for the goal of increased productivity for his business but to give an opportunity for second chance learning to the workers who had experienced very limited formal education provided by the state. However, despite the best of intentions, Molt soon found participation in these classes declining; the workers were not interested in developing themselves beyond the immediate needs of the workplace. Molt came to a realisation that a predisposition for *learning how to learn* was generally lacking in the consciousness and outlook of his employees:

> What soon became apparent was that learning has to be relearned by adults…From this I concluded that one must begin with the young if forces are to be successfully schooled and interests awakened. I became absorbed by the idea of providing for children what was no longer possible in later years, and of opening the door to education for all children, regardless of their parents' income. (Murphy 1991: 136–137)

This realisation led to the founding of the first free Waldorf School in 1919, which will be discussed in more detail in Chap. 10. Meanwhile, this story reinforces another key ingredient in education—the *motivation to learn*. In distinguishing between adult learning and educating children, it will be seen that the difference between *extrinsic motivation* (imposed by rewards, for example, good marks or praise from the teacher) and *intrinsic motivation* (wanting to learn for personal fulfilment) is significant.

3.3   Reciprocity

The concept of reciprocity suggests some kind of learning contract between the individual and society. State-funded public education is therefore seen as an investment in future generations that will benefit both the state and the individuals with returns on this investment. This view has echoes of Friere's 'banking concept' of education—in this case implying that education will be of measurable value to society and generate human and social capital. The definition of education as personal possession or property (such as a degree or diploma) also implies a resource that can be translated into monetary value or wealth, which can contribute to a person's social capital. As will be discussed in Part II, merely by attending an elite school or university can generate personal social capital and greatly improve a person's chances in making their way in the world. In this respect, education can be seen as a form of *currency*. And just like money can be forged, parchments and academic transcripts can be faked, assignments can be bought, false qualifications can be claimed or bought online from dodgy universities (McDonagh 2017), so how does one really 'show one's education'?

> In 2012, every third adult in the OECD had attained a tertiary degree. (Payton 2017: 3)

What we have seen in this capitalist view of education is the value of credentials diminishing over time, so that, for example, a bachelor degree might once have been highly thought of and be the minimum requirement for entry into a profession, whereas now a higher degree such as a master's might be the minimum qualifying degree. This concept of 'credential creep' turns education into an economic commodity, with the laws of diminishing returns, and supply and demand applying, so that in many OECD (Organisation for Economic Co-operation and Development) countries one now finds PhD graduates driving taxis, their qualification almost worthless as a job ticket. Recent developments in the recruitment of graduates in the United Kingdom have even seen university qualifications as irrelevant in assessing new employees by global firms such as Ernst & Young, PricewaterhouseCoopers, and Penguin Random House—with potential, creativity, and subjective qualities like 'strengths and ideas' considered more important. Apparently, Ernst & Young has found "no evidence to conclude that previous success in higher education correlated with future success in subsequent professional qualifications undertaken" and that "screening students based on academic performance alone was too blunt an approach to recruitment" (Sherriff 2015: 1). In Australia, the most recent census data at the time of writing showed that in the five-year period between 2006 and 2011, postgraduate degree completions rose from 413,093 to 631,121, an increase of 52.8%, while the number of people who held a bachelor degree rose by 27.2%, from 1.8 million to 2.3 million (Hall 2012). All of the above begs yet another question:

> *The more qualified a society's citizens become, to what extent does that society become more 'educated'?*

It also leads to the question: What are the reciprocal benefits for society of investing in education? Reciprocity recognises that each individual is unique and this uniqueness will be of value to the community. But uniqueness has no value in isolation—therefore, education must be a process not only of *individuation* but also of *integration*.

> For Plato the supreme aim of education is human goodness, but goodness of a far wider kind than our normal use of the word suggests….the ignorance most fatal to states and individuals is not ignorance in the field of technology or of the professions, but spiritual ignorance. So he conceives education essentially as a training in values. (Livingstone 1959: 118–119)

One of the perceived purposes of education is to socialise our children by integrating them into the values, morals, and rules of our society and culture, as well as ideally turn out individuals who will also benefit society in some way, for example, as workers, parents, and model citizens. This process of *enculturation* highlights the Platonic notion of 'goodness' in the sense that is suggested in the quote above—a type of universal human goodness "intimate with the eternal order of the music of the spheres"

(Plato, Laws, p. 689). Is the purpose of education then, a 'training to goodness'?

Herbert Read noted that "the individual will be 'good' in the degree that his individuality is realized within the organic wholeness of the community", but that there is potential for success or failure in achieving social integration to become a 'good citizen', or not to become a 'bad citizen'…concluding that "education must discriminate between good and evil inclinations, and therefore, in addition to its creative function, it must have a destructive or repressive function" (Read 1948: 5).

Here is a significant observation about the purpose and function of education in maintaining some sort of balance in society, and harks back to the biblical story of the Tree of Knowledge—balancing knowledge of the good with knowledge of the bad. Recognising that education can also have a 'destructive or repressive function' is realistic in terms of the way it can mould young people to a particular way of thinking that may be positive but may also be negative, leading to the kind of bad experiences of schooling that I mentioned in the Introduction, and to the 'potential for failure'. As Gidley notes, "education is both a product of culture and a creator of culture and…it both contributes to psychological development as well as potentially hinders it" (2016: 7). In this respect, we have to acknowledge the *hidden curriculum* as well as the overt curriculum presented in schools.

The hidden curriculum includes those things that are not taught explicitly, but underpin what is presented in the classroom as well as the way it is presented, which subtly and often unconsciously impose values, beliefs, and even ignorance on impressionable young minds. This includes what is left out or left unsaid as well as what is said. For example, a history lesson on Aboriginal Australia may be presented from an entirely Eurocentric view and unwittingly reinforce racism and bigotry. Children who do not see themselves represented in pictures and stories of white, middle-class people may feel excluded. Teachers who pay more attention to the boys in the class can make the girls feel inferior. As will be discussed in Part IV, schoolteachers really do need to recognise the responsibility they have in developing not only the knowledge and skills but the attitudes of young people in their charge. Furthermore, who decides what is taught and what is not taught in schools is a critical question that we will return to in subsequent chapters, as it highlights the need for schools (and teachers) to have an underpinning philosophy of education that defines their purpose.

Finally, the notion of reciprocity is neatly encapsulated in a verse by Rudolf Steiner that is often spoken at the beginning of meetings or group activities in Waldorf School communities, sometimes labelled as his 'Motto of the Social Ethic':

> The healthy social life is only found when in the mirror of each human soul the whole community finds its reflection, and when in the community the virtue of each one is living.

Steiner considered it a "fundamental social law" (1927: 1) that the wellbeing of a community depended on the individuals working towards the greater good rather than for their own personal interests or needs— what we might acknowledge in general as *the whole being greater than the sum of its parts*. Furthermore, however, as a result of every member working towards community wellbeing, an individual's needs may also be satisfied. This dynamic interacting interface between the whole and the parts can be represented organically with the image of the *lemniscate* (from the Greek: *lemniskos*, meaning ribbon). The "wonderful form of the lemniscate" has been used to represent the dialogue and interaction that maintain community relationships (Pietzner 1992: 86):

Individual  Community

3.4   Forms of Education

It is also important to distinguish between forms of education and the range of different learning processes that an individual can experience over time, which in sum total can be considered their 'education'. These will include formal, informal, non-formal, experiential, mandated, self-directed, and even accidental and unconscious learning events. They will include learning from one's family, friends, and peers as well as those who are labelled as 'teachers', from books and the media in all its forms, from institutions other than those labelled as 'schools' (such as the church, the workplace, the sports club, community organisations), in fact learning from life itself. I believe, from personal experience over a lifetime, that the aphorism 'You learn something new every day' is almost always true. It could involve the smallest and most trivial piece of information, often happened upon by chance, but still new and of interest if the information is turned into knowledge by reflecting on it, or associating it within our existing knowledge structures. Sometimes this process involves *re-learning* something that has been forgotten (unfortunately a function of ageing), sometimes it requires *unlearning* something that was based on misinformation or ignorance in the first place. All of these forms and processes will now be briefly discussed.

Formal learning is defined as that which is undertaken within some sort of institutional setting (which could be face-to-face, by distance learning, or online) that is *accredited* to award some form of credential or qualification.

[School of the Air. In Australia, children living in remote and isolated parts of the country are able to attend school via correspondence. This used to occur over the airwaves via radio, and now can also include the internet, email, skype or similar, provided there is internet connectivity].

These institutions could include schools, colleges, universities, training institutes, and professional associations that provide in-service training. In the case of schools, the accrediting body is an external organisation such as a government-sanctioned Board of Studies or Inspectorate, and schools are registered or licensed to deliver the relevant award (such as a Higher School Certificate or A levels). In the case of the International Baccalaureate which is taught in many schools worldwide, the accrediting body is based in the United Kingdom and participating schools must show their ability to meet the teaching and assessment criteria to enable them to offer IB qualifications. Technical training institutes must be closely aligned with the professions and trades for which they are delivering training and apprenticeship programs, to meet the criteria for awarding trade certificates and technical diplomas. Universities are self-accrediting organisations, working within national accreditation frameworks. In Australia, for example, the AQF (Australian Qualifications Framework) sets out a hierarchy of formal qualifications over nine levels—from Level 1 'schools' to Level 9 'doctoral degrees'.

Ideally, formal qualifications should be transferrable across jurisdictions and recognised beyond the state or country in which they are awarded, depending on the accrediting body. However, for example, a pharmacist trained in Australia cannot work as a pharmacist in the United Kingdom without undergoing a further two years of UK-based training on top of their three-year Australian pharmacy degree. In comparison, an Australian trained hairdresser can work anywhere in the United Kingdom on the basis of their three-year Australian trade certificate (as long as they have a working visa). Furthermore, in comparing formal educational awards merely in terms of time served, it is immediately apparent that there is a vast difference in the amount of content, assessment, theory, and practice between, say, a three-year pharmacy degree and a three-year hairdressing apprenticeship. This is starkly reinforced by their differing entry requirements—a matriculation score of 95% or more for pharmacy, no pre-requisites for hairdressing except having completed Year 10 at school.

Non-formal learning is also associated with undertaking some form of learning in an organised, institutional setting, but in this case, the learning is not accredited. Often labelled as *Continuing Education*, examples include *extension* or *enrichment* courses, which by definition offer content that is of interest to people wishing to enrich or extend their knowledge, about topics as obscure as the history and appreciation of coffee, to undertaking guided tours of archaeological sites in Ancient Greece. Participants sign up and pay course fees, and may receive a certificate of attendance or completion, but not a qualification or award in the formal sense. Teachers or tutors need not be officially qualified but usually have significant experience and knowledge in their subject area, and quite often might even offer their services on a voluntary basis, so keen are they to share their interests. Some well-known and established institutions offering non-formal courses include the WEA (Workers Educational Association) and the Volkhochschule (Folk High Schools) of Scandinavia.

The WEA was established in the United Kingdom by Albert Mansbridge in 1903 as another example of providing liberal education to workers who may have received little formal education before beginning their working life in an industrial society. An early example of further education, the WEA evening classes proved to be successful, with the model successfully transplanted to Australia where the WEA also continues to flourish, providing enrichment courses on topics ranging from digital media to dance. Sweden has a rich history of providing non-formal and second chance education for its citizens, and the Volkhochschule are an example of community-based education aimed at increasing the general knowledge, wellbeing, and civic interaction of the population to maintain the Platonic idea of 'the good life' in a social democracy. NFS Grundtvig (1783–1872), the Danish pastor who has been called the 'ideological father of folk high schools', firmly believed that "exams [are] deadening to the human soul" (New World Encyclopedia). Some of the founding principles of the Volkhochschule movement were that there would be no assessment or qualifications awarded for participating in and completing courses, and that class leadership would be shared democratically in a learning model that has led to established adult learning pedagogies today, including study circles and communities of practice.

Informal learning implies a form of self-education—learning that is experienced through daily interactions with people, places, and things. Much formal education can be associated with *surface learning*—information that is retained just long enough to reproduce at an exam, after which it inexplicably recedes into oblivion (contrary to this of course is *rote learning*, such as memorising the multiplication tables in elementary school through constant repetition). By contrast, informal learning can lead to a process of *internalisation*, where deep learning occurs, due to the often surprising and memorable nature of the learning experience. Examples of informal learning include *learning on the job*—which could include workplace learning as well as learning how to cook from your grandmother, coming across a book in the library that changes your whole view of history, visiting an art gallery and finding out about a wonderful artist you never heard of, or surfing the internet and discovering the origins and meaning of your surname. This type of learning could be accidental, by literally stumbling over something—a process of *serendipity*—or even unconscious learning, that is, we are not even aware at the time that we are learning something.

[Serendipity: Making desirable discoveries by accident, good fortune, or luck]

Learning that can have a profound effect on one's world view and meaning perspective has been labelled *transformative learning*. Research by the American educator Jack Mezirow (1923–2014) investigated the extent to which adult women enrolled in a continuing education program, which was ostensibly about something rather mundane, experienced a change in their view of themselves in the world as a result of expanding their educational perspectives—in effect undergoing a transformation from which there was no return. For some of these women it meant the end of a relationship or marriage, as their male partners could not understand or empathise with their new level of consciousness, having not experienced it. A similar process has been observed in the phenomenon of 'Men's sheds'—where mature aged men, often retrenched from work, widowed, or otherwise alone, gather in sheds to make toys or mend things for charity. In the process they find themselves sharing life experiences and supporting each other in what can be a lonely and confusing phase of life transition—so that the shed becomes a site for transformative learning and social support—a happy outcome even though it was not its original purpose.

The process of informal learning is well known in the adult education literature with *self-directed learning* being an accepted pedagogy. This rather self-evidently involves learning that is not directed by a teacher or educator, but by the individual themselves pursuing an interest or knowledge path through a program of study that can range from casual to rigorous. The term *auto-didact* is often applied to this kind of person, with *didactic* meaning 'instructive' (dictionary.com). An auto-didact is literally someone who is self-educating on a voluntary basis, under their own impetus and guided by intrinsic motivation. We can contrast this with education that is *mandated*, for example, by state regulations which mandate that all children up to a certain age must attend formal schooling. Homeschooling is a very interesting take on this idea and will be discussed in Chap. 11. It acknowledges that 'learning on the job' can occur in the home, and that in fact the home is a child's first learning environment, where the meaning of education in terms of 'rearing' first takes place.

Given the fact that learning can be 'credentialled' with a formal credential such as a certificate, parchment, or diploma as its outcome, we must acknowledge that the process or means of leading up to that outcome is just as important as the end itself. In addition, we must also acknowledge the other side of that coin, which is known as *uncredentialled learning*. This is a term to describe and give recognition to all the learning that a person experiences that is not able to be shown by the evidence of a certificate or qualification. It takes into account a person's life and work experience, background knowledge, and demonstrated understanding, and gives authenticity to the concept of learning from life. For many adult learners, uncredentialled learning has been the pathway back into formal credentialled learning—for example, the woman who did not finish school, worked her way up through the fashion industry, then applied to enter art school as a mature age student on the basis of her self-directed learning in art and design, or the early school leaver who was a retail manager for many years and was able to enter university to undertake management studies at degree level on the basis of *recognition of prior learning*.

Finally, all these forms of education imply some sort of *relationship*. The teacher-learner relationship is important and will be discussed further in subsequent chapters. However, relationships also exist among learners, between the learners and the content or curriculum, with educational administrative and regulatory bodies, and even within the learner and their own motivation or reason for engaging in any learning process. While learning as an adult can be *transformative*, the following discussion focuses more closely on the *formative* years of education, in which we inculcate our children into their family, community, and society in a range of ways that are both planned and unplanned. It will be seen that the process of education is not necessarily a linear and sequential one—even though our education systems are structured that way.

3.5   Educational Philosophy

'Education' is a broad concept. It encapsulates everything from structured schooling to unconscious learning. It affects, guides, and influences us on a daily basis. Education as a *discipline*, or field of study however, is a relatively recent category in academic circles.

[Discipline meaning…from disciplere, 'to follow'… compare with the word 'Disciple']

As we have seen, it has grown out of the study of philosophy, as have the other relatively recent disciplines of psychology and sociology, two areas in the social sciences that also inform educational theory. It has really only been since the late nineteenth and early twentieth centuries that we have seen education as a specialised study, with a separate body of literature, university faculties and professors of education, and specialised conferences for educationalists and educators. Scholars labelled as 'educationalists' or 'pedagogues' only appeared as distinct specialists in education in the literature within the last two to 300 years.

Yet we have seen that the concept of educational philosophy has been around for several thousands of years in western history and culture. The question for us in the twenty-first century which we have begun to address in Part I of this book is:

What have we learned from history that will inform and guide us in our relationships with the discipline of education now and into the future?

If the purpose of education is therefore more than just learning to take one's place in society and the workplace, then what is it? Nearly 400 years ago, Comenius clearly stated what he believed to be the purpose of education: that through "teaching all things to all men … a general education for all can lead to commonly shared insights into the True and the Good", and that "this would lead to eternal Peace and a unified world under the government of Wisdom" (Dahlin 2006: 18). If Plato believed that the ultimate purpose of education was 'a training in values', is that still relevant today? Can we develop personal and communal philosophies of education that will build on all that we know so far about humanity and its relationships with education, yet apply them in a way that takes into account the rapidly changing world we live in?

There have always been radical moves to change the education systems that we have inherited, and the early twenty-first century has seen much debate around schools and their purposes, around teachers and their effectiveness, even questioning the need for schooling at all. Continued debate and discourse is healthy and can be informative and even *educative*, but in the meantime, we still have to prepare succeeding generations for future life on the planet. A thorough examination of schooling as a concept follows in Part II, in order to understand where we have come from, where we are now, and where we might be going in the discipline of education.

References

Bloom, B. S., Engelhart, M. D., Furst, E. J., Hill, W. H., & Krathwohl, D. R. (1956). *Taxonomy of educational objectives: The classification of educational goals*. New York: David McKay Company.

Dahlin, B. (2006). *Education, history and be(com)ing human: Two essays in philosophy and education*. Karlstad: Karlstad University.

Gidley, J. (2016). *Postformal education: A philosophy for complex futures*. Basel: Springer.

Goleman, D. (1995). *Emotional intelligence*. New York: Bantam Books.

Hall, B. (2012). Postgraduate numbers double in ten years. *Sydney Morning Herald*. http://www.smh.com.au/national/tertiary-education/postgraduate-numbers-double-in-10-years-20121030-28gz3.html. Accessed 29 Mar 2017.

Livingstone, R. (1959). *The rainbow bridge and other essays on education*. London: Pall Mall Press.

McDonagh, D. (2017, April 16). My PhD is fake. *The Irish Mail on Sunday*, p. 1.

Murphy, C. (1991). *Emil Molt and the beginnings of the Waldorf School*. Edinburgh: Floris Books.

Payton, A. (2017). *Skilling for tomorrow*. Adelaide: NCVER.

Pietzner, C. (1992). Community relations and outreach. In D. Mitchell (Ed.), *The art of administration: Viewpoints on professional management in Waldorf Schools* (pp. 83–97). Boulder: A.W.S.N.A.

Read, H. (1948). *Education through art*. London: Faber and Faber.

Robinson, K. (2006). www.ted.com/talks/ken_robinson_says_schools_kill_Creativity.html. Accessed 14 Apr 2017.

Sherriff, L. (2015). Ernst & Young removes degree classification from entry criteria as there's 'no evidence' university equals success. http://www.huffingtonpost.co.uk/2016/01/07/ernst-and-young-removes-degree-classification-entry-criteria_n_7932590.html. Accessed 28 Mar 2017.

Steiner, R. (1927). Reordering of society: The fundamental social law. http://wn.rsarchive.org/Articles/FuSoLa_index.html. Accessed 23 Mar 2018.

Part II

Schooling Versus Education

4

School: History, Meaning, Context, and Construct

The history, meaning, context, and construct of *schooling* are explored in this chapter, which includes a discussion of definitions, origins, and early examples and investigates the extent to which schools function as social sorting and socialisation agencies as well as knowledge factories. Schools are analysed in terms of their establishment, development, and purpose with case study examples of experimental schools attempting to break the 'factory model' of universal mass education that resulted from the Industrial Revolution.

4.1 Definitions, Distinctions, Developments

Q: *Why are fish so smart?*
A: *Because they live in schools.*

The modern word *schooling* comes from the Greek word *skhole*, which actually meant 'spare time, leisure, rest or ease; idleness' as well as 'learned discussion', implying that initially, learning was not associated with *work*

© The Author(s) 2018
T. Stehlik, *Educational Philosophy for 21st Century Teachers*,
https://doi.org/10.1007/978-3-319-75969-2_4

but was something one engaged in almost as a pastime. This reinforces the fact that schooling is just one aspect of the broader concept of education discussed so far, which includes things like learning on the job and learning from life. The *Online Dictionary* now defines schooling as:

1. the process of being taught in a school
2. instruction, education, or training, especially when received in a school
3. the act of teaching
4. *(Archaic)* a reprimand

How interesting that the archaic form has negative connotations, that once upon a time children were 'schooled' by being told off, and although that form of the word is no longer in common parlance, it would still align with many people's experiences of schooling today. The rather banal joke at the head of this chapter is also there to reinforce the image of schools as places where children and young people are massed together and treated as a collective body, all seen as being able to swim and turn in the same direction at the same time, much like the way a school of fish behaves. Despite what we now know about individual development, different learning styles, and differentiated curricula, we still put children into classes according to their age and expect them to swim as one against the various tides and currents acting upon them. And the question would still remain, does being in school necessarily make all children 'smart'?

As we have seen, the concept of schooling as an *act or process* has a long history, but schools as the institutions that we know today are considered to be a relatively recent construct. In fact, it has been claimed that:

…formal publicly funded universal school education began little more than 200 years ago in Europe. (Gidley 2016: 71)

While schools for the elite, the wealthy, the professions, and the military (and mostly males) had been around earlier in Plato's Athens and also in China and Egypt, by the early 1800s these had morphed into the sort of exclusive private schools that we are familiar with today (rather confusingly known as public schools in Great Britain, for example,

Eton, Harrow, etc.). 'Universal school education', available to all children in a given society, is a concept that has been mentioned as being developed in theory by Comenius back in the 1600s. However, it was not until the early 1800s that his educational theories were put into practice by Wilhelm von Humboldt (1767–1835) in Prussia, now part of Germany. As the Minister for Education, Humboldt developed the Prussian educational system, defined by standardised public instruction, assessed by examinations, and regulated by inspections. This has provided a template that is still in use today. In fact, it is quite interesting to note that when Japan made a conscious effort to modernise and take on western ideas of education during the nineteenth century, they modelled their schooling system on Humboldt's plan—and modern-day Japanese school uniforms still have a Prussian military look about them.

Humboldt was influenced by the idealistic romantic notions of German philosophers such as Hegel, Goethe, and Schiller, as represented by the German word *Bildung*, and his vision for public education was more aligned to the Platonic ideal of 'the good life'. Humboldt would go on to found the Humboldt University in Berlin, providing a template for most modern universities as cultural institutions independent of the state, but equally importantly, introducing the concept of *Bildung* into the educational lexicon has had a lasting legacy not only in the German-speaking world but in the bigger picture of the development of educational philosophy. The word Bildung is not easy to translate directly into English, but it helps to know that *Bild* in German means 'picture' or 'image'. One definition is that "philosophy and education are virtually synonymous… [Bildung is] an ongoing process of personal and cultural maturation" (Gidley 2016: 87). The notion of learning being an ongoing process in which the individual's personal agency is central and incorporates all aspects of personality and identity also distinguishes Bildung from the German word *Erziehung* which refers more to traditional concepts of training. In this sense, Bildung can be conceived as an *outcome* of training and formal education, incorporating the notions of *cultural development and awareness*, and taken together with all other aspects of learning, leading to the formation of an individual's *essence* (Danner 1994).

In Britain meanwhile, the influence of the Industrial Revolution from the early 1880s onwards drove a more mechanistic and instrumental approach to mass public education, according to the increasing demands of industry and the mass migration of working people from the country to cities. The demands of the rapidly developing urban and working class way of life introduced the 'factory model' of schools that we still have today. In fact, many early schools in Great Britain were not established by the state, but by industrialists and factory owners who, out of a sense of responsibility or philanthropy, saw the need for looking after their workers, including their families and their children. The example of Emil Molt founding the Waldorf School for the children of his German workers has already been mentioned. Some captains of industry went as far as building whole towns for their workforce, inclusive of schools, social activities, and community centres, for example, the model village of Port Sunlight built in the 1880s by the Lever Brothers soap manufacturers at Merseyside in the United Kingdom. This occurred in Sweden as well as in England, where the eventual development of 'garden cities' aimed to soften the industrial working life with an environment that was less Dickensian than the smoky grimy cities as characterised by William Blake's 'dark satanic mills' in the poem and anthem *Jerusalem* (Blake 1808).

Speaking of Charles Dickens (1812–1870), his graphic descriptions of schools in books such as *Hard Times* and *Nicholas Nickleby* record the fact that they could also be established by any enterprising person, with little or no educational qualifications or teaching experience required. While some of these private schools were run by 'ladies' for young ladies, the 'schools for boys' described by Dickens were characteristically run by severe men who often mistreated the children and barely provided any real education, being interested only in collecting fees from parents who were quite happy to have the responsibility of their boys taken off their hands and could afford to pay for it. As we shall see later in this chapter and in Part III, children were treated very differently in early Victorian society; educating girls beyond learning how to be a homemaker was not seen as necessary as they would only be married off; and there was no concept of adolescence as children transitioned straight into adulthood, often entering working life at an age when we would consider them to still be teenagers—a term that would not even emerge until the twentieth century.

The link between schools and with industry and the economy is therefore very clear in the early development of universal public education in the English-speaking part of Europe. From this we can see the development of schools and their purposes growing in several different directions, especially in Great Britain. On the one hand, well-endowed elite schools for the wealthy and titled upper class thrived and maintained the hereditary class system embedded in British political and social traditions, as ultimately represented by the House of Lords. The graduates of these schools were able to indulge in a liberal rather than a vocational education as their careers would already be assured in the clergy, the officer class of the military, or through inheritance in business or the land. On the other hand, there was a need for the children of the working class and the rapidly developing middle class to learn basic literacy, numeracy, and general knowledge in order to fill the increasing range of jobs required in the new industrial economy. From this we begin to get a picture of schools as sorting agencies—with children being sorted by class, by gender, by location, and by what we would now know as differences in socio-economic status and equality of opportunity. The gap between those who are included and those who are excluded still exists, even if it is more subtle in many ways, such as in the hidden curriculum. However, school choice is still to a large degree determined by socio-economic circumstance and intergenerational traditions (Figs. 4.1 and 4.2).

4.2   Which School or College Did You Go to?

There can be no doubt that the formative years of a child's life will determine and influence the sort of person they will grow into as an adult—their character, temperament, interests, and life choices, to name a few. While inherited characteristics and family of origin are of course part of the developmental picture (see Part III), there is undoubtedly a direct causal link with a child's experience of formal education, especially if they are going to spend up to 12 years of their developing life in institutionalised schooling. The curriculum, the teachers, the other children, the

Fig. 4.1 Sorting by age and gender began even as the children entered school in 1898. (Greenwich, London, England)

Fig. 4.2 Separate entrances for students and everyone else…but given the placement of the apostrophe, did St Patrick's have only one student?! (Ballycastle, County Mayo, Republic of Ireland)

school environment, the level of involvement of parents—all of these relationships will have a shaping and directing influence on a child's physical and psychological as well as intellectual development.

There is plenty of evidence to support this view. For example, the 'Growing up North' project in the United Kingdom has found empirical data to support what would appear to be obvious anyway, that "growing up in a particular area affects the chances a child has going into adulthood" (Pidd 2017: 10). In this case the project has been comparing children growing up in the north of England with those in the south, finding a general difference in school achievement and development of more than 10%, in favour of those in the south. "These figures are a stark reminder that there are hundreds of thousands of children growing up in the north who are falling behind children in the south – in many cases before they've even started their school lives" (Pidd 2017: 10).

A number of points are raised by this project. Firstly, that *place* is important in terms of access to schooling opportunities. Secondly, that children can be disadvantaged by place and circumstance *even before they have started their school lives.* Rudolf Steiner and Maria Montessori saw schools as places where children could experience a 'remedial effect' from the pressures of modern life and disadvantages of upbringing; however, if those disadvantages and pressures are merely reinforced by the school environment, the child will have even less chances to flourish. Thirdly, in interpreting any such research data, we need to question what is meant in this case by 'achievement and development', and what measures these are determined by, in the light of the bigger picture questions around the purpose of education and the role of schooling in that picture.

While international organisations such as UNESCO and the British Council have recently been promoting the rhetoric of *Education for all*, espousing increased access to schools for more children globally through various international projects, there are still barriers to be overcome in conflict zones and in the many ethnic, cultural, and geographical differences; questions around whether increased school attendance will directly increase learning and life opportunities; and no guarantees that the dominant model of school education that is being subscribed to will actually meet the future needs of the children and their communities (Gidley 2016; UNESCO 2015). 'Education for all' is a noble idea; however, the history and structure of schooling as we know it, and the analysis of education as followed in Chap. 3, mean that 'education' is still not a level playing field or equal experience for all children, that in fact *some are more equal than others*:

> There are still 58 million children out of school globally and around 100 million children who do not complete primary education. Inequality in education has increased, with the poorest and most disadvantaged shouldering the heaviest burden. The world's poorest children are four times more likely not to go to school than the world's richest children, and five times as likely not to complete primary school. (UNESCO 2015: 4)

This inequality is no more obvious in western countries than in comparing private or independent schools with those that are part of a national or state government education system—especially those private schools that are elite, exclusive, well-funded, and well-founded. In Australia, the proportion of students attending a non-government school has now exceeded more than one-third of all school students (Reid 2017).

The reasons for this are as many and varied as are the schools themselves—ranging from wealthy single-sex schools such as Church of England Girls Grammar School in Sydney or Melbourne Grammar, large co-educational Lutheran and Anglican schools, small Catholic Parish schools and Islamic schools, and Montessori and Steiner schools. As will be seen, schools outside state-run systems are either established along religious lines or according to a particular educational philosophy, and sometimes both, presenting a choice to parents for schooling that either aligns with their religious beliefs or is perceived to provide the type of education, ethos, and opportunities not otherwise offered in government schools. The concept of 'the old school tie' is also alive and well in Australia as in other countries, where career opportunities, business networks, family connections, and even which church you attend are seen as giving young people distinct life advantages.

The Catholic Education sector in Australia makes up a large part of the non-government sector alone, reflecting the influence of the early European settlers, many of whom came from countries like Ireland. The tenacity of organised religion to maintain schooling traditions is starkly presented in Irish history, when Jesuit schools were outlawed under Protestant English rule in the early nineteenth century, and the Penal Laws prevented Catholics from openly attending school as well as any religious gatherings such as mass. This gave rise to the Irish 'hedge schools', where clandestine classes would literally gather in secret under the shelter of a hedge or a barn, with a learned person in the neighbourhood providing basic literacy and numeracy to Catholic children. The image of hedge schools highlights the importance of faith and belief in maintaining a community's strong desire to educate its children in the prevailing values and ethos. Even more significantly, this tenacity for education kept the Irish language alive and promoted Gaelic culture and literature, leading to what would eventually be the movement for Irish independence which was finally achieved in 1922 (Foster 1989).

South Australia however saw a large proportion of German immigrants in its early colonial occupation, and the Lutheran tradition is noticeably strong in that state, with the Lutheran education sector still providing specific training for teachers in Lutheran schools, similar to Catholic teacher education. This popularity of religious schools in Australia is despite the fact that the country as a whole does not have an official religion, with census figures showing one-third of Australians have 'no religion', although almost all religions are represented to some extent, with by far the largest cohort being the 25% who identify as Catholic (ABS 2017). Contrast this with countries like Sweden and Finland, which are officially Lutheran, to the extent that all Finns, for example, are automatically born into the Lutheran faith and, if they do not want to be a member of the church, must formally apply to the state for a 'divorce' from it. Yet while religion is a subject in Finnish state elementary schools, it is more concerned with morals, values, and ethics (Plato's 'good life') than the type of dogmatic preaching that occurs in some Australian Lutheran schools. Finland is a very interesting educational case study and is given more attention in Chap. 10.

While still subject to the same rules and regulations in terms of accreditation, mandatory attendance, and teacher registration as state schools, in addition to religious beliefs, private or independent schools can also be established according to particular educational methodologies, philosophies, and pedagogies. Montessori Schools, for example, offer a curriculum founded on Maria Montessori's views of child development based on manual manipulation of objects, embodied learning, and freedom of expression. Steiner or Waldorf Schools are also based on Steiner's philosophy of education and his unique research into child development and teaching-learning relationships, with the first school which opened in Stuttgart in 1919 named the 'Waldorf Free School', in recognition of being free of state control and established educational dogma, which by then was entrenched in the Humboldtian system in Germany. This yearning for freedom from the inherited 'factory model' of schooling which inevitably resulted from centralised and regulated state systems has led to other interesting and ongoing variations on the concept of schooling over time, and still today, as follows.

4.3   Evolution and Revolution

Schooling is a process that has evolved over time, sometimes in a gradually planned and managed way, at other times driven by political, social, or cultural upheavals and *paradigm shifts* in educational thinking. Such revolutions can be characterised by the various experimental schools that have appeared, mostly flourishing briefly before losing momentum (or funding), while others are still with us today. Such a shift occurred at the beginning of the twentieth century when utopian ideals combined with the growing influence of psychological science brought to a head the Enlightenment aim of improving the world, leading to what Dahlin (2006) describes as 'psychological utopianism'. This envisioned not only a new approach to education but a new vision of a reformed society and the transformed human being:

> The basic principle of psycho-utopian thinking is that an ideal society can be created by the application of psychological knowledge in order to transform the human personality, consciousness or psyche. Sometimes this even seems to imply the possibility of a fundamental change in human nature. (Dahlin 2006: 7)

Perhaps the most well-known and enduring experiment in utopian schooling is Summerhill, which was established in 1921 by the Scottish teacher AS Neill (1883–1973), first in Germany and then in England, where it is still functioning to this day. Neill's educational philosophy was based on the 'innate goodness of the child' who could be 'self-regulating' if given the chance to identify their own learning needs and interests (Summerhill website). Rather than being directed by teachers and a set curriculum, children would be free to choose when, where, what, and how they wanted to learn. This methodological approach and an account of the school's first 40 years are set out in Neill's 1960 book *Summerhill: A Radical Approach to Child Rearing*. Even the title of the book suggests that Neill saw his role as *rearing* children, not *teaching* them. As such, the school's website claims it to be 'the oldest children's democracy in the world' and 'the original alternative free school' (Summerhill website). There are always questions about the continued survival of any institution that is founded by a charismatic personality when that individual passes on, that the momentum will fail and the model may not be replicable. In this case, Summerhill is still pursuing its seemingly successful alternative approach, currently and since 1985 under the guidance of Neill's daughter Zoe.

As 'the original', Summerhill has inspired many other such free schools around the world, many of which remain small and struggling with a dedicated teaching staff and parent population keeping them alive, often maintained by pure will and a commitment to providing children with freedom of educational choice. Others however appear to be flourishing and achieving remarkable results, like the Evangelical School Berlin where:

> …there are no grades until students turn 15, no timetables and no lecture-style instructions. The pupils decide which subjects they want to study for each lesson and when they want to take an exam. (Oltermann 2016: 1)

Another famous experiment in elementary schooling was established by the pragmatist John Dewey in 1896, at the University of Chicago. What became known as the Laboratory Schools were founded on an integrated approach to subjects, based on 'real life' activities like cooking, gardening, and crafts, and in an early version of problem-based learning, students were tasked with coming up with creative solutions to set problems. In a comparison with Summerhill, Dewey referred to his laboratory school as an 'embryonic democracy', but the ideal of allowing children to democratically run the school and the curriculum quickly faded to a more structured approach, and gradually the Laboratory Schools at the University of Chicago have evolved into high-status private co-educational institutions that today have over 1700 students enrolled from nursery to Grade 12 (https://www.ucls.uchicago.edu/).

Readers who have gotten this far and remember Chap. 2 will recall that the educational ideal of *freedom* was the central plank of Rousseau's philosophy and ideas about rearing children, showing how such ideals are not new, and persistently surface in the evolution and revolution of schools. Revolutionary ideals however contributed in the early twentieth century to another example of experimental schooling, this time in Ireland.

St Enda's school was founded in Dublin in 1908 by Patrick Pearse, an Irish Republican and activist who was one of the leaders of the Irish Republican movement, eventually executed by the British after the failed Easter uprising of 1916 (Edwards 2006). As an educator, Pearse believed strongly that the movement towards Irish nationalism and freedom would be inspired by the native Gaelic language and culture, and he established St Enda's as an experimental school that would re-create the noble traditions of Ireland's glorious past:

> Here the theories of William Morris and fashionable European ideals of active, open-air education were mingled with Pearse's obsessional Celtic motifs: notable the mythical hero Cuchulainn, pictured by him as a slim, beautiful boy dying happily for Ireland. (Foster 1989: 458–459)

Here we can see the purposes of education being bound up in nationalism, in this case the language of sacrificial politics. As will be seen in Chap. 10, nationalism and maintenance of the 'mother tongue' also drove the development of education in Finland, but in a much more subtle and inclusive way. St Enda's was also an example of schooling taking up 'fashionable ideals' and current theories of the time, such as those of William Morris (1834–1896) who was one of the leading lights in the Arts and Crafts and 'return to nature' movements in late nineteenth-century England, which spearheaded the beginnings of a return to Platonic aestheticism in culture and education. Pearse also attempted to start a school for girls, but St Enda's was established as a Catholic school for boys only, driven by romantic patriotic ideals bound up in notions of manliness, honour, and the glories of self-sacrifice for the higher good, starkly demonstrated by its founder's own martyrdom in 1916—yet ultimately doomed.

> Patrick Pearse had been an essential and irreplaceable part of the school. It limped along until 1935, always operating at a loss, and suffering by competition with other more successful colleges. Numbers were low, ranging between about sixteen and thirty. When the school finally closed, it was tacitly admitted by many of those who had helped in its running that is should have died with its founder. (Edwards 2006: 309–310)

In the example of St Enda's, we see schooling appropriated as a tool—some would say a weapon—and a means to a particular end, in this case political, with children being caught up in the idealism and subject to the educational experiments of obsessive individuals. In a further example, 'active, open-air education' was also a hallmark of National Socialism in Nazi Germany in the 1930s, with the staged athleticism and fitness of the Hitler Youth not only harking back to classical Greek ideals of 'perfection in form' in the beauty of the youthful human body but clearly having a political and nationalistic agenda as well. Hitler also called on 'mythical heroes' and noble deeds as templates for youth to aspire to, although in his case these were Aryan and Wagnerian, not Irish. In Finland, the mythical heroes of the Kalevala folk sagas still provide Finnish schoolchildren with examples and archetypes for moral development and social values; and the importance of stories, myths, legends, and archetypal characters to a child's developing consciousness is a thread that weaves through most educational endeavours throughout history, to be further explored in later chapters.

One hundred years ago when Waldorf Schools first appeared, they were also be considered as experimental schools driven by utopian ideals and a vision for social renewal through education. As discussed in more detail in Chap. 10, they introduced radical new pedagogical approaches and teaching methods and pursued an independent form of governance aimed at being self-regulated rather than externally controlled. However, their ethos, while also being child-centred, was highly structured and far from the kind of approach taken at Summerhill where children were free to learn what they felt like. Steiner actually developed a formal and detailed curriculum that provided definite and prescribed subjects and topics which progressed in a logical sequence from year to year according the child's developing needs. The fact that Waldorf Schools have spread worldwide and continue to be one of the fastest growing independent school movements in the world proves that there is room within the concept of 'schooling' for many and varied educational philosophies, ranging from almost total freedom to virtually total control, with many possibilities in between.

While we can see that the basic concept and structure of schooling has remained almost unchanged, experimentation within that structure in terms of curriculum, pedagogies, and methodologies continued through the twentieth century and continues today. In South Australia, for example, the 1960s saw the introduction of 'Demonstration Schools'—primary schools which introduced and experimented with teaching methods and ideas that were driven by an increased interest in educational theory and research, and also borrowed from trends in other countries and from alternative education movements. As a child during the 1960s, I attended several different primary schools, as my parents moved house a lot. One of these schools was Rose Park Demonstration School.

To all intents and purposes, it operated as a primary school with classes from Grades 1 to 7, but the South Australian Education Department identified the school as one of several in the metropolitan area of Adelaide where teachers were expected to test various 'new' teaching methods and resources in different subject areas. In English we had 'Reading Laboratory', and rather than reading whole books, we worked through selected extracts of comprehension exercises which were sequenced in a lockstep fashion according to vocabulary, with our progress recorded and compared with the whole class. In mathematics we had 'attribute blocks'—pieces of wood in various different shapes and colours—that we were supposed to manipulate and arrange in various patterns as a way of understanding geometrical forms. We also went out into the quadrangle and drew intersecting circles of chalk on the asphalt and stood in them in various configurations, which is where I first learned about Venn diagrams. (This idea of a hands-on rather than a purely abstract approach to maths is taken directly from the Montessori Method, where the use of colour, shape, and embodied experience in learning is central.)

While experimenting with new methods, teachers at Rose Park were also locked into educational traditions that can be traced back to the nineteenth-century 'cellular classroom' in which "students were not randomly distributed within the rank and file structure of the classroom but were rather placed according to a variety of well-defined criteria such as their ability, their behaviour, or diligence" (Schratzenstaller 2010: 25).

For example, every Friday we would have a test of the week's work, and each child's test score would determine where they would sit for the coming week. The top scoring students would sit right at the back, and so on down to the lowest achievers who ended up in the front row right in front of the teacher's desk, where their behaviour could be 'managed'. In this way it was immediately obvious not only to the children but to anyone coming into the class who were the 'bright good kids' and who were the 'dumb naughty kids'. This odd mixture of new-fangled and old-fashioned pedagogical methods was represented by the diversity of the teaching staff. Some of the teachers were young and embraced the new ideas, while others were entrenched in the traditional methods of chalk-and-talk, speak-only-when-spoken-to, and corporal punishment administered by 'cuts' to the hand or legs with a cane. These experiments with method did not yet extend to more enlightened approaches to behaviour management or discipline, and it was at a time when physical punishment of children was accepted and even seen as necessary.

At Rose Park Demonstration School, children were also assessed for any musical ability and those who were deemed as having some talent were then given instruments and music lessons which regularly took them out of the mainstream classroom, leaving those of us who were left behind feeling somehow left out. This notion of 'special treatment' was an early indication of the policy of treating 'gifted children' differently from the rest of the class, which continues to be an issue within the traditional schooling model of a classroom of 25 or so children who are not necessarily at the same level of development just because they are in the same age group. This also applies to the other end of the spectrum in consideration of children who would be considered as slow learners, with remedial learning needs and other developmental issues. For those children with serious intellectual disabilities, Rose Park had a special 'Opportunity Class', operating out of a transportable building on the edge of the campus, in an early approach to working with children with special needs. Everyone referred to these kids as 'the Oppos', and the threat of ending up with the Oppos was tacitly used as a way of getting some of the more recalcitrant children to 'pull their socks up'.

This duality between 'mainstream' and 'alternative' approaches to schooling, which could be inclusive of any of the examples given so far above, highlights a constant quest within the traditional model of schooling to address the need for universal mass education on the one hand and on the other hand to accommodate various specialisations in ability, interest, outcome, and method that constitute the reality of the reciprocal needs of individuals and the society in which—and for which—they are being educated. This differentiation has been addressed in a number of ways over the evolution of schooling and has led to these various evolving and developing experiments, some of which have been quite radical, while others have just tinkered around the edges. Some have been passing fads, while others have endured. Demonstration schools still exist, for example, in New South Wales where they "provide evidence based and innovative teaching practices to ensure a quality 21st Century *education for all*" (www.nthsyddem-p.schools.nsw.edu.au, my italics). But in some parts of the world, whole education systems have actually developed along different pathways according to perceived ideas about the purpose of education, creating, for example, the entrenched dual systems to be found in Germany, Sweden, and other European countries.

4.4   Differentiation and Dual Systems

We *explain* nature, but we *understand* the inner life. (Wilhelm Dilthey 1894, cited in Biesta and Tröhler 2008: 10)

When we refer to someone colloquially as a 'Renaissance man or woman', what is meant by the description is that they are interested/educated/involved in a number of diverse subject areas ranging widely across the arts and sciences, in comparison to someone who is a 'specialist' or 'expert' in one particular field, and labelled as such: for example, an astrophysicist or a pharmacist. The subdivision of knowledge and occupations into increasingly narrow and specialised areas is a relatively recent development. Isaac Newton (1643–1727), for example, is famous for his law of gravitation, but it is only in hindsight that we label him a 'scientist'; he saw himself more as a natural philosopher interested in a wide range of interests and observations of the natural world, which he saw as interconnected. Johann Wilhelm von Goethe (1749–1832) was a celebrated poet and writer but was also keenly interested in nature and made a number of important scientific discoveries. However, both of these men would be considered part of the

Enlightenment era, when we have seen that science gradually came to dominate intellectual life through the application of technology and the resulting industrialisation of society.

During this era the gradual separation of the arts and sciences became entrenched and manifested in the way that universal mass education began to diverge into separate and distinct pathways. As mentioned above, the modern system of education we have inherited can be traced back to Comenius in theory and Humboldt in practice, through the concept of *Bildung*. However, Bildung in its pure form can be seen as *apolitical*, in which knowledge is presented uncritically and theoretically in ways that may be disconnected from the realities of daily life (Siljander et al. 2012). This can be seen in the Humboldtian model of liberal education in which Bildung was represented by the 'Seven Liberal Arts': grammar, rhetoric, logic, geometry, arithmetic, music, and astronomy. Harking back to the educational ideals of the Ancient Greeks and entrenched in Medieval Philosophy, these seven arts (some of which we would now consider to be sciences) represented higher forms of knowledge that were associated with higher status and of relevance only to those who could afford to indulge in them without having to worry about where their next meal was coming from—in other words, the elite of society. In this sense then, during the nineteenth century, *education did become politicised* as it contributed to the formation of the middle classes:

> *Bildung* had become a code word for a newly emerging social class. In the German language, this social class became known as "the educated class" [representing] the urban bourgeoisie that had attended a higher school or had undertaken an academic course of study (Konrad 2012: 109)

In Europe, this educated class attended schools that were known as *Gymnasia*. Again, the word comes from the classical Greek 'Gymnasion', which was the name of an exercising ground in ancient Athens and from which the use of the word to describe a place of sport and exercise still applies. The concept of the Gymnasium as a place of learning was revived during the Renaissance and became the universal title for a secondary school that would specifically prepare young people for higher education, by order of the Austro-Hungarian, German, and Russian Empires during the nineteenth century. Today, young people in Germany, Sweden, and many other European countries still attend a Gymnasium if they aspire to go on to a university education.

Contrast this with the development of education for purely vocational purposes, which also evolved from the Industrial Revolution and the need for skilled labour in the new trades and professions that were emerging. In educational terms, the German word *Erziehung* describes vocational learning as a distinctly separate construct from Bildung, and refers to skills training as a specifically different type of learning process that is not so bound up in higher ideals or associated with identity and personal development. Erziehung is the pragmatic, applied, and practical side of education and provides the balance to the liberal arts approach to education, reminding us of the duality of *contemplative and practical activity* as discussed in the previous chapter. Here we really see differences in the purpose of education—on the one hand, to develop citizens within a civil society, and on the other to train workers who would keep the machinery of the civil society turning.

This differentiation has led to dual education systems and pathways through school which channel young people either into an academic higher education pathway or into a vocational pathway. In some countries like Sweden, this occurs within a unified education system with high schools specialising in either academic or vocational subjects, while in Germany secondary education is very complicated and actually includes five types of schools. After elementary school German children are more or less channelled into three pathways according to their grades—the Gymnasium is the highest form and leads to university, the Hauptschule the 'lowest' form and generally leading to vocational school, and the Realschule somewhere in between. Contrast this with the concept of a *comprehensive high school* which aims to educate students of all abilities and does not sort them according to some form of examination or grading; this is the system that is mostly adopted in the United States.

Historically, Australia featured an approach to sorting secondary students not only by achievement but by gender, with Boys' Technical High Schools being a feature until the late 1960s, and high schools for girls concentrating on vocational subjects relating to commerce, such as typing and shorthand. Most of the larger comprehensive co-educational high schools now offer vocational pathways within the senior secondary certificate, often based on industries associated with the local region. A perceived 'skills gap' in Australia in the early 2000s saw history repeating itself with the establishment of a new form of technical high school called vocational colleges. At the same time, initiatives under the banner of *Social Inclusion* saw early school leaving and student disengagement being addressed through alternative approaches to schooling based on vocational, adult learning methodologies outside of the traditional school structure (see Chap. 11).

Further back in history, from 1857 onwards we find *Industrial schools* established in England for homeless children aged between 7 and 14. By the end of that century, there were around 275 such schools in England and Scotland. In Ireland Industrial schools were established from 1868, to care for neglected, orphaned, and abandoned children, or children whose parents deemed them 'uncontrollable', with over 5000 children living in these schools by 1884 (Ryan 2009). Modelled on German, Swiss, and Scandinavian farm schools, these were an early example of vocational training, as they not only dealt with the 'problem' of abandoned and uncontrollable children but provided:

> …practical training which would equip the children for employment rather than academic learning. This approach fitted with the Victorian idea of utilitarian progress and also helped provide skills to fuel the Industrial Revolution. (Ryan 2009: 36)

Originally intended so that boys would be 'trained to be industrious' by learning woodwork, shoemaking, and other trade skills, separate schools were established for girls who were trained in housework duties with the clear intention that they would then go into domestic service as housemaids. These children were lodged, clothed, and fed, but also 'reformed' as it was believed that for many of them, "home was a bad influence" (Ryan 2009).

This gap between 'home' and 'school' has hopefully closed since the 1800s. However, as recently as the 1980s, these two dominant influences in a young person's life and upbringing were still in danger of being completely out of step with each other. As English farmer and author James Rebanks recollects:

> The whole time I was at school, I wanted to be at home on the farm. I was convinced then, and still am, that home was a more interesting and productive place to be for me. Making anyone do something they don't want to do with thirty other bored kids seemed to me absolutely pointless. (Rebanks 2016: 90)

Rebanks writes of learning more practical and useful life skills from his father and grandfather while working alongside them on their farm than what was on offer at school, which he left as soon as he was able to at the age of 15. Apart from painting a picture of 'thirty bored kids' which is every teacher's nightmare, this passage really begs a question of great import to the consideration of educational philosophy:

> *At what point in our lives are we able to take responsibility for our own education rather than be subjected to what someone else believes we should be learning?*

The whole notion of *compulsory education* suggests that we put our children under compulsion to attend school until a certain age that has been defined by legislation, varying from 15 to 17 depending on where you happen to live. Proponents of public education in South Australia, for example, suggest that "ever since the late 19th century… there has been community agreement that education is so important that it should be compulsory to a certain age" (Reid 2017: 4). While the important relationship between school and community will be discussed in the next chapter, at this point we also should question how this particular 'community agreement' has been maintained since the late nineteenth century, and whether it is well over time in the early twenty-first century for society to re-visit this agreement and question whether it is still valid, or whether we are simply taking it for granted based on tradition.

The negative aspects of compulsion are represented by the sort of 'factory' approach to schooling which not only channels young people into life pathways according to such variables as gender, place, religion, socioeconomic status, or parental influence but also produces potentially harmful effects on the developing child and adolescent who is *compelled to be there by society*, with some of these effects being introduced at the beginning of the following chapter.

In closing this chapter, a brief mention must be made of *postcompulsory education*, which necessarily follows on from the compulsory years. As a distinct sector of education, this suggests a phase in one's life where one is no longer under compulsion to attend an educational institution but instead can attend one by choice. By definition it includes everything post-school: universities, colleges, adult and community education centres, professional institutes, and so on. Postcompulsory education also brings with it a completely different approach to pedagogy, associated with adult teaching and learning methodologies in which the student is there (generally) because they want to be, and has had some choice in the matter including making a conscious decision about why they are there.

Malcolm Knowles (1913–1997) popularised the term *andragogy* to make a distinction between the types of learning undertaken by adults in post-compulsory settings with that of pedagogy, which he argued applied more to the formative years of teaching children than to the type of transformative learning that could be facilitated with adults. Knowles' definition of andragogy, *the science of understanding and supporting lifelong education of adults* (Merriam 2001), includes informal and self-directed learning processes, as described in Chap. 3. Although the separation between andragogy and pedagogy has been critiqued as too simplistic, the main difference between the two concepts relates to intrinsic self-motivation in comparison with the types of extrinsic motivation associated with compulsory schooling. However, the point at which pedagogy might merge into andragogy could be seen as the process of 'education' morphing into 'lifelong learning'. It is important to the theme of this book which suggests that, in the end, *learning must be a self-directed process* (Fig. 4.3).

Fig. 4.3 Post-compulsory education: specialisation of schools, Amos sports college

References

ABS. (2017). *Australian Bureau of Statistics, Religion in Australia.* www.abs.gov.au. Accessed 17 May 2017.

Biesta, G., & Tröhler, D. (2008). Introduction: George Herbert Mead and the development of a social conception of education. In G. H. Mead, G. Biesta, & D. Tröhler (Eds.), *The philosophy of education.* London: Paradigm Publishers.

Blake, W. (1808). *Milton: A poem.*

Dahlin, B. (2006). *Education, history and be(com)ing human: Two essays in philosophy and education.* Karlstad: Karlstad University.

Danner, H. (1994). Bildung: A basic term of German education. *Educational Sciences,* 9/1994.

Edwards, R. D. (2006). *Patrick Pearse: The triumph of failure.* Dublin: Irish Academic Press.

Foster, R. F. (1989). *Modern Ireland 1600–1972.* New York: Penguin.

Gidley, J. (2016). *Postformal education: A philosophy for complex futures.* Switzerland: Springer.

Konrad, F.-M. (2012). Wilhelm von Humboldt's contribution to a theory of Bildung. In P. Siljander, A. Kivela, & A. Sutinen (Eds.), *Theories of Bildung and growth: Connections and controversies between continental educational thinking and American pragmatism* (pp. 107–124). Rotterdam: Sense Publishers.

Merriam, S. (2001). Andragogy and self-directed learning: Pillars of adult learning theory. *New Directions for Adult and Continuing Education, 2001*(89), 3–13.

Neill, A. S. (1960). *Summerhill: A radical approach to childrearing.* Middlesex: Penguin Books.

Oltermann, P. (2016, July 1). No grades, no timetable: Berlin school turns teaching upside down. *The Guardian*, www.theguardian.com/world/2016/jul/01/no-grades-no-timetable-berlin-school. Accessed 22 Aug 2016.

Pidd, H. (2017, March 30). Schoolchildren in northern England falling behind south. *The Guardian.*

Rebanks, J. (2016). *The shepherd's life: A tale of the Lake District.* London: Penguin.

Reid, A. (2017). *Public education in South Australia.* Adelaide: SA Department of Education and Child Development.

Ryan, S. M. J. (2009). *Report of the Commission to inquire into child abuse* (Vol. 1). Dublin: CICA.

Schratzenstaller, A. (2010). The classroom of the past. Chapter 2, In K. Mäkitalo-Siegl, J. Zottman, F. Kaplan, & F. Fischer (Eds.), *Classroom of the future: Orchestrating collaborative spaces.* Rotterdam: Sense Publishers.

Siljander, P., Kivelä, A., & Sutinen, A. (2012). *Theories of Bildung and growth: Connections and controversies between continental educational thinking and American pragmatism.* Rotterdam: Sense Publishers.

UNESCO. (2015). *Education for all 2000–2015: Achievements and challenges.* Paris: UNESCO.

5

School: Rhetoric, Reality, and Revisionism

In this chapter I compare the rhetoric of school with the reality of what children experience, then query how, why, when, and where we educate our children, arguing that school choice should be an informed decision but has become an emotionally charged and hotly debated issue in a commodified educational marketplace. The massification and marketisation of education are examined in the light of such trends as globalisation and the Global Education Reform Movement (GERM), accountability standards for teachers, and a curriculum focused on narrowly defined vocational outcomes. Responses to these trends are examined, including the alternative view that 'It takes a whole village to raise a child'. How do we understand and work within these opposing positions in the twenty-first century?

5.1   Schools as Places and Spaces

The physical manifestation of 'the school' as a building or structure looms large in the history and mythology of schooling and has a profound effect on the teaching-learning relationship as well as the socialisation of the occupants.

© The Author(s) 2018
T. Stehlik, *Educational Philosophy for 21st Century Teachers*,
https://doi.org/10.1007/978-3-319-75969-2_5

> The school we go to is called Burnham High School. It's recently built, oblong in shape, flat-roofed, undecorated, unrevealing, sort of like a factory. It's the latest thing in modern architecture. (Atwood 1988: 218)

Margaret Atwood's description of a Canadian high school from the early 1950s in her novel *Cat's Eye* (1988) gives a classic visual image of the physical reality of post-World War II universal mass education; the bland building that resembles a factory where education has become a commodified product, just another outcome of modernism and suburban planning. This bricks-and-mortar reality can be seen repeated endlessly in the planning and architecture of not only Commonwealth and other 'western' countries, but in Eastern Europe too: in Russia, for example, schools were so numerously mass-produced on an industrial scale that they are still designated only by a number, not even by a name.

In Atwood's novel, the brutal blandness of the school's façade only serves as an allegory for what actually goes on inside its walls. The main character Elaine experiences all of the horrors that school in the 1950s could deliver: sadistic and cruel teachers, discrimination by gender, corporal punishment, organised bullying by other girls, loneliness, fear, insecurity, and desperate attempts to fit in and appear 'normal', eventually leading to self-harm. This is fiction but it is based on fact, and many people could relate to these experiences. And while it is hard to believe that we would put our children through this sort of thing in public, state-funded and government-sanctioned schools, the experiences of children in Catholic institutions are also unfortunately well known:

> From the age of ten, I was taught by the Christian Brothers: the carrot and stick method of education, but without the carrot. (McCarthy 1988)

It reminds me of that awful saying: 'Spare the rod and spoil the child'. I am sure that many children survived such schooling and possibly even enjoyed it, growing up to be happy and normal people; but from an educative point of view, what does this approach tell us about how we treated our children (and ourselves) in the past, and how we treat them now? On what educational qualifications and theories did such teachers base their practices of literally beating children into becoming submissive learners?

For those working under some form of religious dogma, one could say their philosophy of education was based on their faith. One would hope that things have improved in terms of pedagogy and methodology, and one of the aims of this book is to show that *trust* is emerging as a better educational paradigm than *faith*; but in terms of children experiencing bullying, it has probably gotten worse—and not only since the concept of cyberbullying has been identified as an unfortunate twenty-first-century phenomenon.

The other side of this coin which highlights the extremes that can be experienced in institutionalised education is the fact that schools can also be *places of refuge* for children coming from domestic family situations that are dysfunctional, abusive, and even dangerous. It is a sad fact that in many documented cases, children and young people are living in domestic environments that expose them to neglect, physical, psychological, and sexual abuse, drug abuse, hunger, deprivation, and situations of extreme squalor. This may be due to poverty, unemployment, overemployment, family breakdown, criminal activity, and just plain ignorance on the part of adults who are given the responsibility of looking after the wellbeing of the children in their care. For example, children could be disadvantaged simply by not having a quiet place or space to do their homework. In extreme cases, children may experience a home environment where they are not protected from strangers or relatives exposing them to alcohol, drugs, pornography, or inflicting abuse (Barnes 2016). For these children, school is a safe haven and a place where they might be fed and protected and even experience love. A close friend recalled to me her own upbringing in a dysfunctional family of seven children where the home environment was chaotic and disorganised, with the parents often absent or disengaged, while she and her siblings were just left to fend for themselves—even in finding something to eat and somewhere clean to sleep. After her oldest sister started school, she immediately began to play 'schools' at home with her younger siblings, who loved this game and played it continually as it provided some order and stability in their otherwise chaotic home life—even when their big sister always insisted on being the teacher and controlled them with a childish iron fist. (This sister grew up to become a teacher and then a school principal, possibly a common story!)

Child development and parenting practices will be addressed in Part III and teacher education in Part IV. In this chapter, I want to tease out where we have gotten to in the twenty-first century, given the weight of historical experience, theoretical experimentation, and cumulative everyday practices that continue to drive the global education project along like 'a giant oil tanker':

> In education, you can only create change from the bottom—if the orders come from the top, schools will resist. Ministries are like giant oil tankers: it takes a long time to turn them around. What we need is lots of little speedboats to show you can do things differently. (Oltermann 2016: 3)

Do we need to create change? In education, some things evolve as has been shown, while others have stayed remarkably the same since the concept of schooling began. Some of these changes have been positive, others have been driven by agendas that are perhaps outside the best interests of those for whom education is apparently for—current and future generations.

5.2   The Massification and Marketisation of Education

Globalisation is a phenomenon that Gert Biesta has defined as being "about the creation of interdependence and at the same time about the creation of new dependencies", further suggesting that it is "the contemporary face of colonialism" (2006: 104).

However, globalisation is nothing new. During the Roman Empire, humans were very mobile and established trading and migratory patterns along with the conquest and occupation of countries and regions in the known world at the time. We can see archaeological evidence of this with, for example, Syrian artefacts turning up in places like Bath in England, where the Romans established public baths which must have attracted tourists from all over Europe, North Africa, and the Middle East around 2000 years ago. The age of exploration and global navigation that took western civilisation to the Far East, the East Indies, the Americas, and eventually Australia also established the image we now take for granted of the earth as a sphere with a fragile surface containing the finite environments in which we now live, defined as continents, countries, nations, and oceans.

While the reality of our planet as a defined ecosystem has driven environmental awareness with local and global movements in conservation and sustainability increasingly recognising the fragility of this system over the last century, the image of the world as a whole and the human race as a global tribe has been brought into stark focus by technology. With a computer and a fast internet connection, one can cruise the globe in the comfort of one's living room simply by manipulating Google Earth. One can communicate with people on the other side of the world in real time via email, Skype, Facebook, Twitter, and a range of other ICTs (Information and Communication Technologies). International air travel has created the greatest and fastest mobility yet available to humans; on any given day there are between 1 and 2 million people up in the air flying in commercial, military, or private aircraft. Online media can broadcast news, information (and advertisements) in real time all over the world as it happens; so that whether we want to know or not, we are only too aware of what is happening in places far away from where we actually live. In fact, the 24-hour media cycle has contributed to the information society that we now live in, with a concomitant result of conflating and confusing information with knowledge (refer to the image in Chap. 2). Again, it is a matter of being able to discern between what we need to know and what may just be nice to know—as well as all the things we just don't even need or want to know!

This mobility across borders, communicating in cyberspace, being involved in virtual communities, in fact being a *global citizen,* has been characterised by what contemporary sociologist and philosopher Zygmunt Bauman has termed *liquid modernity.* Bauman (2012) uses the term to describe a modern way of life in which change is so rapid that social institutions which we have previously relied on to maintain a predictable and firm foundation no longer have time to 'solidify':

> The most successful people nowadays are flexible and rootless; they can live anywhere and believe anything…liquid modernity is a more or less unstoppable force—in part because capitalism and technology are unstoppable. (Rothman 2017: 48)

In the field of education, this liquid modernity can be seen in the massification, commodification, and commercialisation of education as a global economic phenomenon, what has in fact become known in general terms as the *knowledge industry*. In higher education, universities are now competing for market share in a global market that transcends borders, as exemplified by MOOCs (Massive Online Open Courses) that can be taken online from anywhere in the world and have seen institutions such as Melbourne and Harvard Universities enrolling literally millions of 'virtual' students in topics ranging from financial analysis to the French Revolution (www.edx.org/school/harvardx; www.unimelb.edu.au). In Australia, education has for a long time been one of the country's largest export 'products', at the time of writing coming fourth in export revenue after primary resources such as iron ore, coal, and natural gas (dfat.gov.au). This has occurred as a result of the targeted marketing of higher education to overseas countries, mainly from the South East Asian region, attracting a continual influx of international students who are paying high tuition fees as well as living and travel expenses to study in Australia.

As courses that are generally not accredited or assessed, MOOCs are a form of non-formal learning and could be seen as an example of 'Education for all' according to the UNESCO agenda discussed in the previous chapter. However, they also exemplify the notion of *massification*—which simply means delivering a service or product on a mass scale—as well as turning education into a *commodity* that can be commercialised and sold, resulting in the increasing need for educational institutions to market themselves aggressively, relying on status and prestige, often creating niche products in an attempt to carve out a distinct market edge, or even undercutting entry requirements and course fees. Massification also implies a transformation from an elite form of education to one that provides wider access to universities and colleges for more and more applicants, with the resulting credential overload and overcrowded labour market for the increasing number of university graduates as discussed in Chap. 3.

The blurring of commerce and higher education can be no better exemplified than in the phenomenon of the 'McDonald's Hamburger University', which by 2002 had produced over 70,000 graduates of *hamburgerology* who went on to work in outlets of the fast food chain that established the institution (Hayes and Wynyard 2002). This has led to the term the 'McDonaldisation of higher education', coined by George Ritzer in 1998 to refer to the general and pervasive trend for the rationalisation of university education according to commercial interests and the financial power and influence of consumer society.

School education has also experienced McDonaldisation. In America, this has now been branded as 'Pearsonisation' (Ravitch 2010) for the multinational company Pearson that owns papers like the *Financial Times* and respected textbook imprints like Addison-Wesley, Prentice Hall, and Longman, and which, from being the world's largest education publisher, has since moved aggressively into the education provision market, in particular online testing.

> Today standardized testing seems to many to have become the goal of education—as embodied in the [American] No Child Left Behind program and the new Common Core standards—rather than a means of implementing it. Add in the increased use of technology to teach students, government cutbacks, and the private-sector-funded reform movement, and companies have more clout than ever when it comes to what and how kids are taught. (Reingold 2015)

Pearson is one of the largest and most visible of those companies, and its perceived control over school education has received strong criticism from parents, principals, and teachers, particularly in America where Pearson now controls much of the process of high-stakes testing (60% of the market in 2015) and has plans to own and operate its own education institutions. Again, it is being sold as an inevitable outcome of globalisation, and not just a corporate grab for profits in an emerging online education market, according to Pearson's chief education advisor, Michael Barber:

> "It's not remotely true to say we are setting the global standards," he says. "What is happening is a global economy and technological change and that affects every walk of life. It's not caused by Pearson. It's caused by globalization. Students are going to be part of a global labor market." (Cited in Reingold 2015)

A similar trend has been observed in the United Kingdom, where the policy response to globalisation and international comparisons of student performance led to the Blair Labour government advocating in the late 1990s for the creation of 'Academy Schools'. These schools are a kind of public/private partnership. Academies are independent, state-funded schools which receive funding directly from central government, rather than through a local authority, but the big difference is that they are allowed to be run by charitable bodies known as 'academy trusts'. The trend towards Academy Schools in the United Kingdom has snowballed under subsequent conservative governments, so that at the time of writing 60% of secondary schools and 12% of primary schools are now academies (bbc. com). So far they have achieved mixed results, but much of the criticism is based on concern about the extent of control over schools by interest groups who qualify for charitable trust status—such as evangelical Christian groups—and the growth of 'academy chains' in which schooling has become a sort of franchise for particularly large and ambitious providers.

Microsoft Corporation has also stepped into the global education business. "Microsoft has been working with schools across the globe for the past decade", with some newly established schools no longer using textbooks in favour of all resources and content created in a virtual learning environment "with all students and teachers using Microsoft Surface devices" (Irish Times 2017: 6). The perceived benefits of a virtual learning environment are that parents can also log in to the system, and that by learning this way the students are being prepared for careers that 'don't exist yet'. These are possibly good things but are as yet untested and assumed and will require not only ongoing evaluation to determine if this is the right track to take education in the future but also imply that education of the future will undoubtedly look very different.

5.3   The Global Education Reform Movement

Policy is multidimensional and multilayered and occurs at multiple sites. Globalised discourses and agenda setting and policy pressures now emerge from beyond the nation … Global agents and agencies, both public and private, are now often involved in the gestation and establishment of education policy agendas. (Rizvi and Lingard 2010: 14–15)

All of these trends related to the globalised influence on education including privatisation, massification, and marketisation can be summarised and explained by what has been termed the *Global Education Reform Movement* by the Finnish educator Pasi Sahlberg, with the intentional acronym of *GERM* (Sahlberg 2012). This movement, which has gained traction and momentum since the late 1980s, parallels other developments in politics and policies such as economic rationalism and neo-liberal agendas which have laid the ground for such concepts as McDonaldisation and Pearsonisation to emerge. The Global Education Reform Movement can be defined in terms of five key characteristics which have consistently taken hold in education policy and practice in western capitalist societies.

These five globally common features are:

1. *Standardisation of education*—Based on measurable outcomes; setting performance standards for schools, teachers, and students; test-based accountability
2. *Focus on core subjects*—Such as literacy and numeracy and STEM (science, technology, engineering, and maths) at the expense of subjects which become marginalised, for example, social studies, arts, and music
3. *Low-risk ways to reach learning goals*—Minimising experimentation, creativity, and alternative pedagogies in teaching and learning methodologies, with a defined focus on 'guaranteed content'
4. *Corporate management models to drive improvement*—Policies and ideas borrowed from the business world, including managerialism, key performance indicators, accountability requirements, and so on
5. *Test-based accountability policies*—School performance closely tied to processes of accrediting, inspecting, and rewarding or punishing schools and teachers, based on high-stakes testing and national and international comparative data (Sahlberg 2012)

Processes that drive the GERM agenda include PISA, the Program for International Student Assessment, a triennial international survey which aims to evaluate education systems worldwide by testing the skills and knowledge of 15-year-old school students living in countries that are part of the OECD (Organisation for Economic Co-operation and Development). To date, students representing more than 70 economies have participated in the assessment, with the most recent round occurring in 2015 (oecd.org). Countries and schooling systems can compare their results across a range of literacy and numeracy indicators, and as never before in the history of education, countries like Australia can compare their students' achievements with countries like Singapore and Finland, which, although having completely different education systems, cultures, and even languages, are held up as benchmarks as if there was a level international playing field. Other international comparative surveys of educational achievement include TIMSS (Trends in International Mathematics and Science Study) and PIRLS (Progress in International Reading Study).

To further unpack the GERM agenda, the five features are now discussed in more detail, with acknowledgement to Pasi Sahlberg (2012).

1. *Standardisation of education*

- Outcomes-based education reform became popular in the 1980s, followed by standards-based education policies in the 1990s, initially within Anglo-Saxon countries
- These reforms, quite correctly, shifted the focus of attention to educational outcomes, that is, student learning and school performance
- Consequently, a widely accepted—and generally unquestioned—belief among policy makers and education reformers is that setting clear and sufficiently high performance standards for schools, teachers, and students will necessarily improve the quality of expected outcomes
- Enforcement of external testing and evaluation systems to assess how well these standards have been attained emerged originally from standards-oriented education policies
- Since the late 1980s centrally prescribed curricula, with detailed and often ambitious performance targets, frequent testing of students and teachers, and test-based accountability have characterised

a homogenisation of education policies worldwide, promising standardised solutions at increasingly lower cost for those desiring to improve school quality and effectiveness

2. *Focus on core subjects*

- Basic student knowledge and skills in reading, writing, and maths are elevated as prime targets and indices of education reforms
- As a consequence of accepting international student assessment surveys, such as PISA, TIMSS, and PIRLS as criteria of good educational performance, reading and mathematical and scientific literacy have now become the main determinants of perceived success or failure of pupils, teachers, schools, and entire education systems
- This is happening at the expense of social studies, arts, music, and physical education that are diminishing in many school curricula

3. *The search for low-risk ways to reach learning goals*

- This minimises experimentation, reduces use of alternative pedagogical approaches, and limits creativity and risk-taking in schools and classrooms
- Research on education systems that have adopted policies emphasising achievement of pre-determined standards and prioritised core subjects suggests that teaching and learning are narrower and teachers focus on 'guaranteed content' to best prepare their students for tests
- The higher the test-result stakes, the lower the degree of freedom in experimentation and risk-taking in classroom learning

4. *The use of corporate management models as a main driver of improvement*

- Educational policies and ideas are often borrowed from the business world, and often motivated by national hegemony and economic profit, rather than by moral goals of human development

- Faith in educational change through innovations bought and sold from outside the system undermines two important elements of successful educational change:

  – First, it often limits the role of national policy development and enhancement of an education system's own capabilities to maintain renewal
  – Second, it paralyses teachers' and schools' attempts to learn from the past and also to learn from each other

5. *Test-based accountability policies for schools*

  - School performance—especially raising student achievement—is closely tied to processes of accrediting, promoting, inspecting, and, ultimately, rewarding or punishing schools and teachers
  - Success or failure of schools and teachers is often determined by standardised tests and external teacher evaluations that devote attention to limited aspects of schooling, such as student achievement in mathematical and reading literacy, exit examination results, or intended teacher classroom behaviour

5.4   Responses to GERM

In Australia, one of the most visible and controversial responses to this global trend is the introduction of national high-stakes testing for all Australian school students: the National Assessment Program—Literacy and Numeracy or NAPLAN. Since 2008, students in Years 3, 5, 7, and 9 are assessed annually via a series of tests developed by an independent statutory body specifically set up to manage this process—the Australian Curriculum, Assessment and Reporting Authority (ACARA).

> NAPLAN tests the sorts of skills that are essential for every child to progress through school and life, such as reading, writing, spelling and numeracy. (ACARA 2017)

At the same time, the federal government set up a system whereby the results of the NAPLAN tests would be required by all schools to be made publicly available on a website entitled 'My School'. This website also contains detailed information of school finances, student characteristics, staffing, and other quite confidential information which is readily available to anyone able to log on (http://www.myschool.edu.au/).

The result of all this has been that Australian schools are now exposed 'warts and all' to scrutiny not only by government inspectors but by parents who are making choices about schools, producing a sort of leagues table where the 'high performing schools' (according to NAPLAN results) are able to market themselves as academic success stories at the expense of those which do not perform so well, for a range of reasons. Of course the NAPLAN is a blunt instrument and does not measure other important considerations like student wellbeing, the health of the school community, or successes in other not-so-academic areas (arts, music, sports, and so on). In fact, the test creates so much stress for children that it can negatively impact on their wellbeing. Teachers and principals realise that so much is at stake that they also stress about their schools' performance and how they will be judged on the My School data. Instances of manipulating test scores to try and make them look better have been reported, but the main criticism of mandatory testing like NAPLAN is that teachers 'teach to the test', with the analogy of the *tail wagging the dog* in terms of curriculum delivery.

A review of NAPLAN after its first four years of implementation found a number of problems with the approach (Polesel et al. 2012):

- NAPLAN data is not a reliable measure of a school's performance, as it is only a measure of performance at the time of testing
- Due to the five-month lag between testing and the receipt of results, data cannot be used as a diagnostic tool to improve student performance until the following year
- Teachers may focus on tested areas, perhaps reducing the time spent on curriculum areas not tested
- The publishing of testing data puts pressure on schools to perform—in extreme cases, meaning that schools may deter low-performing students from sitting the test

Apart from the dubious effects on teaching and learning, the other outcome from the introduction of responses to the GERM such as

NAPLAN and My School has been the reality that public as well as private schools are now competing with each other in an open and aggressive education market.

In the United States, a similar response saw the George W. Bush administration's *No Child Left Behind Act* introduced in 2001. This required districts to measure student and school progress through increased testing. "The viewpoint was clear: Schools were failing their students, and the best way to improve was to understand—and measure—what teachers and students were getting wrong" (Reingold 2015: 1). The view that 'schools were failing their students' also put the spotlight (or blowtorch) onto teachers, with 'teacher quality' now becoming an issue and another area of reactive policy with consequences for teacher training programs, national teaching standards, and teacher performance measures.

It was not surprising then that also in 2001, the Australian Institute for Teaching and School Leadership (AITSL) was set up by the federal government as a body charged with the oversight of developing and administering standards for teachers and school leaders as a response to concerns about 'teacher quality'. As a result, all teachers in Australia, whether public, private, pre-service, or in-service, are now accountable to the *Australian Professional Standards for Teachers* (https://www.aitsl.edu.au/). There are seven standards in three domains:

Domains of teaching	Standards
Professional knowledge	1. Know students and how they learn
	2. Know the content and how to teach it
Professional practice	3. Plan for and implement effective teaching and learning
	4. Create and maintain supportive and safe learning environments
	5. Assess, provide feedback, and report on student learning
Professional engagement	6. Engage in professional learning
	7. Engage professionally with colleagues, parents/carers, and the community

These accountability requirements include the need for all teachers to be annually assessed against the standards by their principal or school manager, and to demonstrate that they have undertaken a certain prescribed amount of approved professional development. Principals in turn can be assessed and appraised against the *Australian Professional Standards for Principals*, also developed and administered by AITSL. As a clear example of the standardisation of education under the GERM agenda, the way in which these developments are playing out will be discussed in more detail in Part IV.

Finland is a nation that has been able to resist succumbing to such accountability agendas, yet retain a very high performing education system that has become the envy of other western countries. According to Sahlberg, it appears that:

> …the Finnish education system has remained quite uninfected to viruses of what is often called the **global education reform movement** or GERM. And the reason for that is clear: professional strength and moral health of Finnish schools. (Sahlberg 2012)

What Sahlberg means by *professional strength* and *moral health* is outlined in some detail in the case study of Finland in Chap. 10, but suffice to say that high-stakes testing is voluntary not compulsory, teachers and principals are not measured against performance standards, with high academic outcomes resulting from a central focus on student wellbeing in all pedagogical activity rather than the reverse approach of 'teaching to the test'. What Finland has achieved is equality of educational opportunity across the country, with all schools being fully funded and supported so that "parents don't have to shop around for schools…they are all the same" (Finnish teacher cited in Moore 2015).

5.5   It Takes a Whole Village to Raise a Child

In concluding this section on 'schooling vs education', the story of Finland is appropriate in leading into a consideration of how schools operate within and are influenced by the community in which they are located, since another 'secret' to the Finnish success story is that the whole country, culture, and society is united in supporting education as the key to developing a modern civil society in which both the individual *and* the community benefit.

The word *community* implies a group that has something in *common*. It is a widely used—and often abused—term and could apply to humans, plants, animals, or insects, in contexts that are social, geographical, eco-logical, and even virtual. We talk about the community in which we live as somehow being more immediate and localised than the *society* in which we live. Yet we may also be members of a work community, a sporting community, a musical community, or an online community—all outside the immediate geographical area where we live. We speak of having a sense of community, feeling part of a community, of community values, of communal interests and the common good. Community permeates our lives:

> We are fortunate, because adults are community-forming beings. Our capacity to create social coherence is always there. We need community to find security, identity, shared values and people who care about us and about whom we care. (Wlodkowski 1999: 91)

Humans needing to find security and identity in community groups can be traced back to earlier times, when survival depended on coopera-tion and organisation in tribal or kinship groups, and being ostracised or excluded from the community meant certain death. Even now, we can see how social exclusion can lead to a struggle for survival in the modern world and *social inclusion* has become a policy agenda for some govern-ments. The notion of *individualism* however is a relatively recent histori-cal construct.

The concept of individuality can be considered to be culturally con-structed and not an absolute state, having evolved in western civilisation to the point where modern society is more than ever geared towards meeting the rights of the individual, in contrast to feudal society, for example, where the masses were not considered to be individuals in con-trol of their own destiny. In medieval times, institutions such as the church, the state, or the monarchy had absolute power over individuals whose destinies were entirely determined by limitations imposed by class structures and accidents of birth.

The rise of individualism in the twentieth century can be seen in the development of a competitive free market economy, broadcast media, the cult of the personality, the notion of everyone experiencing '15 minutes of fame', the idea of the 'star' (e.g. rock star, film star), concepts such as the tall poppy, the overachiever, the genius, and so on. Most recently, social media truly has enabled global exposure for anyone with a computer, iPhone, or tablet to have their own profile or blog with any number of 'followers' or 'friends' in a virtual community. Our identities, therefore, are also not absolute but established in relation to significant others and our various roles as parent, sibling, child, friend, worker, teacher, learner, citizen….all defined by some form of community, whether they are intentional, random, determined by birth or joined by choice.

The idea of *schools as communities* emerged in the 1970s when, according to Merz and Furman, a gradual shift in thinking occurred in relation to schools as communities rather than as bureaucratic organisations, with more of a focus on relationships and values as well as academic outcomes and structured learning, or what could be generalised as "a sense of community" about the school (1997: 68). To extrapolate, the concepts of *school* and of *community* can be defined in terms of social relationships, roles, and situations as much as by organisational frameworks, physical boundaries, and hierarchical structures. The functional and brutalist architecture of the school described in the quote that opens this chapter reinforces the 'bricks and mortar' image that we might have when the word *school* is mentioned. However, the example of the Irish hedge schools mentioned in the previous chapter shows that school can occur anywhere, even in the open air as long as the tenacity and desire are there for teaching and learning.

A school therefore could also refer to the *idea* of a school—the non-physical aspects including the people, the ethos, and the philosophy of the school. For example, when we say that 'the Australian artist Tom Roberts was a member of the Heidelberg School', we are referring to an ideated construct, a movement in art that can be represented as a *school of thought* or a *school of practice;* not a physical edifice. When we refer to any organisation, we often think in terms of its physical presence or spatial aspects, but it is the *people* who actually make up the organisation. 'Organisation' really means people coming together to organise themselves around a common interest or endeavour.

As organisations, schools are in danger of being viewed and managed as corporate bureaucratic entities, as if education were a commodity or product, according to trends identified in the GERM agenda outlined above. It is more important than ever then, to keep the image of schools as communities alive. Diane Ravitch, the American educator and former Assistant Secretary of Education who became a vocal critic of the US *No Child Left Behind* agenda in her book *The Death and Life of the Great American School System* (2010), believes that standardised testing and the marketing of education create unhealthy competition between schools.

"Schools operate fundamentally—or should operate—like families," author Diane Ravitch said in a Morning Edition interview. "The fundamental principle by which education proceeds is collaboration". (Inskeep 2010)

The image of schools operating like families is an attractive one, especially if we believe that the values and beliefs that we would want to develop in our families of origin should align with those of the schools our children attend. As shown in the previous chapter, the gap between home and school can still be unfortunately wide. However, taking a bigger picture view, if we consider that home and school are both part of the wider community in which children live, then this leads to the realisation that a child's education consists of a lot more than what they might experience at school.

Lo Shan (2000) notes that this has both positive and negative aspects:

The most illuminating and the most troubling Platonic lesson is that a well-formed education involves nothing less than a well-formed *politeia*. ("It takes a whole village to raise a child"). If education is to promote *eudaimonia*, if it is to form sound habits of perception and thought, desire and action, it encompasses the smallest details of the political system. In short, the ethos and *nomoi* of a polity, its economic and family arrangements, its popular arts and even its architecture are the fundamental educators of the city. (LoShan 2000: 45)

The Greek word *politeia* incorporates the notions of citizenship, a form of government, and the constitution of a polis, or state. *Eudaimonia* is a wonderful word that translates as wellbeing, having a good spirit, and general human flourishing. *Nomoi* translates as laws, customs, or what we might now understand as norms. So the Platonic lesson is that in order to promote wellbeing in our children and society, the whole state or polis and the norms of society are involved in the education process, proving a context and environment which cannot be discounted in their potential overt and covert influences. That art and architecture are considered just as important as economic arrangements reinforces the discussion in Chap. 2 around the importance of *aesthetics* in education. Therefore, the 'whole village' is part of the picture of a child's education, or putting it another way: the community in which the child, the home, and the school exist.

While there are great examples of how this works in practice, some of which will be presented on the case studies in Part V, the 'troubling' aspect of it can be illustrated by the trends discussed in this chapter, which reinforce the fact that the involvement of the state in education can be overdone to the point of legislative control over social institutions and practices such as schools, governed by rigid and extensive rules and regulations. As Dahlin notes, "it is not so much 'the smallest details of the political system' that is of crucial importance as the basic constitutional laws" (2006: 65). Aristotle identified that *the moral condition of a society depended on a good constitution*, and there is no reason to think this does not hold true for modern society as it did for the Ancient Greek republic. It therefore suggests that in the bigger picture of the education movement, we could take a leaf from the conservation movement in *thinking globally and acting locally*: to be aware of global trends but also work to ensure the constitutional state in which we live supports and encourages *Eudaimonia*. The task for us all will be to address the question: *What is my village?*

This chapter concludes the section that discusses *schooling* as a distinct and historical form of *education*, addressing the overall question that considers the present and the future in the light of the past: *How have we applied what we have learned from history?* Chapters 6 and 7 in the following section now focus on the education and development of those members of society who have the most to gain or lose from education and schooling while at the same time being the most disempowered in terms of being able to make decisions about what their education and schooling look like—our children.

References

ACARA. (2017). https://www.acara.edu.au/. Accessed 19 May 2017.

Atwood, M. (1988). *Cat's eye*. New York: Doubleday.

Barnes, J. (2016). *Working class boy*. Sydney: Harper Collins.

Bauman, Z. (2012). *Liquid modernity*. Cambridge: Polity Press.

Biesta, G. (2006). *Beyond learning: Democratic education for a human future*. London: Paradigm Publishers.

Dahlin, B. (2006). *Education, history and be(com)ing human: Two essays in philosophy and education*. Karlstad: Karlstad University.

Hayes, D., & Wynyard, R. (2002). *The McDonaldization of higher education*. London: Sage.

Inskeep, S. (2010). Former 'No Child Left Behind' advocate turns critic. http://www.npr.org/templates/story/story.php?storyId=124209100. Accessed 20 May 2017.

Irish Times. (2017, March 30). Tablets help school cure problem of rote learning. *The Irish Times, Business Technology and Innovation*.

Lo Shan, Z. (2000). 'Plato's counsel on education', chapter 3. In A. Oksenberg Rorty (Ed.), *Philosophers on education, historical perspectives*. London/New York: Routledge.

McCarthy, P. (1988). *McCarthy's bar: A journey of discovery in Ireland*. London: Hodder & Stoughton.

Merz, C., & Furman, G. (1997). *Community and schools: Promise and paradox*. New York: Teachers College Press.

Moore, M. (2015). *Where to invade next*. IMG Films.

Oltermann, P. (2016, July 1). No grades, no timetable: Berlin school turns teaching upside down. *The Guardian*, www.theguardian.com/world/2016/jul/01/no-grades-no-timetable-berlin-school. Accessed 22 Aug 2016.

Polesel, J., Dulfer, N., & Turnbull, M. (2012). *The experience of education: The impacts of high stakes testing on school students on their families: Literature review*. Sydney: University of Sydney Whitlam Institute.

Ravitch, D. (2010). *The death and life of the Great American School System: How testing and choice are undermining education*. New York: Basic Books.

Reingold, J. (2015). *Everybody hates Pearson*. Fortune. http://fortune.com/2015/01/21/everybody-hates-pearson/. Accessed 16 May 2017.

Rizvi, F., & Lingard, B. (2010). *Globalising education policy*. Oxon: Routledge.

Rothman, J. (2017, May 1). The seeker. *The New York Times*, pp. 46–55.

Sahlberg, P. (2012). https://pasisahlberg.com/. Accessed 17 May 2017.

Wlodkowski, R. (1999). *Enhancing adult motivation to learn*. San Francisco: Jossey Bass.

Part III

The Kingdom of Childhood

6

Development over the Life Span

Paedology: *The study of the character, growth, and development of children*
Dictionary.com

This chapter provides an overview of development over the life span, with reference to key educational theorists whose work has influenced contemporary thinking and practice around human physical, mental, emotional and spiritual development. It refers to the early work of Friedrich Froebel who recognised that *play is a child's work*, and to the work of Jean Piaget and Rudolf Steiner in child development and human development. The debate about the influence of nature vs nurture in child development is examined with reference to the literature on 'wild children'.

6.1   The Kingdom of Childhood

The term 'Kingdom of Childhood' which is the overarching theme of Part III has been deliberately taken from the work of Rudolf Steiner, specifically his lectures on education and child development which were

© The Author(s) 2018
T. Stehlik, *Educational Philosophy for 21st Century Teachers*,
https://doi.org/10.1007/978-3-319-75969-2_6

given in England in 1924 and subsequently published under that title (Steiner 1982). The term provides a strong picture of that precious and special time in an individual's life when the world is new and the realities and responsibilities of 'grown up' life are still a long way off. In recognising this 'kingdom' as a special place and time that needs to be respected, protected, and nourished, several important consequences become apparent: that forcing formal instruction too early can be damaging to a child's development, that what occurs in the early years can manifest later in adult life in both positive and negative ways, and that the years before a child even experiences any formal schooling will be crucial to their socialisation and development as an individual. It is no wonder that the period from birth to seven or eight years of age is referred to by Steiner Early Childhood Educators as *the vital years*.

Steiner gave a picture of the child *incarnating* into the physical world in a gradual process that recognises the child as a threefold human being—body, soul, and spirit. The physical *body* reflects an earthly stream in terms of the laws of biology and heredity—the genetic history the child inherits from its parents. The *spirit* is subject to the laws of reincarnation and karma and represents a cosmic stream which presumes that the individual not only has a spiritual history which it brings with it to its earthly incarnation, but will have a future spiritual potential. The *soul* then is the expression of the meeting of these two streams in the present, the higher self and the physical self which create an individual identity, or psyche (remember, psyche = Greek for soul). While the concept of destiny is acknowledged in this view, past lives plus spiritual potential create a certain choice or freedom in the present. Teachers are concerned with the soul of a child in this sense of the word, but must recognise and work with the fact that each child has a spiritual history and that very young children are still incarnating until about their third year.

This view of the child as a being that incorporates a cosmic history was not new—in fact Steiner acknowledged that this was part of the classical Greek ideal of education:

Up to the seventh year of life, the Greek child was brought up at home. Public education was concerned with children only after the age of seven. They were brought up at home, where the women lived in seclusion, apart from the ordinary pursuits of social life, which were an affair of the men. This in itself confirms a truth of education, without knowledge of which one cannot really educate or teach, for the seventh year of life is an all-important period of childhood. (Steiner 1981: 54)

The all-important characteristic of the seventh year that Steiner was referring to is the change of teeth. During the sixth year of life, the nature-forces of growth which replace infant teeth with adult teeth culminate with an incarnation process that is significant, since this happens only once in our lives, around the seventh year (the appearance of wisdom teeth is an exception!).

> What did the Greek see in the little child from birth to the time of the change of teeth? A being sent down to earth from spiritual heights! He saw in man a being who had lived in a spiritual world before earthly life. And as he observed the child he tried to discover whether its body was rightly expressing the divine life of pre-earthly existence. It was of importance for the Greek that in the child up to the seventh year he should recognise that a physical body is here enclosing a spiritual being who has descended. (Steiner 1981: 56–57)

When applied to an educational philosophy, this creates a picture of the child as an "unfolding personality" who "requires nourishing by caring adults" (Miller 1997: 5), according to certain pre-destined rhythms and patterns. While this is important for teachers, it can also be a revelation for parents, particularly for the nursing mother to realise that her infant's soul has a 'dreamlike consciousness' which is still in the realm of the angels and therefore should be regarded with reverence. However, the most important aspect of child development, both from a parenting and teaching point of view, is the recognition of the rhythmic progression of the unfolding soul in accord with the "rhythmic processes of the universe" (Childs 1991: 39), and the importance of understanding the appropriate ways of responding to a child's needs at particular stages in this process.

This philosophical idea holds that as we observe children going through the bodily phases of growth from newborn, to infant, to toddler, and so on, at the same time they are experiencing soul development and changes in their consciousness. Consistent with a biological science view that the body cells are 'replaced' every seven years, a way of mapping and understanding this developmental process in consciousness can also be viewed as a seven-year cyclical pattern. The first seven years are characterised by rapid growth of the physical body and learning by imitation and play, in which the child largely relates to the world through its *will*. Around the age of six or seven, the change from milk teeth to adult teeth signifies a change in consciousness that goes beyond dependence on immediate experience to an ability to create mental pictures and to interpret concepts through *feeling*. This phase continues until the next great physical change, the onset of puberty around the age of 13–14 when a capacity for abstract *thinking* and an ability to make meaningful judgements unfolds, leading up to the full development of the individual ego by the age of 21. These first three phases can therefore characterised by the progressive development of the three 'soul forces'—*willing*, *feeling*, and *thinking* (Easton 1997; Childs 1991; Ruenzel 1995).

These seven-yearly milestones continue throughout life and can similarly be mapped against phases of development in adult life that coincide with major life transitions. For example, 'coming of age' is associated with the age of 21 in many societies, not coincidentally also the age at which the physical body is deemed to be anatomically fully formed. The age of 28 is associated astrologically with the 'Saturn return' experience, when the planet Saturn returns to the position it occupied in the heavens at birth, a time in an individual's life often characterised by an emotional or spiritual upheaval such as a relationship, career, or life change. The ages of 42 and 56 are also significant in similar ways, although all of these should be seen as "milestones, averages, ideal distances around which individual development moves" (Lievegoed 1993: 42), and not absolute fixed dates.

In the book *Phases* (1993), Bernard Lievegoed examines in some detail the literature on the division of human life into phases, also noting that the seven-year cycle schema which is fundamental to Steiner's educational philosophy originated in classical Greek times. He is careful to make the point that while it may be apparent that an individual develops through clearly definable phases of life such as childhood to adolescence, adolescence to adulthood, and so on, the transition from each change is gradual and will differ according to social and environmental contexts. At one end of this interpretation of the process of gradual change is the view that the course of life evolves in a continually unfolding series of developments in an almost seamless way, making the notion of separate phases redundant. A more critical view suggests that "the concept of self-development over the life course, with its putative phases and stages of development, is itself a social construct", and that individuals actually live out expectations placed upon them at particular ages and phases in a predictable fashion (Tennant and Pogson 1995: 4).

Another approach to contextualising personal identity as a social construction is the understanding of development as an ongoing dialectical process, in which "the person is construed as a changing person in a changing world", and is not only created by the society in which they live but also contributes to its creation (Tennant 1997: 54). Tennant further suggests that a view of the life course as evolving in predictable stages also presumes movement towards some end goal, whereas change can be irregular and unpredictable and does not necessarily imply improvement or progression to higher levels of development.

Linked to this is the recognition that the meaning of the word *development* itself can also be contested, as a social as well as a psychological construct. That is, what it means to be 'developed' may differ according to whose interests are being served, much the same way as the distinction between 'developed' and 'developing' countries is based on a western capitalist perspective of economic growth, which tends to devalue and ignore cultural and spiritual development. Therefore, development, as applied here to the individual, is distinguished from *change*, a term which merely signifies that nothing is static, and *growth* which describes a quantitative increase in size or number. Development is defined as "growth in which structural changes occur at critical points throughout the system" (Lievegoed 1993: 18).

It follows then that for the individual, these structural changes at critical points are more than just physical. While physical changes can be an indicator of critical points of development, such as the change of teeth in the developing child, it is self-evident that biological development is only one aspect of human development. Based on the previously discussed picture of the threefold nature of the human being as body, soul, and

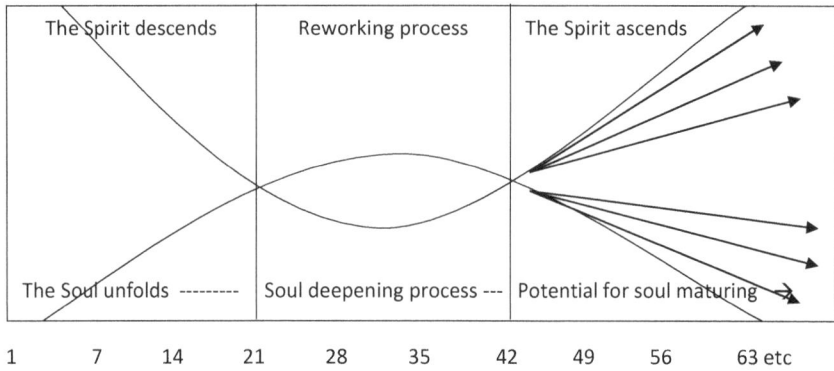

Fig. 6.1 The threefold development of life over seven-year cycles

spirit, Lievegoed (1991, 1993) clearly identifies three human development patterns in the course of the life span—biological development, psychological development, and spiritual development. This schema is represented in Fig. 6.1 and overlaid over the seven-year cycles. The diagram represents this linear model of development as 21-year phases and shows how in the first 21 years the body is growing up while the spirit is descending or 'incarnating', while the soul, which represents the meeting of these earthly and cosmic streams, is unfolding. In the second 21-year phase, the body has reached maturity and is physically 'stable', giving the opportunity for 'true psychological development' or soul deepening. Around the age of 42, when physical-biological development decreases, soul-spiritual development may become the focus of an individual's personal life journey.

An archetypal illustration of this spiritual searching is the metaphor of the Holy Grail, which has been recognised as representing the universal search for meaning in the context of western culture. This eleventh-century narrative story of Parsifal was considered by the psychologist Carl Jung to be an important allegorical myth, informing the psychological development of western consciousness in the past millennium with symbolism and archetypes which can be related to the individual's quest for knowledge, understanding, and identity. The young hero of the story is confronted with the question of what it means to 'know thyself' (Von Eschenbach 1980).

Lievegoed goes on to suggest that this ongoing development of the spirit (which he also terms the 'mind' and equates with the Jungian notion of the higher ego) occurs in the polarity between extroversion and introversion, manifested in creativity and wisdom. Creativity represents the outward expression of the ego and a person's individuality, and plays a major role in spiritual development during youth and the expansive period of adulthood. He also suggests that wisdom does come with age, from being able to reflect and learn from life, and characterises such development in the later period of life:

> Wisdom is based on *inspiration*, and inspiration, literally, means 'breathing in'. Wisdom is breathing in, filling oneself with spirit, with norms and values, with meaning, with humanity. (Lievegoed 1993: 24, original emphasis)

This analogy of the rhythm of breathing, of expiration and inspiration, is a powerful metaphor for the balancing forces of earthly and cosmic development and is representative not only of the development of an individual but of organisations, communities, and humanity in general. It is a fundamental natural process that can be observed in the rhythm of the seasons in a literally global sense; for example, mid-winter can be seen as the deepest in-breath of the earth, while mid-summer is conversely the extent of nature's out-breathing. In his 1922 book *The Aims of Education*, Alfred Whitehead also stressed the importance of the cyclical, rhythmic nature of education:

> There are also subtler periods of mental growth, with their cyclical recurrences, yet always different as we pass from cycle to cycle, though the subordinate stages are reproduced in each cycle. That is why I have chosen the term 'rhythmic' as meaning essentially the conveyance of difference within a framework of repetition. Lack of attention to the rhythm and character of mental growth is a main source of wooden futility in education. (Whitehead 1922: 226)

A fundamental aspect of this theory of the unfolding being is the significance of the effects of education and upbringing on an individual's later development in body, soul, and spirit, which is encapsulated in

William Wordsworth's well-known aphorism—'The child is the father to the man'. The meaning of this saying can be interpreted as:

Everything that the child experiences will affect the way in which the adult relates to the world later in life

Or more literally:

Children bear the seeds of that which they will become within themselves.

The task for parents and educators is to nourish this seed and allow it to grow naturally, in order to lay the foundation for effective learning throughout life.

Allowing children *to simply be children* is a simple yet significant realisation in acknowledging and nurturing the Kingdom of Childhood. Yet in modern western societies, this has not always been so self-evident, with an increasing focus on institutionalising children from a very early age and exposing them in infancy to cognitive stimulation based on theories of psychological development and more recently technological innovations whose long-term effects are yet to be assessed. As noted, the field of psychology developed into a coherent discipline in the early twentieth century and then proceeded to dominate thinking around child development and consequent educational responses, with the influence of theorists like Jean Piaget, Jerome Bruner, and Lev Vygotsky now deeply embedded in contemporary approaches to education and particularly teacher education.

Piaget in particular, "who is widely regarded as 'the father of developmental psychology' particularly as it applies to children and adolescents" (Gidley 2016: 48), was responsible for the theory of cognitive development developed in the 1930s that was taken up with alacrity in the 1970s so that it is still taught in universities and teachers' colleges today. It is so pervasive that readers may well be very familiar with it. In brief, his four stages of human cognitive development are set out as:

1. Sensori-motor stage, up to two years old (pre-language, non-representational)

2. Pre-operational stage, from two to seven years (language acquisition, symbolic play, mental imagery)
3. Concrete operational stage, from 7 to 11 years (logical reasoning based on concrete objects or events)
4. Formal operational stage, from adolescence to adulthood (higher order and hypothetical reasoning)

Although still popular enough to be taught in university subjects in educational psychology, Piaget's model has come in for some criticism. One criticism concerns the limitations of such 'stage theories'. Piaget himself acknowledged that transitions between stages can be blurred and gradual rather than abrupt, and the same could be said of the seven-year cycle model. Of more concern perhaps is the idea that 'cognitive development' ends with the formal operational stage which then presumably is the state in which an individual stays from adolescence to death, resulting in further research which suggests that "the formal operations stage is not the highest point in human development" (Souvaine 1990, cited in Tennant and Pogson 1995: 26).

This has led to the identification of *postformal* stages of cognitive development, in line with trends in holistic thinking, integrated knowledge, and a move away from focussing purely on *cognition* in development and education to acknowledge the affective domain, emotional intelligence, and higher levels of consciousness. Jennifer Gidley notes that the Piagetian notion of formal operations comes directly from Aristotelian categorical logic:

> The binary categorical nature of formal operations leads to dissection, specialisation and fragmentation of knowledge rather than synthesis and integration. The failure of much contemporary psychology, and indeed education, is that it is based on the primacy of formal operations and that it tries to emulate natural science in its approaches to the psyche, which cannot be measured in the same way as physical objects. (Gidley 2016: 56)

A scientific/psychological view of human development is therefore bound to be fragmentary and not inclusive of a holistic perspective that should recognise traits such as imagination, inspiration, creativity, and artistic ability which are not simply cognitive processes and as Gidley says difficult to measure, therefore requiring subtler approaches to teaching and learning than relying on standardised content delivery and testing.

This leads to the age-old question of whether such character traits are inherent and latent within the developing child, only needing to be 'drawn out' through effective education, or whether they can be inculcated and transmitted as if all children were a 'blank slate' or an empty vessel waiting to be filled, as suggested by Locke's theory of *tabula rasa*. Not surprisingly, the 'nature vs nurture' debate has also been presented and analysed as a binary 'either/or' categorical dilemma: between either genetic heredity or environment and upbringing.

6.2   Nature or Nurture?

The history of educational theory is marked by opposition between the idea that education is development from within and that it is formation from without; that it is based upon natural endowments and that education is a process of overcoming natural inclination and substituting in its place habits acquired under external pressure. (Dewey 1963: 17)

The classic experimental approach to determining the extent to which children are a product of their natural environment or their upbringing includes the literature on 'wild boys and girls'—those who have been found running with wolves or brought up by animals other than humans, then captured and brought into some form of civilisation with attempts to tame and teach them (Newton 2002). One of the first documented and published cases was that of 'Victor – the wild boy of Aveyron', a wolf-child found in the forests of France at the end of the eighteenth century (Itard 1802; Lane 1976; Malson 1972). At the time—well before Charles Darwin—contemporary debates ignited by the Enlightenment included questions around what distinguished the human animal from all other animals, with one of the most significant factors considered to be the ability to learn language. As such, the physician and psychologist Jean Itard (1774–1838) took on this feral child when he emerged from the woods at about the age of 11 or 12, treating him as an experiment in education to try and prove some of the latest theories around knowledge being empirical rather than inherent, as well as the importance of sociali-sation and civilisation in being able to learn.

By "awakening the boy's mind" (Malson 1972: 72), Itard hoped to disprove prevailing views that the child, who he named Victor, was a congenital idiot who had been abandoned by his parents for this reason and was therefore uneducable. Over a five-year period, Itard was partially successful in his quest—'taming' Victor and teaching him some very basic living skills and a few words, although he never gained speech or understood language even though he lived to the age of 40. As psychol-ogy was seen with suspicion at this time as a new and untested form of social science, many critics pointed to the failure of Victor to be fully rehabilitated into civilised society as proof that Victor's nature "destined him to be a savage" and that he had suffered "arrested development" not only at birth but in spending the majority of his early life in the wild (Malson 1972: 78–79).

Itard however continued to work at the Deaf and Dumb Institute in Paris for almost 40 years and established himself as a pioneering peda-gogue and the founder of education for what were known as 'backward children', based on some of the novel techniques he had invented for working with Victor. His work and his writings were later taken up with keen interest by Maria Montessori in Rome, after she too had been work-ing with children regarded as 'mentally deficient' and after achieving suc-cess in teaching them, had applied her remedial methods to the teaching of 'normal' young children, resulting in the Montessori method now active in many countries. In 1907 when Montessori was working with these culturally deprived children in San Lorenzo, Italy, she also aimed to disprove the prevailing view among educators and psychologists that "intelligence was still thought to be determined by heredity" (Kramer 1976: 375).

> Other studies have shown that while intellectual capacity may be geneti-cally determined, interaction with the environment – early stimulation – has a great deal to do with whether an individual will realise his full potential or not. Enriched environments in the preschool years are now seen as possible antidotes to cultural deprivation – just what Montessori was providing in her work with the children in San Lorenzo in 1907. (Kramer 1976: 376)

Enriched environments for very young children are today seen as normal and necessary aspects of the education and socialisation process, yet around 100 years ago this was still an emerging educational philosophy, and was even vigorously criticised and resisted by establishment authorities, under the prevailing Victorian mindset of the purposes of public education. This was partly an economic argument—why spend public money on three-year-olds?—and partly to do with the place of children in society at the time. In fact, only a century earlier, at the beginning of the nineteenth century "it was generally believed that human infants, with the rare exception of those with physical defects, were miniature adults already fully equipped for life" (Malson 1972: 77).

The 'miniature adult' paradigm gradually gave way during the nineteenth century to the concept of *childhood* as a distinct and different phase of life, but not before the dreadful exploitation of children in factories, mines, and industries that fed the new industrial society and sent them to do the same work as adults at a very young age. As we have seen in Chap. 4, school was reserved for the few and privileged. Kindergartens were yet to be conceived and established. Books for children were rare and children's literature slowly developed during the 1900s, with some early didactic and strident attempts to educate children in Victorian morals and values by scaring the daylights out of them, for example, the German *Struwwelpeter* stories that featured—with graphic pictures—the girl who played with matches and burnt herself to death, the boy who sucked his thumbs and had them cut off by the scary Scissor Man, and so on (Hoffmann 1845). The well-known folk tales collected and published by the German Grimm brothers appeared in 1812 in a first edition which was not 'sanitised' like later versions that watered down to some extent the scenes of cruelty and violence deemed inappropriate for children.

It was a German educationalist, Katharina Rutschky (1941–2010), who introduced the idea of 'poisonous pedagogy' in her 1977 book *Schwarze Pädagogik* (literally black pedagogy), to describe child-raising approaches that damage a child's emotional development. Psychological, physical, and emotional abuse or manipulation is unfortunately still a feature of some children's upbringing and will be discussed further in the following chapter. However, this comes from a long history starting with original sin, and in the eighteenth century, children were actually seen as inherently 'evil' and therefore needed to be 'tamed like animals', so that the *Struwwelpeter* and Grimm stories then appear to be unremarkable in the context of a society in which a German child-raising book advised parents that:

> These first years have, among other things, the advantage that one can use force and compulsion. With age children forget everything they encountered in their early childhood. Thus if one can take away children's will, they will not remember afterward that they had had a will. (Sulzer 1748)

So even though it was recognised that *will* was the guiding soul force in early childhood, it was seen as something that should be conquered with *force and compulsion,* not nurtured as a precious gift of individuality. The Polish/Swiss psychologist Alice Miller (1923–2010) went even further to suggest that German traumatic childrearing was responsible for producing such a damaged character as the dictator Adolf Hitler (Miller 1980).

Having no rights and no voice in society and no real identity as a vulnerable group needing protection and nurturing under the responsibility of society and the state, children in Victorian times were at worst exploited in Dickensian fashion in the workforce, relegated to industrial schools as orphans or 'uncontrollable children' (see Chap. 5), or at best expected to be 'seen and not heard' by the emerging middle class in both private and public situations.

How contrary then that by the second half of the nineteenth century and into the twentieth, a vision of childhood as a romantic ideal gradually emerged, popularised, and sentimentalised by fantasy fiction such as Lewis Carroll's *Alice in Wonderland* (1865), Edward Lear's nonsense stories (1846), and culminating in JM Barrie's *Peter Pan*, 'the boy who wouldn't grow up' (1904). Influenced by Romantic poets such as Wordsworth, and strangely curtailed by Victorian morals and Edwardian values, these books, followed by Kenneth Grahame's *The Wind in the Willows* (1908) and AA Milne's *Winnie the Pooh* (1926), created an idealised view of perpetual, pastoral childhood innocence that not only spawned a genre of children's literature but "lay at the core of a powerful fantasy [that] adults worked out in response to their own hopes, fears and doubts about themselves and their world" (Wullschlager 1995: 13). Adult parents living vicariously through their children is a theme that is explored further in Chap. 7.

It is not surprising then that the 'nurture' side of the binary argument about nature vs nurture was confused and divided and while gaining traction over the last 200 years or so is still the subject of inquiry and research.

Much like wild children, twins have provided opportunities for social researchers to test various theories around the development of intelligence and character, with the possibility of comparing identical (monozygotic) twins who are considered to have exactly the same genetic and hereditary characteristics with variables such as having experienced the same environmental upbringing; or even better, though rare, having been separated at birth and experiencing differing upbringings. The University of Minnesota Twin Family Study conducted from 1979 to 1999 is one of the more well-known studies:

> A 1986 study that was part of the larger Minnesota study found that genetics plays a larger role on personality than previously thought. Environment affected personality when twins were raised apart, but not when they were raised together, the study suggested. (Lewis 2014)

Of interest is the general finding already established in the 1960s that "identical twins show far fewer psychological than physiological similarities" (Malson 1972: 21), because physiological development is also undoubtedly influenced by environment and upbringing as well as by genetic inheritance. This is clearly apparent in countries where children suffer malnutrition as a result of growing up in situations of poverty or famine, and fail to thrive physically due to deprivation. The link between intellectual and physiological development is harder to establish because lack of educational opportunity goes hand in hand with socio-economic disadvantage.

Recent research by the Murdoch Children's Research Institute has shown that even in a developed country like Australia, poverty affects physiological development. A longitudinal survey of 3700 children found significant differences in the age that they reached puberty depending on their socio-economic circumstances:

Boys who grow up in hardship are more than four times at risk of starting puberty aged 10 than those who grow up in safer, wealthier households. And girls who grow up disadvantaged are twice as likely to start puberty earlier than others. (Spooner 2017)

The findings go on to discuss some of the reasons for early maturation—associated with emotional, behavioural, and social problems during adolescence—and some of the consequences, including health problems in later life (Sun et al. 2017). Adolescence itself, however, is a relatively recent social construct, as discussed in the following chapter.

To conclude this brief discussion on nature vs nurture, it is apparent that a binary oppositional view of genetic heredity on the one hand and environmental influences on the other is too simplistic in considering the possible effects on the developing child and adult, which literally cannot be generalised but are unique to practically every individual case—much like an individual's fingerprints are unique. However, one could think of the two sides of this coin more as two ends of a spectrum or continuum, along which one could be placed according to situation and opportunity. Returning to the threefold picture of the human being presented earlier in this chapter, it also needs to be pointed out that the individual has some agency as well, that life is not entirely pre-destined by the inheritance of the *spirit* and the physical manifestation of the *body*, but can be shaped and developed by consciously working on the *soul*—by the individual from within and by society, through education, from without.

Man's genetic inheritance is quite formless until it has been given a shape by social forces, yet the direction of these forces themselves may always be changed by the intervention of consciousness. (Malson 1972: 24)

6.3   Play Is a Child's Work

Enforced learning will not stay in the mind. So avoid compulsion and let your children's lessons take the form of play. (Plato, *The Republic*)

From being considered as 'miniature adults', to being recognised as unique entities with emerging consciousness, physical and intellectual developmental needs, very young children have gradually established a place in society as needing a different form of educational approach, leading to the specialised field of Early Childhood Education. In line with the developmental theories discussed in this chapter, this roughly equates to the first seven or eight years of life, from birth until the time that a child is deemed ready for formal education. In those first few years, children experience a whole world of learning long before they encounter formal schooling and a place where adults are referred to as *teachers*. A child in its first three years of life learns to walk, talk, comprehend, and communicate with others all by the process of imitation and experiment—not by formal schooling. What the young child learns about the world into which it is born, it learns from its significant kinship relations—parents, siblings, grandparents—and "it is important to realise that cultural learning begins at birth, is mostly non-verbal and 90% unconscious" (Khoshkhesal 1995: 14).

Just as a child's physical body is developing unconsciously according to the laws of nature, so are their other faculties developing without their conscious input. Recognising and working with this unconscious development and allowing it to blossom naturally, rather than forcing abstract adult-oriented thinking and rational-logic expectations onto the child too soon, is a significant realisation for parents and educators. Pestalozzi and Froebel, introduced in Chap. 2, were pioneers in early childhood education, recognising this significant reality about young children at a time when mainstream society still viewed them as miniature adults. Pestalozzi was influenced by Rousseau and the ideal of 'the natural life', establishing a school in rural Switzerland for poor country children, with a radical (for its time—the end of the eighteenth century) curriculum based on training the senses through natural activity and observation of concrete objects before moving onto abstract concepts.

Friedrich Froebel was one of Pestalozzi's student teachers, who went on to become famous as "the German schoolmaster who gave the world the kindergarten" (Kramer 1976: 65). Froebel became interested in the pre-school years, eventually establishing a school for very young children in Thuringia which, in an inspired moment, he named a *Kindergarten*—literally a garden where children would be allowed to grow like unfolding flowers. A radical and innovative move at a time when early childhood education was not yet institutionalised, the kindergarten movement only flourished because it was taken up as a cause by a wealthy German patroness—Baroness von Marenholtz-Bülow—who spread the word abroad, opening the first kindergarten in London in 1851. Charles Dickens was impressed and helped to raise public awareness of kindergartens through his writings in the popular press, which at the time was emerging as a platform for more broadly promulgating influential ideas about education. By 1873, kindergartens had become part of the public school system in the United States, with Dewey incorporating the philosophy into his Laboratory Schools at the University of Chicago.

> The Froebel society, founded in 1875, spread the kindergarten philosophy. In a context of romantic mysticism in which growing children were described as flowers unfolding, Froebel presented his contributions to educational thought. He saw all education as basically a process of self-activity, the natural endowments of the individual unfolding according to the universal laws of organic development. Convinced of the value of play in early childhood learning, he introduced a series of toys or apparatus he called the "gifts", to stimulate learning through play. (Kramer 1976: 66)

The *value of play in early childhood learning* is one of the enduring legacies of Froebel's philosophy, in addition to the fact that the kindergarten is now a well-established and embedded aspect of formal education systems. In Edwardian England, the social reformer Margaret McMillan, influenced by Froebel and also William Morris (see Chap. 4), championed the role of nature play for very young children (McMillan 1919). In the field of early childhood education, free play is now a recognised activity and play-based learning an accepted methodology. Anyone watching young children engrossed in play activity will realise that for them, it is a lived experience, being in the moment, and very often incorporating all their sense faculties to the extent that the real and the imagined are merged. In this respect, we could say that *play is a child's work*—they are actively working out their identities and relationships with the natural world and with others through exercising imagination, creativity, negotiation, and empathy.

> Van Hoorn et al. (2011) summarised play as the fundamental driver that fosters physical, social-emotional, linguistic and intellectual development, as well as personality and sense of self in the child. (Pryor 2014: 34)

Adventure playgrounds were established in Britain in the years after World War II, in recognition of the need for children to be able to experience outdoor activities that involved some form of risk and therefore self-regulation, and initially utilising vacant land that had been bombed or made derelict by the conflict. Providing children with cast-off goods that were considered junk but could be recycled into resources for creative play, these playgrounds became hugely popular and have influenced a resurgence in community-based pop-up play spaces in the United Kingdom, the United States, and Australia (https://www.popupplay.net/; http://www.playwales.org.uk/eng/home).

Play is a subtle construct. It should be spontaneous, voluntary, and intrinsically motivated in order to be meaningful and satisfying for the child—so what is the role of the parent, play worker, or early childhood educator in encouraging play, and how do we know if play is meaningful and beneficial, not just random and trivial?

Firstly, play in a pre-school or kindergarten setting can be seen as a continuum, with spontaneous child-directed 'free play' at one end, moving to teacher-guided play, and continuing to the other end of the spectrum where play is teacher-directed (Pryor 2014; Van Hoorn et al. 2011). Knowing when and how to negotiate this continuum is part of learning to be an effective parent and educator; providing a safe but enriching learning environment is a vital first step, with attention to detail such as the kindergarten in a Waldorf School (Fig. 6.2):

> Round in form and soft in feel, to support the oneness of the group, the Kindergarten building has a soft inner space devoid of detail – the room, without corners, is filled with warm, low light. The roof is domed completing the gesture of gentleness. (Keyte 2010: 68)

Fig. 6.2 The kindergarten at Willunga Waldorf School—a safe, nurturing, and enriching environment

The 'toys' that Froebel introduced in the first kindergartens need not be anything manufactured or even educationally significant—children will make use of chairs, sticks, bits of wood, cloth, or stones to invent imaginative play objects.

Secondly, play is all about the *process and the activity*, and unlike most other forms of education, not concerned with any perceivable *outcome or product*. The same game may be played over and over again, the same cubby house constructed and pulled apart and re-built again. The end result is not important, it is the lived moment that matters.

The fragile and delicate nature of play as a spontaneous child-centred activity is therefore open to being rationalised, commodified, commercialised, and over-regulated just like other aspects of education. The cultural historian Howard Chudacoff published a history of child's play (2008) in which he points out that:

…for most of human history what children did when they played was roam in packs large or small, more or less unsupervised, and engage in freewheeling imaginative play. They were pirates and princesses, aristocrats and action heroes…they spent most of their time doing what looked like nothing much at all. "They improvised their own play; they regulated their play; they made up their own rules". (Speigel 2008)

Chudacoff then argues that during the second half of the twentieth century, this kind of play changed radically:

Instead of spending their time in autonomous shifting make-believe, children were supplied with ever more specific toys for play and predetermined scripts. Essentially, instead of playing pirate with a tree branch they played Star Wars with a toy light saber. Chudacoff calls this the commercialization and co-optation of child's play – a trend which begins to shrink the size of children's imaginative space. (Spiegel 2013)

So began the influence of popular culture, advertising, commerce, and the emergence of children as a cohort who could be aggressively targeted as a distinct sector of the consumer market, effectively reached through the growth and exploitation of mass media, especially television. In this milieu, the twenty-first-century child now finds itself as never before confronted with a modern world bombarding it with stimuli that increasingly needs to be mediated by discerning parents, guardians, and teachers, making it even more important to respect the sanctity of the kingdom of childhood so that children do not grow up 'too fast'. Chapter 7 considers these issues and further addresses the key question: *How should children learn?* as well as the coterminous question for those of us tasked with their wellbeing and education: *How should adults learn?*

References

Childs, G. (1991). *Steiner education in theory and practice*. Edinburgh: Floris Books.
Chudacoff, H. (2008). *Children at play: An American history*. New York: New York University Press.

Dewey, J. (1963). *Experience and education*. New York: Collier Books.

Easton, F. (1997). Educating the whole child, "Head, heart and hands": Learning from the Waldorf experience. *Theory into Practice, 36*(2), 87–94.

Gidley, J. (2016). *Postformal education: A philosophy for complex futures*. Switzerland: Springer.

Hoffmann, H. (1845). *Lustige Geschichten und drollige Bilder mit 15 schön kolorirten Tafeln für Kinder von 3–6 Jahren*. Frankfurt am Main: Literarische Anstalt.

Itard, J. (1802). *An historical account of the discovery and education of a savage man, or of the first developments, physical and moral, of the young savage caught in the woods near Aveyron, in the year 1798*. London: British Museum.

Keyte, J. (2010). Metamorphosis in building design. In F. Hickman, M. Huxholl, & K. Kytka (Eds.), *Weaving threads of community: A patchwork history of Willunga Waldorf School*. Adelaide: Willunga Waldorf School.

Khoshkhesal, V. (1995). Grace before meals. *Education Australia, 32*, 13–15.

Kramer, R. (1976). *Maria Montessori: A biography*. Oxford: Basil Blackwell.

Lane, H. (1976). *The wild boy of Aveyron*. Cambridge, MA: Harvard university Press.

Lewis, T. (2014). *Twins separated at birth reveal staggering influence of genetics*. http://www.livescience.com/47288-twin-study-importance-of-genetics. html. Accessed 24 May 2017.

Lievegoed, B. (1991). *Developing communities*. Stroud: Hawthorn Press.

Lievegoed, B. (1993). *Phases: The spiritual rhythms of adult life*. Bristol: Rudolf Steiner Press.

Malson, L. (1972). *Wolf children*. London: NLB.

McMillan, M. (1919). *The nursery school*. London: Dent and Sons.

Miller, A. (1980). *For your own good: Hidden cruelty in child-rearing and the roots of violence*. New York: Farrar, Straus, Giroux.

Miller, R. (1997). *"Partial vision" in alternative education*. http://www.dandugan.com/waldorf/articles/partial_vision_in_altern.htm. Accessed 22 June 1999.

Newton, M. (2002). *Savage boys and wild girls: A history of feral children*. New York: Picador.

Pryor, W. (2014). The power of play. Chapter 4, In T. Stehlik & L. Burrows (Eds.), *Teaching with spirit: New perspectives on Steiner education in Australia*. Murwillumbah: Immortal Books.

Ruenzel, D. (1995). The Waldorf way. *Teacher Magazine, 7*(2), 22–27.

Spooner, R. (2017, May 24). Poor children face higher risk of early puberty, Murdoch Children's Research Institute says. *Sydney Morning Herald*. http://

www.smh.com.au/national/health/poor-children-face-higher-risk-of-early-puberty-murdoch-childrens-research-institute-says-20170523-gwb90u. Accessed 25 May 2017.

Speigel, A. (2008). Old-fashioned play builds serious skills. https://www.npr.org/templates/story/story.php? storyId=19212514. Accessed 23 Mar 2018.

Steiner, R. (1981). 'Greek education and the middle ages', a modern art of education. London: Rudolf Steiner Press.

Steiner, R. (1982). *The kingdom of childhood*. London: Rudolf Steiner Press.

Sulzer, J. (1748). *Versuch von der Erziehung und Unterweisung der Kinder*.

Sun, Y., Mensah, F., Azzopardi, P., Patton, G., & Wake, M. (2017, May). Childhood social disadvantage and pubertal timing: A national birth cohort from Australia. *Pediatrics*. http://pediatrics.aappublications.org/content/early/2017/05/19/peds.2016-4099. Accessed 25 May 2017.

Tennant, M. (1997). *Psychology and adult learning*. London: Routledge.

Tennant, M., & Pogson, P. (1995). *Learning and change in the adult years: A developmental perspective*. San Francisco: Jossey Bass.

Van Hoorn, J., Scales, B., Nourot, P., & Alward, K. (Eds.). (2011). *Play at the centre of the curriculum*. Upper Saddle River, New Jersey: Prentice-Hall.

Von Eschenbach, W. (1980). *Parzival*. London: Penguin.

Whitehead, A. (1922). *The aims of education*. New York: Free Press.

Wullschlager, J. (1995). *Inventing wonderland: The lives and fantasies of Lewis Carroll, Edward Lear, J. M. Barrie, Kenneth Grahame and A. A. Milne*. London: Free Press.

7

The Twenty-First-Century Child

This chapter unpacks the notion of the 'twenty-first-century child' in the light of contemporary and often challenging and complex contexts in which children are now growing up. Children and young people are now labelled as 'digital natives', tangled up inextricably in the world wide web, with toddlers, tweens, and teens seen as consumers of education as well as consumers of goods and products. As a result, education has also become a commodity. Reactions and responses to these modernist trends driven by information technologies and the media include various 'back to nature' initiatives such as the Forest School movement in the United Kingdom and Europe and bush kindergartens in Australia. This chapter also addresses those who are charged with the care, support, and upbringing of our children—parents, guardians, and families. *Parenting as a vocation* is introduced and discussed, in the light of the various roles that parents have in educating their children and managing their own learning about parenting.

© The Author(s) 2018
T. Stehlik, *Educational Philosophy for 21st Century Teachers*,
https://doi.org/10.1007/978-3-319-75969-2_7

7.1   From Infancy to Adolescence and Beyond

From occupying a place in society as miniature adults who should be seen and not heard, to being placed within an idealised picture of fantasy and innocence, to today's view of the child as a yet unformed individual, children now find themselves in the twenty-first century being represented and categorised in complex and contradictory ways based from a bewildering variety of adult and societal perspectives, not only educational but economic, psychological, sociological, medical, legal, and familial.

This can be no better illustrated than in pointing out the variety of labels applied to children in various stages of development, partly as a result of the sort of psychological stage theories described in the previous chapter, but also driven by progressive policy shifts in thinking about childhood and an apparent desire to pigeon-hole children into cohorts as convenient units of analysis. Even in the *pre-natal* period before birth, children have an identity, with ultrasound images of the developing foetus now forming part of the suite of baby photos displayed and shared by proud parents, increasingly via online platforms such as Instagram, Twitter, and Facebook. In its first month of life, the baby is medically labelled as a *neonate* (Latin for newborn), after which it is generally referred to as an *infant* up until about one or two years of age, then perhaps a *toddler* when it starts to walk. The term *infant* can also be applied to children between the ages of four and seven, and there are still schools in England and parts of Australia catering to this age group known as *infant schools*. In the English legal system however, the period of *infancy* has an entirely different meaning and continues from birth until the age of 18.

Kid, when referring to a child, is a colloquialism and a pejorative use of the word for a baby goat. It does not help in defining what the age of the child might be and has a range of connotations including negative implications, as exemplified by sayings such as 'kid stuff', 'kidding around', 'acting like a kid', and so on. There seems to be no actual term to cover those first seven years of life that were considered by Plato to be significant, at a time in history when we could say that from being a *child* in the context of the family and household, at seven the young person became the responsibility of the state and a *student* in the more general sense: that is a student of the world.

The related terms of *teenager* and *adolescent* have become well known as representing important stages of childhood for consideration in modern western society, yet are relatively recent concepts in child and human development. Adolescence comes from the Latin *adolescere*, meaning 'to grow up', and is understood to represent a transitional period of physical and psychological development generally occurring from puberty to legal adulthood, which in most cases is at the age of 18.

As we have seen in the previous chapter however, the age at which puberty can occur is not necessarily fixed and can be affected by environment (Sun et al. 2017), and over the centuries the onset of puberty has gradually been observed to happen at an increasingly earlier age, due to a number of factors that are thought to include improved nutrition and the increasing presence of hormones in the environment and food chain. Moreover:

> The concept of adolescence, as generally understood and applied, did not exist before the last two decades of the nineteenth century. (Demos and Demos 1969: 632)

Demos and Demos (1969: 632) further claim that adolescence "was on the whole an American discovery", related to broad changes in American life such as changes in the structure of the family as part of the new urban and industrial order, as identified and popularised by the work of American psychologist G Stanley Hall from the 1890s into the early twentieth century. Other sources such as the Oxford Dictionary, however, suggest that the word and the concept of adolescence, to mean 'young adult', was in use as early as 1762.

The associated concept of the *teenager* is also credited as having first appeared in America during the 1920s and 1930s, and in this case specifically referring to the teen years from 13 to 19, rapidly becoming associated with a specific *adolescent culture* as well as a developmental stage. Interestingly, it is suggested that:

The dramatic rise in high school attendance was the single most important factor in creating teenage culture ... The proportion of fourteen- to-seventeen-year olds in high school increased from 10.6 percent in 1901 to 51.1 percent in 1930 and 71.3 percent in 1940. (Encyclopedia of children and childhood in history and society http://www.faqs.org/childhood/So-Th/Teenagers.html)

The experience of secondary education with its increased focus on abstract and critical thinking, plus the close proximity of adolescent girls and boys in social groupings that encouraged the development of peer relationships, reshaped the experiences of 13–18-year-olds and led to the development of adolescent identity. In America, the word *teenager* was first applied to young girls who were identified as a cohort influenced by romantic ideals as fed by popular culture and the emergence of the popular male idol, and rapidly targeted by marketing, manufacturing and retail companies as a new consumer cohort with disposable income fuelled by increasing affluence, followed later by the same targeting of teenage boys.

The result was that for the first time, adolescents could see themselves represented as having a collective identity and a collective strength, eventually leading to the 'rebellious' teenager image that arrived in the 1950s with cultural icons like James Dean, films such as *Blackboard Jungle*, and the emergence of a new musical style and associated sub-culture—rock and roll. Children's literature also caught up with the trend, with books like JD Salinger's *The Catcher in the Rye* addressing teenage angst, alienation, and emotional turmoil in a story that resonated with American youth and eventually became a hugely popular, while controversial, part of mainstream studies in high school English literature, along with other similar titles that are now considered as adolescent literature (Salinger 1951). Adolescent angst and teen relationships in literature, however, were nothing new—early examples include Shakespeare's 'star-crossed lovers' *Romeo and Juliet* (1597) and the unrequited love and suicide of the hero of Goethe's book *The Sorrows of Young Werther* (1774).

Cultural theorists such as Neil Postman (1994), however, consider that the 1950s also heralded the 'disappearance of childhood' in modern western society, with the advent of television which became the dominant source of information and did not discriminate between the ages and genders of those to whom programs, news, and commercials were broadcast.

> Television… requires no specialized learning, further diminishing the distinction between children and adults. Some television content adultifies and eroticizes children; some television infantilizes adults. (Postman 1994: 99)

Fashion is a good indicator of cultural shifts, and the fact that grown men can be seen wearing sneakers and shorts while little girls wear high heels and make-up reinforces Postman's argument that the lines between child and adult boundaries are increasingly blurred. It is not surprising then that one of the more recent appellations to be applied to a stage of childhood is the word *tween*. This is defined as "a youngster between 10 and 12 years of age, considered too old to be a child and too young to be a teenager" (Online Dictionary), and literally comes from a conflation of the words *teen* and *between*, first appearing in popular parlance in the 1980s. It is representative of the early exposure of 10–12-year-olds to fashions, fads, and products that would normally be targeted at older teenagers and shows not only the increasingly tight focussing and labelling of the marketing and media worlds but the ever-increasing incursion of consumerism, popular culture, and social stereotyping into the realm of the kingdom of childhood.

7.2   The Millennial Child

Concurrent with changes in how we think about childhood have been changes in how we think about and label generations, according to recent periods in history. The post-war *baby boomer* generation, which includes those born somewhere between the mid-forties and mid-sixties, was so named because of the increased birth rates that occurred after the trauma and mass casualties of World War II. This generation is characterised in modern western societies by increased economic prosperity and opportunity, but also by disaffection and turning away from establishment traditions fuelled by threats of nuclear war as well as counterculture ideals. *Generation X* was so identified as those children born from the early 1960s, when the birth control pill became commonly available, through to about the early 1980s. Consequently this generation is characterised by lower birth rates, but also by increased migration and border crossing, resulting in a more ethnically and culturally diverse demographic cohort.

The children of baby boomers and older Gen X parents were therefore labelled as Generation Y, also known as *millennials*: those born from the early 1980s through to the beginning of the twenty-first century. Depending on social and economic conditions, millennials are generally characterised by increased familiarity with and use of media, communication, and digital information technologies, but also have been affected by global financial recessions resulting in less stable employment opportunities and conditions. Millennials are more likely to be working in what has been termed the 'gig economy', in which full-time permanent employment is replaced by part-time, casual jobs that offer more work-life balance but consequently less opportunity to generate savings and be able to afford to enter the housing market (Baldwin 2016). The higher cost of housing—and also higher education in those countries where university fees are not subsidised by the state—means that millennials are more likely to be delaying adult 'rites of passage' such as marriage and starting families and as a result are more likely to still be living at home with their parents. However, some American studies have shown that those in the millennial age group, currently 18–34, are consciously making choices such as favouring career and education over families and children and are so far the most educated generation (US Census Bureau 2017).

As *millennial children* however (Schwartz 1999), this generation was the first to be globally recognised as having basic human rights and needing special protection under the Universal Declaration of Human Rights, leading in the late 1980s to the *United Nations Convention on the Rights of the Child* (UNICEF 1989). Everyone under 18 years of age has rights under this convention, by definition enshrining the notion that childhood ends, and adulthood begins, at the age of 18. The convention has 54 articles, many of which relate to a child's health, safety, right to privacy, and protection from abuse. Articles 28 and 29 relate to education:

Article 28: Children have the right to an education. Discipline in schools should respect children's human dignity. Primary education should be free. Wealthier countries should help poorer countries achieve this.

Article 29: Education should develop each child's personality and talents to the full. It should encourage children to respect their parents, their cultures and other cultures. (UNICEF)

Of interest is the fact that education as a pathway to jobs, careers, and individual economic prosperity is not stated in the convention. The main focus of the most of the articles in the convention is on a child's *wellbeing*, and by association the purpose of education for young children begins to hint at this being a central and global concern, rather than a focus on academic achievement, cognitive development, and intellectual capacity. This is a feature of education for millennials and beyond and will be discussed further later in this chapter, but it is interesting to note the 1989 convention appearing at about the same time that the *Global Education Reform Agenda* was also beginning to take effect, creating a tension that is now apparent in considering the purpose of education and the way young people are caught up in this tension: between education to develop each child's personality and talent on the one hand, and education to be measured against global academic benchmarks on the other.

Also of interest however is the international agenda implicit within the convention, for respecting all cultures and for sharing educational funding between the poorer and wealthier countries. UNICEF itself was established in 1946 as the United Nations International Children's Emergency Fund, in response to post-war re-development and re-settlement needs. Seventy years later, it is still a non-profit body dedicated to raising funds for international programs and advocating for children's rights in 63 countries.

The current (at the time of writing) 'post-millennial' generation is still establishing an identity, but indicative of the way in which these demographic cohorts are associated with marketing and branding, the label which has gained traction is *Generation Z*. Born anywhere between the early 2000s and 2010s, Gen Z children are also referred to as the iGeneration or the Internet Generation for obvious reasons and are also considered, like most millennials, to be *digital natives*—a term attributed to Marc Prensky (2001). They are, however, the first generation to have widespread access to Internet technology at a very early age and to have been exposed to an unprecedented amount of technology in their upbringing. As a cohort that has experienced access to and the regular use of personal devices such as i-phones, laptops, and tablets on a daily basis not only in the home but in the school setting, it will be interesting to see how this generation of digital natives respond to the world of work and the world in general, and whether their technological-educational experiences will result in different outcomes to those of previous generations.

Early indications show that they have however developed a social conscience, perhaps through the regular use of social media and constant peer-to-peer interaction, for example, the Gen Z girls at a 14-year-old birthday party who agree to put their phones in a pile on the table so they won't be distracted and can 'talk to each other'. The negative effects of such online activity and connectivity of course include cyberbullying, sexting, and other abuses of privacy and trust at worst, but also an unhealthy focus on the virtual world at the expense of the natural world. Gazing at screens with images and information that are not direct experiences of the real world but representations of it can be seen as just a modern digital version of looking at the shadows on the wall in the allegory of Plato's cave.

The digital age however is upon us, and is an undisputed phase in human and social development. From an evolutionary perspective, computers and other ICT devices could be seen as just another more sophisticated tool, and from an educational perspective as just another teaching resource; in other words they are means to various ends and not ends in themselves. Early in the twenty-first century, social commentators were coming up with other descriptive labels for the emerging 'e-Generation', including the rather clever *screenagers*, and the even more anthropological-sounding *Homo Zappiens*:

> They are young. They seem inattentive. They do seven things at the same time. They communicate continuously. They are Homo Zappiens. (Veen 2004; cited in Dahlin 2006: 27)

Without doubt we have evolved from the modernity of an industrial society which was characterised by the constructability of the world, to the post-modernity of an information society. One could say that the natural world is no longer mechanised; it is digitised (Dahlin 2006). Children growing up in this brave new world will know no other environment and so will only have subjective experiences of living in a digital world. Those of us from previous generations are able to make objective comparisons of what life was like before, but our children cannot. It has been ever thus with intergenerational change, as has been the inevitable trend for subsequent generations to reject or rebel against the fashions, values, and ideals of the previous generation.

At the same time, those of us from previous generations find it difficult to look outside our own subjective experience of what education and learning should look like, and by extension project that assumed logic onto the current generation. If the millennial and Gen Z students seem inattentive, distracted, and unable to concentrate on one thing during a 40-minute lesson at school, it is because they cope with information and communication in a different way:

> Homo Zappiens has learnt to deal with information overload by clicking and zapping. It has learned how to navigate efficiently and effectively through information, how to communicate, and how to build effectively on a network of peers. (Veen 2006: 2)

Rather than force traditional teaching methodologies onto this mind-set therefore, it makes sense to build on the strengths and skills of this approach to dealing with information, through encouraging an exploratory learning approach, and even focussing on play and gaming as a positive and effective way of problem-solving and developing strategies. Figure 7.1 summarises the different learning approaches between Homo Sapiens and 'Homo Zappiens', adapted from Veen (2006).

While this is important to recognise in terms of the characteristics of the current generation of school students, there is also a danger in putting all of the eggs in one basket and completely embracing the digital online world, losing sight of the human and social traditions that still occur 'outside the cave'. In education, for example, some schools have reacted

Homo Zappiens	Homo Sapiens
High speed	Conventional speed
Multi-tasking	Mono tasking
Non-linear approaches	Linear approaches
Iconic skills first	Reading skills first
Connected	Stand alone
Collaborative	Competitive
Learning by searching	Learning by absorbing
Learning by playing	Separating learning and playing
Learning by externalising	Learning by internalising
Using fantasy	Focussing on reality

Fig. 7.1   Homo Zappiens vs Homo Sapiens

to these trends by removing all books from their libraries, arguing that everything their students need is available online via e-books and the internet, accessible via their own personal tablets. This seems a rather short-sighted over-reaction to the digital world and what Merga and Roni (2017) call the 'myth' of the digital native, pointing to research that shows children prefer to read books on paper rather than screens. The 'death of the book' was predicted because of such practices, but books are more popular than ever and thankfully do not look like disappearing any time soon as many people still appreciate holding a hard copy object in their hands when reading for pleasure or information. Furthermore, old, rare and interesting books do not always become digitised or available online, and there is nothing like coming across an interesting and exciting text just by trawling through the shelves of a library or bookshop.

7.3   The Quantified Self

In addition to being tangled up in the world web, another feature of the millennial generation is the unprecedented focus on their health and wellbeing, as shown in the articles of the Convention on the Rights of the Child. While this is a positive trend, concern for their wellbeing has partly arisen as a response to alarming developments in the increasing exposure of children to physical, sexual, and psychological abuse, neglect, or manipulation; to increased pressure from peers, parents, and schools to perform and conform; and to an ever-growing number of children and young people presenting with medicalised and diagnosed disorders such as attention deficit hyperactivity disorder (ADHD), autistic spectrum disorder including Asperger syndrome, anxiety, depression, and mental health problems sometimes leading to self-harm and even suicide.

ADHD in particular has been the subject of controversy with debates around its causes, diagnosis, and treatment, and detailed discussion of this is to be found in literature elsewhere than space in this book allows (Hicks 2013; George Washington University Milken Institute School of Public Health 2015). However, it is symptomatic of the way in which the fields of medicine, psychiatry, and psychology are overlapping with the field of education, in a medicalised model of the child that some critics believe leads to over-diagnosis and places too much emphasis on a 'deficit' approach to child behaviour. This can be clearly seen in the kind of education policy in which parents receive extra funding or support for a child exhibiting behavioural and learning difficulties if they receive a formal diagnosis of autism or ADHD from a health professional. Again, there are many and varied consequences of this sort of policy, for example, on the one hand a tendency for over-using the diagnostic approach, while on the other hand a reluctance from parents to seek such diagnoses because they perceive it will label their child as 'backward', 'remedial', or 'special' and therefore stigmatise them.

Of similar concern is the number of young people presenting with a range of other mental health disorders, ranging from actual depression to unspecified anxiety issues which can affect not only their education but their self-esteem, socialisation, and life trajectory. Certainly in the university sector, I have personally observed an increase in the number of young students—mostly young women—presenting with such issues and applying for a 'disability access plan' for special consideration in attendance, time management, and engagement in class. If an undergraduate teacher education course causes anxiety, one wonders how these young people will cope in the real world of school and classroom environments, with timetables, deadlines, responsibilities, and challenges when—or if—they graduate. But more of this is in the next section.

Young people can put themselves under pressure to achieve, either from personal ambition and motivation, or to please their parents and even their teachers who may have high expectations of them. Peer pressure can also create competition to perform which can be healthy and, in a classroom, on the sports field, or in ensemble situations such as musical or dramatic performances, may push individuals to aim higher or at least conform to the norm. Peer pressure can also cause individuals to disengage and under-perform in order not to appear 'too smart' or stand out from others. This has especially been shown to affect teenage girls, and in co-educational high schools where girls generally achieve better academic outcomes, they have been observed to hold themselves back in order not to 'show up' the boys, to whom they often defer. This may be due to the hormonal processes that are taking place in adolescence, but also no doubt to an ingrained patriarchy in the system and to the additional observation that boys tend to receive more attention from teachers in class because of their attention-seeking behaviours. While these are perhaps generalisations, there is some basis in fact, and one of the central arguments for single-sex schools is that girls perform better without this gendered influence, free from the distractions of boys, and vice versa.

Negative peer pressure also takes the form of bullying, an unfortunate reality in schools, and in my opinion a result of putting children and young people together in age-specific groupings, every day of the school week, competing with and comparing each other against norms that are often established outside of their control through institutionalised school and social systems as well as the media, often influenced by the sort of values, attitudes, and behaviours that have been inculcated in the home, in those vital seven years before schooling even starts. In a kind of herd mentality, it seems to be very similar to the sort of pecking order that establishes itself in any grouping of animals or birds in a confined space. I wonder if such bullying occurs among children growing up in what might be called 'tribal' situations: for example, in mixed age groups where the older children look out for the younger ones? As a baby boomer, I and my peers experienced bullying in school, not only from other children but from teachers, which shocks me to think of it even now. Yet at least we were not subject to the kind of cyberbullying, online stalking, and 'Facebook friending and un-friending' that our millennial children can suffer.

Facebook did not exist before 2004. Over a decade later, there were two billion users signed up to this social media site, which according to its founder Mark Zuckerberg "stands for bringing us closer together and building a global community" (cited in Hopkins 2017a: 13). The problem in having such a vast virtual community is regulating what gets posted on the site, and determining what is acceptable according to the values and standards of such a diverse global population. The guidelines that Facebook uses to moderate content attempt to strike a balance between allowing free speech and limiting censorship while also being concerned about issues such as violence, hate speech, terrorism, pornography, racism, and self-harm. There are some real concerns however, in guidelines which state that:

> Some photos of non-sexual physical abuse and bullying of children do not have to be deleted unless there is a sadistic or celebratory element. (Hopkins 2017b: 1)

How such qualifying criteria are determined is obviously a very grey area and open to subjective opinion. Critics argue that Facebook should be subject to the same scrutiny and regulations as other publishers and broadcasters, but its management believes it is "a new kind of company. It's not a traditional technology company. It's not a traditional media company…We don't write the news that people read on the platform" (cited in Hopkins 2017b: 13).

So we are in a new kind of territory with this new kind of media, one that is very difficult to regulate and also to predict how it will evolve. As a new 'platform' for instant communication and venting of opinions, images, and casual remarks, it has the potential to be informative but also to be damaging, especially to children. It is like a genie that has been let out of a bottle. How do we control something like this? How do we know how much impact social media has on the kinds of increased anxieties and pressures that children and young people are experiencing?

Social media is one of the many external factors that the education system has to deal with in the twenty-first century. Within the education system itself however, the kind of high-stakes testing discussed in Chap. 5 is an internally imposed pressure. Putting children under such pressure contributes to anxiety to perform that is now being seen in children as young as ten years old (Reingold 2015). We have also seen how early physiological maturation can be one of the consequences of invading the kingdom of childhood with adult expectations such as academic success based on examinations and tests. In China, this pressure is so embedded in parental and societal expectations that an alarming number of students suffer extreme psychological distress and even take their own lives if they do not do well in the *Zhongkao* (Senior High School Entrance Examination) or the *Gaokao* (National Higher Education Entrance Examination).

These examples of measuring, testing, analysing, and sorting children according to statistically based standardised instruments and formulae are part of the mega-trend for gathering data on every aspect of our lives, which seems to have grown exponentially with the ability to capture, store, and manipulate detailed information with computer technology. We are in an age of *Big data* and the *Quantified self.*

[Big data: extremely large data sets that may be analysed computationally to reveal patterns, trends, and associations, especially relating to human behaviour and interactions. (Dictionary.com)]

Everything from people's browsing history, email traffic, credit card payments, mobile phone logs, down to their shopping habits in the local supermarket can be captured and manipulated to reveal highly personal information in a complex matrix of data. Another genie that is difficult to control, big data require big hardware and software systems to control and manage. Regular hacking of supposedly secure databases such as the May 2017 incursion into the data files of the United States National Security Agency and the United Kingdom National Health System shows how difficult it is to keep such personal information secure from international 'cyber extortionists' (Corderoy 2017).

In the education sector, big data has become manifest in the concept of *learning analytics.* The rise of online education and virtual learning environments using learning management systems such as Moodle and

Blackboard has resulted in the ability to capture every interaction and log on between and among students and their online instructors. For example, in my online university classes I have access to detailed information for every student including the number of times they have logged on to the course home page. This does not mean, of course, that they have actually engaged with and understood the content or completed the activities required, nor does it assess the depth or meaningfulness of their learning, but it gives some very convenient statistics that can then be used to make decisions about course content and delivery at a management level, since this big data is available to the university's Business Intelligence Unit. This means educational institutions can now:

> ...let the algorithms do the work...because statistical correlation tells us what we need to know; and that scientific or statistical models aren't needed because, to quote "The End of Theory", a provocative essay published in *Wired* in 2008, "with enough data, the numbers speak for themselves". (Harford 2014: 1)

Learning analytics allows for the profiling of students and monitoring of their study habits and also monitoring of teaching staff and their teaching habits. It can be used as a carrot and also as a stick. It gives a completely quantified and empirical slant to the concept of assessment of learning, a sort of 'learning by numbers', and an assessment of teaching performance based entirely on statistics. This has obvious implications for the teaching-learning relationship and the role of the teacher, which can be compromised and sidelined by the sheer weight of the trends discussed so far in this chapter.

> Education has now undergone the digital turn and to a large extent been captured by big data systems in administration as well as teaching and research. Criticality has been avoided or limited within education and substituted by narrow conceptions of standards, and state-mandated instrumental and utilitarian pedagogies. (Peters 2017: 565)

Peters places these shifts in criticality within the context of the 'post-truth' era that we currently find ourselves, with *post-truth* defined as "relating to or denoting circumstances in which objective facts are less influential in shaping public opinion than appeals to emotion and personal belief" (Oxford Dictionaries). Peters argues that in a post-truth era, facts and evidence have become replaced with feelings and emotions in the political media landscape, with the result that "the role of teachers as arbiters of the truth has become challenged" (Peters 2017).

We now have so much data available on ourselves that we refer to the *Quantified Self*. In addition to big data being captured by external means, we can now capture it for ourselves. Those people who wear a 'Fitbit' or similar activity tracker will know exactly how many steps they take every day, exactly how long they have slept every night, and what their heart rate is at any given moment. They can share this information and challenge and compete with other people who are similarly inclined or obsessed with personal fitness and/or measuring everything. Such wireless-based wearable technology has been with us for a while, and being able to track biometric data has benefits for medical conditions such as diabetes—but it still feels like something from a futuristic science fiction trope. Smart phones, even smart televisions, can track our movements and our personal devices can track our spending habits. Can we harness this sort of technology in a positive way for education in the future? Will the corollary of machines becoming 'smarter' mean that humans will become less smart?

7.4   Nature Versus Technology

A number of reactions and responses to these post-modernist trends driven by information technologies have emerged however as a kind of balance to the ubiquity of the high pressure machine world. In the field of psychology, the positive psychology movement has found its way into school curricula through a focus on student wellbeing, with its main theorists suggesting that depression and suicide are linked to a lack of ability to imagine a positive future, which can be developed through learned optimism (Seligman 1995; Seligman and Csikszentmihalyi 2000). Mindfulness meditation has similarly become popular in school settings since 2000, especially in America, where its practice is said to reduce anxiety and stress in students (Zajonc 2016); and in Australia mindfulness training for teachers is a growing trend, as well as showing some success in clinical therapy for children on the autism spectrum (Albrecht 2014; Burrows 2017). It is interesting to note that mindfulness is based on Buddhist meditation practices and is part of the emerging philosophy of *wellness*—"the quality or state of being healthy in body and mind, especially as the result of deliberate effort" (Dictionary.com).

In education, we have also seen various 'back to nature' initiatives emerge and become globally popular in response to the technologisation of education, such as the Forest School movement in the United Kingdom and Europe and bush kindergartens in Australia. As an example of *education outside the classroom*, the idea behind Forest Schooling is literally to take children into the outdoors and use the natural environment as a stimulus for learning, building on the work of theorists like Froebel whose work influenced the English sisters Margaret and Rachel McMillan, who founded outdoor nurseries in the first decade of the twentieth century in response to their observations that young children in industrial settings were not thriving due to lack of fresh air and outdoor exercise (Knight 2017; McMillan 1919). The Rachel McMillan Open-Air Nursery School in Deptford became the template for subsequent nursery schools, and laid the foundation for the recognition of the importance of play in early childhood, as discussed in the previous chapter, as well as the health-giving aspects of outdoor environments. Since the 1950s, forest schools have been a feature in Scandinavia, and also in Germany where they are recognised as an official form of childcare.

Since the 1990s, the UK Forest School movement has grown in response to contemporary issues around children's health and wellbeing; for example, statistics quoted from the 2013 Health Survey for England by Sara Knight in her book *Forest School in Practice* show that up to 30% of English children aged 2–15 were identified as obese or overweight (2017: 17). The movement also appears to be a response to the GERM outlined in Chap. 5, as suggested by UK early childhood teacher Emma Harwood who left the schooling system to establish Dandelion Forest School:

> "I love teaching reception but we're closing the door – literally – and moving towards more testing. It doesn't feel child-centric enough anymore." After taking primary schools on weekly forest school sessions, Harwood noticed a huge difference in pupils' "self-esteem and ability to assess risk and make their own decisions". (Barkham 2014: 1)

Forest school is also a response to an increasing risk-averse culture generated by concerns about safety and the fact that as a society, we don't feel comfortable letting our children ramble and play outdoors away from adult supervision as once was the case. For city children who have been described as 'cotton-wool kids', the opportunity to run around, light fires, cook outdoors, climb trees, and make mud pies can be a novelty and a liberating way to learn through play. The American founder of the *Children and Nature* movement Richard Louv goes further to suggest that children need such experiences to counter 'nature deficit disorder' (Louv 2005).

While outdoor learning can be successfully applied with primary and secondary schoolchildren (see Adventure Playgrounds in Chap. 6 and the case study of Green School Bali in Chap. 10), part of the theory and philosophy behind the forest school method is that it works best with pre-school children because they are still in an early stage of cognitive development (the *vital years* before age seven) when particular habits of mind can still be formed:

> Being outside regularly and being free to stretch and grow makes a child *want* to be outside regularly and be free to stretch and grow. It is much easier to create these healthy ways of being while the brain is young and plastic. (Knight 2017: 18)

In Australia, a similar movement for pre-school children has developed under a different name: *bush kindy*. Bush kindergartens are a feature of some Waldorf Schools as many of them have been established in natural or bush settings rather than in urban environments, and an appreciation for nature and a respect for the environment is already part of their ethos. Bush kindy has followed the same approach as that of the forest schools; to provide a safe but engaging environment in which to explore and learn from the natural world according to the children's own interests and play activities. Whole group co-operative play appears to develop and unfold spontaneously, which is often found as a feature of outdoor education.

> From the abundance of experiences at bush kindy it is evident that each child is enveloped in health-giving sense impressions, stimulating the development of their sense of touch, life, movement and balance. They are

developing an intimate knowledge of nature through their senses and in turn their senses are stimulated in a truly wholesome and life-giving way. (Pridham 2014: 21)

Anecdotal evidence from parents includes comments that their children eat and sleep better and tend to play outdoors more often when at home while attending bush kindy. The time spent outdoors will of course vary according to climate, geography, and age group. In Queensland, where it can be hot and dusty, two to three hours outdoors is enough before needing to go indoors to wash up, eat, and rest (Kearney 2014). In Sweden and Finland, I have observed young children wanting to run out of doors between lessons for 15 or 20 minutes of play, even when it is below zero and snowing (see Chap. 10).

Research cited in the *Journal of Biological Psychiatry* supports this need for exposure to the outdoors and links it to factors that may explain the increase in medical diagnoses as discussed above, suggesting that in America:

…living in states with greater sunshine (solar intensity or SI) may protect against the development of ADHD. There is a wide variation of reported attention deficit disorder from a low of 5.6% in Nevada to a high of 15.6% in North Carolina. Some of this can result from differences in diagnostic practices, but something else may be going on as well…The authors believe that use of modern media, including iPads and mobile phones shortly before bedtime, results in delayed sleep onset, shorter sleep duration, and melatonin suppression. Natural light may counteract the effects of modern media in the evening. (Hicks 2013)

In Japan, the concept of 'forest bathing' (*shinrin-yoku*—walking and/or staying in forests in order to promote health) has been shown to promote positive health benefits for people of all ages and fitness levels, with empirical research into reduced stress levels and increased wellbeing concluding that "forest environments can be viewed as therapeutic landscapes" (Morita et al. 2007: 54).

Even without adopting a 'nature deficit disorder' perspective on the health benefits to young children from being outdoors, the positive effects on the cognitive development of all children have been linked with direct experience with nature, an example of *experiential learning*:

Theories of experiential education contend that cognitive learning in early and middle childhood can be more effective if preceded by spontaneous play, free exploration, and direct personal discoveries in nature. (Moore 2014b: 17)

An interesting point arises from this move to get our children 'back to the woods' and links not only with Rousseau's theories about nature but with the discussion of feral children in Chap. 6. Here we saw that wild children who were brought up by animals ranging from wolves, bears, monkeys, and dogs (Newton 2002) and then emerged from the woods or the forest back into civilisation represented some form of human innocence and a *tabula rasa* or blank slate that the philosophers of the Enlightenment saw as a natural state of childhood grace. The symbolism of the Tree of Knowledge and humanity in a state of innocence before the Fall must also have been in their minds when confronted with these children in their absolute natural state. *The wood* or *the forest* is also a significant and symbolic image in European history and mythology—a place where children can become lost, where witches or trolls live, where the trees themselves can have magical powers, and characterised by darkness, mystery, and danger. The Grimm Brothers story *Hansel and Gretel* is a moral fable that warns children not to wander into the woods and become lost as they may be cooked and eaten by a witch, but it also represents the abandonment of children by society, since it was Hansel and Gretel's parents who took them into the woods with the *intention* of abandoning them (Creed 2017). Have we now come full circle by seeking outdoor play for our children and taking them back to the woods because we have 'abandoned' them to the technological age?

7.5   The Millennial Parent

No formal or legal requirements exist that require parents to instruct their children. However, common cultural assumptions regarding child-rearing infer that parents will guide and prepare children for life in a community. (Barbour and Barbour 1997: 97)

Becoming a parent is a significant life event, and for me, being a parent has been the most informative and educative life experience, over and above all of the formal learning I have done, such as the four degrees I completed at university. Children are like a mirror held up to you, in which you see yourself reflected in this remarkable being who is a part of you but also a unique individual. Watching them grow and develop into adulthood is a precious experience, at times challenging depending on the temperament of the child and how they relate to—or clash with—your own temperament. But it is always a learning experience, and the most important lesson to be learned is that you as the parent or guardian responsible for this incarnating soul will influence and direct the very way in which they grow and develop. You are, in fact, your child's first teacher.

It still amazes me then that there is very little formal training or education in how to do this extremely important job, let alone how to do it well. Parenting skills are acquired through learning by experience, by repeating role models from childhood, by observing and taking advice from other parents, from books or other 'expert' sources, and sometimes through non-formal educational programs—but mainly it is learning by doing. Public opinion also strongly dictates how we raise our children, and while this is now heavily influenced by popular media, even back in the 1860s, the English philosopher Herbert Spencer noted that "men dress their children's minds as they do their bodies, in the prevailing fashion" (Spencer 1860; cited in Gross 1963: 81).

So when my daughters began attending a Waldorf School, I noticed that a lot of attention was being paid by the school, in particular the kindergarten teachers, to supporting and educating parents in childrearing, and in gently suggesting ways to create a home environment that was in harmony with the type of environment and ethos they were trying to create with the children. This impressed me so much as an adult learning model that I began to document my own learning through my children and then started to research other parents' learning journeys, a project that became my doctoral thesis, later published as a book (Stehlik 2002, 2015).

During my research I came across a book popular in Waldorf circles that explores this perspective and is actually entitled *You Are Your Child's First Teacher* (Baldwin 1989). The book validates the important role of parenting as real work in educating children in their pre-school years, in contrast to the dominant paradigm which views teaching as a profession while parenting has lower status, and mothers especially are often labelled as 'homemakers'—a role that is non-paid, non-professional, and not recognised as real work, when it is probably the single most important and responsible role an adult could have, contributing immeasurably to the social fabric.

This paradigm represents a general shift away from recognition of the family as the basic unit of socialisation and placing that expectation upon schools, and to a certain extent on popular culture and the media. Barbour and Barbour consider that child-raising practices have become much less influenced by extended family and the wider community in a modern world where "daily lives now are more frenetic, and all too often families come close to abandoning responsibilities for a home curriculum in favor of that offered by the entertainment industry – a community force that is not always appropriate" (1997: 97). In other words, busy working parents who park young children in front of the television or tablet while trying to make dinner or do the chores might once have had the help of a grandparent, aunt, or uncle with this. The combination of the nuclear family model plus both parents working plus technology has been embedded in our society for some time, and is the current situation now being experienced by many millennial parents. In addition, couples in the twenty-first century are delaying having children until later in life, with the average age for a first-time mother in Australia now being over 30 (ABS). Older parents are more independent and bring their own experience but also their own 'baggage' to the job of parenting. How to proceed?

Creating an appropriate home environment is a recurring theme not only in the literature but in the discourse of Waldorf School communities, as parents are drawn to an understanding of the importance of supporting the ethos and environment that the teacher seeks to create in the classroom, especially in the early years. For example, not exposing very young children to television is one of those very basic changes that parents can make in the home. A typical Waldorf kindergarten in turn seeks to re-create the environment of the home. The kindergarten teacher, almost always a woman, represents a mother figure who does not 'teach' in a formal sense but creates form and rhythm and a nurturing environment by leading activities that would also take place in the child's home—storytelling, painting, cooking, singing, playing games, and allowing the children to play freely and imaginatively. As documented above, bush kindy can be a part of this picture.

Maria Montessori recognised the important link between the home and early learning centres, and in particular the way in which formal structured learning could influence and inform approaches to parenting and mothering:

> Not all mothers, she felt, understood how to care for their children. The experience of the Case dei Bambini showed that children could develop outside their homes, and in fact that when the children returned home their mothers and families were *educated through their children*. The important thing was that mothers and teachers should cooperate in helping the child to become independent. (Kramer 1976: 190, my italics)

The more consistency there is between the child's world at home and in the kindergarten, the more secure they can feel about the school environment and be able to grow into an attitude that will prepare them for the more formal schooling that should begin around the child's seventh year. In the secure and almost domestic situation in the kindergarten, the 'teacher' is playing out the role of 'homemaker', to the extent that the distinction between the two roles is so diffuse as to be almost blended.

> Parenting is one of the most important jobs, but perhaps the most undervalued. It really is a vocation, and one that takes constant work, both inner and outer. (Dowling 1999; cited in Stehlik 2015)

This is an interesting notion as it gives rise to the idea that if *vocational training* is linked to a work-specific job role, then *parenting as a vocation* also requires the acquisition of work-related skills and knowledge. If we further consider the classical rather than the contemporary meaning of vocation, as "a divine calling" (Dictionary.com), then we can see the connection with parenting as a higher calling and even a spiritual task.

Even more curious then that parenting is not recognised as a vocation or acknowledged as a skill that could be taught during the compulsory years of schooling. A broader curriculum focus on relationships and how to maintain them would at least be more practical, especially for teenagers experiencing relationship conflict with parents and/or first-time romantic relationships. Sex education as part of the Health and Physical Education curriculum can attempt to address some of these issues; however, in reality it is in the realm of self-directed adult learning that parenting education occurs, requiring individuals to engage in *constant inner and outer work.*

The 'outer work' of parenting involves many practical factors such as learning about feeding and caring for infants, establishing sleep patterns, doing lots of washing, and guiding their development in addition to looking after their wellbeing. The 'inner work' involves coming to terms with the responsibilities of parenting and making sacrifices of lifestyle, of one's personal space and time, of being able to spend time with partners, friends, and maybe other children. This does require constant work, as the developing child has increasingly different wants and needs; for example, a toddler requires stimulation, interaction, and interest and can't just be put down in one place while you get on with the housework—which is also constant. Not attending to this inner work can result in problems such as post-natal depression, not being able to bond with one's child, relationship issues, or just general fatigue and negativity about the pressures of parenting.

A lot of parenting education is done by trial and error, and the first child can often be a bit of a 'guinea-pig' while first-time parents figure out what to do and what works best, so that by the time the second or third child comes along, they have more experiential learning to draw on. However, the second (and third, and so on) child may have a completely different temperament and character and what worked for number one may not work for others. Back to the drawing board! Here is another reason why parenting *takes constant work*—it is an ongoing individual process of self-education and part of lifelong learning. Even with adult children, one is still their parent and the relationship still requires some form of continuing maintenance.

Parents are therefore partners in the process of teaching children. We have seen that the first vital three years of life represent the foundation of the child's life ahead, and those formative years are critical in developing language, social and behavioural skills for life. By the time children get to the age where it has been recognised since classical Greek times that they need some more formal schooling, parents still need to see themselves as partners in the education project.

> Parents need guidance in directing their children on the road that leads to responsible educational independence. (Illich 1971: 69)

Sometimes parents do not want to 'let go' of their children as they reach school age. Homeschooling, for example, has become an increasing trend, with an estimated 50,000 Australian children being educated at home by their parents—usually the mother (ABC TV 2017). Reasons for parents making the decision to homeschool and the effects on children will be discussed in more detail in Chap. 11. Another phenomenon that has been observed among millennial parents is the tendency to 'hover' over children with overly high expectations of their performance, pushing their development with a full timetable of extracurricular activities in addition to schoolwork, homework, and housework. Hence the term 'helicopter parents' to describe those who have probably read a lot of self-help books about childrearing, perhaps believe their child is above average or gifted, and are often projecting their own educational ambitions onto their children. The ease in which this label has entered the popular lexicon is demonstrated by Lancaster University sponsoring an online quiz in which you can find out in eight questions: *Are you a helicopter parent?* (theguardian.com/parents-guide-to-uni).

The book *Battle Hymn of the Tiger Mother* published in 2011 by Amy Chua coined the term 'tiger mums' to describe the type of mothers who practice intensive parenting and adopt a strict academic regime for their children. Interestingly, such women are generally highly educated and qualified themselves, but have been shown to suffer lower levels of happiness and satisfaction as well as higher levels of stress and tiredness (Bennett 2016). At the same time, it has long been established that there is a positive correlation between academic performance at school and parental education levels. Supporting children without smothering them is a fine balancing act and also suggests that parents who do not necessarily have high levels of social, cultural, and economic capital also need support.

Who will provide this—schools, the community, the state… or is it an expectation for self-education?

Recent US research has further suggested that such micromanaging parenting approaches can cause children to become anxious and actually diminish their academic ability and performance (Young 2017). One could make the connection between this sort of parenting approach and the pressure that millennial children face, leading to the increase in the types of childhood disorders discussed in this chapter.

> Not only does intensive motherhood mean less leisure time for the mothers, it also generates pressure … Young children often do not want to sit down at a table with a book when they could be running around and older children can be reluctant to do homework after a long day at school. (Bennett 2016: 1)

It highlights the fact that encouraging independence in children is also an important part of their development, and the eventual ability to enable the next generation to stand in the world on their own two feet with confidence is actually one of the main goals of parenting. Psychologist Erik Erikson used the term *generativity* to describe the need for parents to work selflessly towards leaving something for future generations. "Generativity has the benefit of helping your personality flourish, even while you provide vital sustenance and support to the next generation" (Whitbourne 2013). It also reinforces the fact that parents should not lose sight of the preciousness of the kingdom of childhood in developing an attitude of generativity.

When my eldest daughter was in Year 11, we sent her on a student exchange to Sweden for six months. She was 16 and seemed very young to go far away from us and live on the other side of the world with a strange family. She had a great time but I missed her terribly. I found the verse by Kahlil Gibran *On children* to be immensely comforting in explaining what my role as a parent actually was. I remember when my daughter returned, she had turned 17 and had changed. She actually told me: "I'm independent now".

> Your children are not your children, they are the sons and daughters of Life's longing for itself

They come through you but not from you, and though they are with you yet they belong not to you (Kahlil Gibran, The Prophet, 1923)

As parents, how do we know when to support our children and when to let go? When they are of school age it is important to realise that there is a certain partnership with their teachers in working with each individual child. This chapter has highlighted the important influence that the environment and technology can have on the developing child, but also the importance and lasting influence of positive relationships with peers and particularly with adults responsible for nurturing the child and its development, then knowing how and when to guide the child into a transition from dependence to independence. These relationships are critical but need to be clear: *parents have children; teachers have students.* Parents have been addressed in this chapter; Chap. 8 now addresses teachers.

References

ABC TV. (2017, June 3). School's out. *Compass*. Australian Broadcasting Corporation.

Albrecht, N. (2014). Wellness: A conceptual framework for school-based mindfulness programs. *The International Journal of Health, Wellness and Society, 4*(1), 21–36.

Baldwin, R. (1989). *You are your child's first teacher*. Berkeley: Celestial Arts.

Baldwin, R. (2016). *The great convergence: Information Technology and the new globalization*. Cambridge, MA: Harvard University Press.

Barbour, C., & Barbour, N. (1997). *Families, schools and communities: Building partnerships for educating children*. Upper Saddle River: Prentice-Hall.

Barkham, P. (2014, December 10). Forest schools: Fires, trees and mud pies. *The Guardian*.

Bennett, R. (2016, September 12). Tiger mums are unhappiest parents. *The Australian*. http://www.theaustralian.com.au/news/world/tiger-mums-are-unhappiest-parents/news-story/b092b9ed68ad1c69b5814ef783cde4ea. Accessed 5 June 2017.

Burrows, L. (2017, May 30). Children benefit from mindful teachers. *The Advertiser*.

Corderoy, J. (2017). Massive cyber attack creates chaos around the world. http://www.news.com.au/technology/online/hacking/massive-cyber-attack-creates-chaos-around-the-world/news-story/b248da44b753489a3f207dfee2ce78a9. Accessed 2 June 2017.

Creed, B. (2017). *Stray: Human-animal ethics in the anthropocene.* Sydney: Power Publications.

Dahlin, B. (2006). *Education, history and be(com)ing human: Two essays in philosophy and education.* Karlstad: Karlstad University.

Demos, J., & Demos, V. (1969). Adolescence in historical perspective. *Journal of Marriage and Family, 31*(4), 632–638.

George Washington University Milken Institute School of Public Health. (2015, December 8). New report finds 43 percent increase in ADHD diagnosis for US schoolchildren: Girls showed a sharp rise in ADHD diagnosis during eight-year study period. *ScienceDaily.* www.sciencedaily.com/releases/2015/12/151208150630.htm. Accessed 3 June 2017.

Gibran, K. (1923). *The Prophet.* New York: Alfred A Knopf.

Gross, R. (1963). *The teacher and the taught.* New York: Dell Publishing Co.

Harford, T. (2014, March 28). Big data: Are we making a big mistake? *Financial Times.* https://www.ft.com/content/21a6e7d8-b479-11e3-a09a-00144feabdc0. Accessed 21 July 2017.

Hicks, M. (2013, August). Why the increase in ADHD? New research reveals causes for ADHD type behaviors. *Psychology today.* https://www.psychology-today.com/blog/digital-pandemic/201308/why-the-increase-in-adhd. Accessed 3 June 2017.

Hopkins, N. (2017a). Social giant faced with difficult balancing act. *The Guardian Weekly, 26*(05), 17.

Hopkins, N. (2017b). Revealed: Facebook's rules on sex, racism and violence. *The Guardian Weekly, 26*(05), 17.

Illich, I. (1971). *Deschooling society.* New York: Marion Boyars.

Kearney, V. (2014). Bush kindy as a childcare centre. Chapter 3, In T. Stehlik & L. Burrows (Eds.), *Teaching with spirit: New perspectives on Steiner Education in Australia.* Murwillumbah: Immortal Books.

Knight, S. (2017). *Forest schools in practice.* London: Sage.

Kramer, R. (1976). *Maria Montessori: A biography.* Oxford: Basil Blackwell.

Louv, R. (2005). *Last child in the woods: Saving our children from nature-deficit disorder.* New York: Algonquin Books.

McMillan, M. (1919). *The nursery school.* London: Dent and Sons.

Merga, M. K., & Roni, S. M. (2017, March 10). Children prefer to read books on paper rather than screens. *The Conversation.* http://theconversation.com/

children-prefer-to-read-books-on-paper-rather-than-screens-74171. Accessed 3 June 2017.

Moore, R. (2014b). *Nature play and learning places: Creating and imagining places where children engage with nature.* Raleigh: Natural Learning Initiative and Reston/National Wildlife Federation.

Morita, E., Fukuda, S., Nagano, J., Hamajima, N., Yamamoto, H., Iwae, Y., Nakashima, T., Ohira, H., & Shirakawa, T. (2007). Psychological effects of forest environments on healthy adults: Shinrin-yoku (forest-air bathing, walking) as a possible method of stress reduction. *Public Health, 121*(1), 54–63.

Newton, M. (2002). *Savage boys and wild girls: A history of feral children.* New York: Picador.

Peters, M. (2017). Education in a post-truth world. *Educational Philosophy and Theory, 49*(6), 563–566. Special Section: History Education.

Postman, N. (1994). *The disappearance of childhood.* New York: Vintage.

Prensky, M. (2001). Digital natives, digital immigrants. *On the Horizon, 9*(5), 1–6.

Pridham, B. (2014). Bush kindy. Chapter 2, In T. Stehlik & L. Burrows (Eds.), *Teaching with spirit: New perspectives on Steiner education in Australia.* Murwillumbah: Immortal Books.

Reingold, J. (2015). *Everybody hates Pearson.* Fortune. http://fortune.com/2015/01/21/everybody-hates-pearson/. Accessed 16 May 2017.

Salinger, J. D. (1951). *Catcher in the rye.* Boston: Little, Brown and Company.

Schwartz, E. (1999). *Millennial child.* Great Barrington: Anthroposophic Press.

Seligman, M. (1995). *The optimistic child: A revolutionary approach to raising resilient children.* Sydney: Random House.

Seligman, M., & Csikszentmihalyi, M. (2000). Positive psychology. *American Psychologist, 55*(1), 5–14.

Stehlik, T. (2002). *Each parent carries the flame: Waldorf Schools as sites for promoting lifelong learning, creating community and educating for social renewal.* Flaxton: Post Pressed.

Stehlik, T. (2015). *Each parent carries the flame: Waldorf Schools as sites for promoting lifelong learning, creating community and educating for social renewal* (2nd ed.). Adelaide: Mylor Press.

Sun, Y., Mensah, F., Azzopardi, P., Patton, G., & Wake, M. (2017, May). Childhood social disadvantage and pubertal timing: A national birth cohort from Australia. *Pediatrics.* http://pediatrics.aappublications.org/content/early/2017/05/19/peds.2016-4099. Accessed 25 May 2017.

UNICEF. (1989). *United Nations convention on the rights of the child*. https://www.unicef.org.au/Upload/UNICEF/Media/Our%20work/childfriendly-crc.pdf. Accessed 30 May 2017.

US Census Bureau. (2017). *The Changing Economics and Demographics of Young Adulthood: 1975–2016*. https://www.census.gov/library/publications/2017/demo/p20-579.html. Accessed March 22, 2018.

Veen, W. (2006). *Homo Zappiens and the need for new education systems*. https://www.oecd.org/edu/ceri/38360892.pdf. Accessed 30 May 2017.

Whitbourne, S. K. (2013, June 2). The joys of generativity in midlife. *The Huffington Post*. http://www.huffingtonpost.com/susan-krauss-whitbourne/generativity_b_2575916.html. Accessed 16 Sept 2017.

Young, J. (2017, January 25). The effects of "helicopter parenting". *Psychology Today*. https://www.psychologytoday.com/blog/when-your-adult-child-breaks-your-heart/201701/the-effects-helicopter-parenting. Accessed 5 June 2017.

Zajonc, A. (2016). Contemplation in education. In K. A. Schonert-Reichl & R. W. Roeser (Eds.), *The handbook of mindfulness in education*. New York: Springer.

Part IV

'I Always Wanted to Be a Teacher'

8

Teaching the Teachers

Teaching the teachers is a critical aspect of the whole education system, but one where educational philosophy has taken a back seat to educational pragmatics. Pre-service teacher education is regularly under the media spotlight in terms of concerns about teacher quality, lowering standards and ideological biases. A brief history over time shows that 'teacher training' in teachers colleges has gradually been replaced by 'teacher education' in universities, where educational theory is meant to inform educational practice and vice versa. The perennial question of whether teachers are sufficiently prepared to meet the challenges of the profession on graduation is still debated and remains largely unanswered, while approaches to their education and development continue to be largely based on historical tradition:

> There has been remarkably little change in the ways in which teachers work in classrooms and schools, or in the ways in which teachers are educated for a lifetime of preparing young people for their future worlds. (Menter 2016: 1)

At the same time, in-service teacher education and ongoing professional development of teachers should be given just as much attention.

© The Author(s) 2018
T. Stehlik, *Educational Philosophy for 21st Century Teachers*,
https://doi.org/10.1007/978-3-319-75969-2_8

With a move towards continual reflective practice and professional learning communities among beginning as well as experienced teachers, a consideration of personal and professional educational philosophies becomes paramount, as argued in this chapter.

8.1   'I Always Wanted to Be a Teacher…'

The university where I taught for 25 years has one of the largest schools of education in the country, and every year I saw hundreds of young people enrolling in the teacher education programs, either the four-year undergraduate Bachelor of Education or the two-year postgraduate Master of Teaching. Each year I asked the students in my classes the same question: *Why do you want to become a teacher?*

I found that the responses generally fell into two camps: those who were inspired by a great teacher or teachers during their own school days and want to follow in their footsteps; or those who had negative experiences at school and believed they could do a better job, sometimes wanting to get into the profession to 'change the system' for the better. Often there was a family member who was a teacher and influenced the young person's career choice, and in addition there were many who had always wanted to be a teacher, identifying teaching as a preferred vocation because they liked the idea of working with children as well as being involved in what is seen as one of the *helping professions* (like social work, nursing, etc.). By the time the pre-service teacher experiences their first practicum placement in a school however, the romantic idea of working with children may quickly fade with the reality and responsibility of being in a classroom with up to 30 students.

My first placement after graduating and qualifying as a secondary English teacher was to a high school in the outer northern suburbs of Adelaide, in an area that was developed as a 'satellite city' in the 1950s and populated largely by migrant families who had been lured there by the South Australian government with promises of work, sunshine and big backyards for the kids to run around in. It was promoted as 'The City of Tomorrow' (Barnes 2016: 82). By the late 1970s, it had become a working-class, low socio-economic area with a reputation for social problems including intergenerational unemployment, alcohol and drug abuse, dysfunctional families, domestic violence, and disengaged youth. The high school buildings were 'the latest thing in modern architecture'; that is, bland brick monolithic structures resembling a factory. There were over 1000 students enrolled. On my first day, the headmaster took me aside and instructed me 'not to smile or be nice to the kids for at least six weeks or they will take advantage of you…'. He himself was a very severe and unsmiling character whose actual name I can't remember as he was known universally by the students as well as the staff as 'Spike'.

I found myself trying to teach poetry and literature to '30 bored kids' who had other things on their minds—mainly hormones, since they were Year 9 students aged around 14 and dealing with puberty, adolescence and teenage hopes, dreams and dramas. Most of the time was spent just trying to keep a lid on their behaviour, as conflict between students and the gangs that operated outside of the school sometimes got out of hand—one memorable day the school was in lockdown because a student had come to school with a firearm. There were many such *critical incidents*, but the one that really affected me as a beginning teacher and educator had to do with my own attitude towards these kids.

I had set an assignment task to the Year 9 class to write an essay. One female student had written a page and a half on the topic but her spelling, grammar and punctuation were very poor, and being the pedantic English teacher that I was, I used my red pen to make a lot of corrections before returning the paper with a low mark. I was then very surprised to receive a request from the girl's mother for a meeting, since parents were generally not at all interested in or engaged with what went on at the school. At the meeting, the girl sat there while her mother angrily waved the assignment in front of me. It was covered in red marks and slashes, words were crossed out, sentences re-written, exclamation and question marks stood out, and the final comment was not very encouraging. What did I mean by doing this to her daughter's paper? She had worked hard on it only to have it returned looking like a dog's breakfast. What about the content? I had only focused on the presentation and given it a low mark as a result. Who did I think I was just because I had been to university? And so on and so forth … I was mortified and apologised profusely. Ever since then I have never used red pen to mark student work on hard copy assignments—I always use pencil, which looks softer and also allows me to erase a comment that might have been written in undue haste!

But there were several other lessons for me to take away from this critical incident in my first teaching job. Firstly, I realised that behind every student in the class was a mother, father, guardian, or other adults who I needed to take into consideration as *stakeholders in the education contract*. Secondly, I needed to consider *each individual student's perspective* on their efforts and not apply a one-size-fits-all perspective based on my own middle class ideas about what constituted good work and appropriate writing. Thirdly, assignments, tests, and written work should be secondary to the primary consideration in teaching, which was *developing good relationships* with the students—including a consideration of each student's family situation. In this instance, for example, the poor girl was trying to communicate something in her writing which I had completely missed in my focus on the mechanics of the language, rather than its meaning or message.

Since then just about all of my practical experience and theoretical research in education have reinforced the importance of the teaching-learning relationship. As a teacher and an adult, one tends to assume a position of authority and even superiority over students, especially children, sometimes just by the nature of the situation but often through personal conceit and hubris. What I did not learn in my university pre-service teacher education course was that becoming a teacher would require continual questioning of my own assumptions, preconceptions, and value judgements about the characteristics of students that I would be *working with*, when the course mainly focused on *delivering content to them* in an expository one-way fashion. In other words, assuming that you have learned everything there is to know about teaching when graduating from a teacher education course is a big mistake.

Another critical incident that still stays with me occurred after I made the transition from schoolteacher to university lecturer. Early on in that career, I was delivering a lecture to a room full of adult education students—mature-age learners who were educators themselves. Right in the front row of the lecture theatre were students gazing at me intently as I read from my lecture notes and emphasised words and phrases with gesticulations and hand movements. One woman was nodding every time I made a point, which encouraged me no end. Another woman however would agitatedly wave her hands every now and then and point to her mouth. I could not figure out what was going on, but at the end of the lecture she came up to me and informed me that she was almost deaf and relied on lip-reading in order to clearly understand people speaking. Apparently I had a habit of putting my hands in front of my mouth when speaking. This was another revelation! Firstly, to assume that all of the students in front of me had the same abilities, secondly that some disabilities are not visible, and thirdly that unless one finds out whether all students are able to participate fully in the learning process, some of them may be excluded.

These critical incidents give examples of two fundamental beliefs that I still hold in my own teaching as well as in working with pre-service teachers—the importance of developing meaningful teaching-learning relationships with students and the recognition that within any group of students there will be differences of ability, background, interest, and motivation requiring an understanding of *differentiated learning*. Over and above these beliefs is the 'meta belief' that *a teacher must model being a learner until they finish teaching*. This not only means undertaking continual professional development and being accountable to external regulations like the teaching standards mentioned in Chap. 5 (AITSL) but adopting an attitude of lifelong learning that is driven by internal curiosity and a desire to keep growing and developing as a person as well as an educator. What then are we teaching the teachers in our pre-service programs if they are not the be-all and end-all of teacher education? Why do a large proportion of beginning teachers drop out of the profession in the first five years after graduating? What is the best way to prepare for the profession of teaching?

8.2   History of Teacher Education

The history of teacher education in Australia makes an interesting case study as it reflects trends and developments in education that were occurring internationally. As a British colony, early influences on Australian teacher education mainly included practices imported from Great Britain, such as *normal schools* and the *pupil-teacher system*. 'Normal schools' were so named to reflect the fact that they not only taught children but established *teaching norms* which could be imparted to the teachers as a form of initial training. The term is still in use in Finland where the teacher training schools attached to universities are known as *Normaalikoulu* (translation: normal school—see Chap. 10). The pupil-teacher system was basically an apprenticeship model, in which promising school students were recruited at age 13 or 14 by the 'Master teacher' who modelled basic teaching competencies that they were expected to learn over a period of several years.

Given the fact that the pupil-teacher model was really a form of cheap labour, in which the young apprentice was paid a pittance to look after junior classes while supposedly in training, this approach was more popular and was exploited in Great Britain and also in Australia from the 1860s until early into the twentieth century, by which time it was apparent that some system of dedicated teacher training institutions was needed to service the growing population and expanding schooling sector. Prior to federation in 1901, the various Australian colonies (now states and territories) had developed differing approaches to institutionalised teacher education, and this continued into the new century with the emerging teachers colleges being funded and directed at state level, compared to the federally funded universities. This distinction remained right up until 1988 when a unified national tertiary system was established, resulting in teachers colleges being subsumed by universities, or amalgamating to form new universities (Dawkins 1988). The university where I teach is one such latter institution, established in 1991 with the amalgamation of three state Colleges of Advanced Education with an Institute of Technology, creating the largest but youngest university in the state of South Australia. The first university in the state had been established way back in 1874 and still enjoys status as the 'Ivy league' or 'Sandstone' university compared with the 'Gumtree' universities of the 1960s (usually established on the metropolitan fringes of capital cities) and the 'Bessa brick' universities of the 'post-Dawkins' 1990s.

However, this historical two-tiered system created a perception that teacher training was a lower status, practical, and craft-based learning process that belonged in the vocational category, compared with the higher status of university education that was seen as more theoretical and research based.

> A pronounced binary system of education emerged in Australia between the two world wars. An elite university system remained essentially disconnected from teacher education which, in turn, became firmly embedded in training colleges which ranked as second-tier institutions. (Aspland 2006: 146)

As outlined in Chap. 3, here was a classic example of a distinction being made, at the level of higher education, between *practical and contemplative activity*. There have been variations to this model over time, such as initial university study followed by pedagogical studies in a teachers college, but this 'theory vs practice' divide is still prevalent today, not only in teacher education but in higher education more generally. Historically, university lecturers have not required formal teaching qualifications in order to teach in higher education; expertise and content knowledge based on studies in their particular field or discipline were seen as sufficient to impart that knowledge on to their students. So, for example, an Astrophysicist might be an expert in astrophysics based on empirical research and peer-reviewed publications, but not be very good at actually teaching the fundamentals of their subject to undergraduate students. While many universities have implemented some sort of tertiary teaching credential requirement for academic staff, it still begs the question as to why schoolteachers need a formal teaching qualification and many regulatory requirements such as state registration, national teaching standards, and so on when educators in the vocational and higher education sectors do not. Even when teachers colleges were first established, the lecturers were initially former schoolteachers themselves without requiring higher qualifications, further reinforcing this theory/practice divide.

Students in those early teachers colleges were taught with the same practice-based teaching methods regardless of whether they were training to become primary or secondary teachers. They were very conservative institutions, reinforcing the curriculum that was controlled by the state, and the attitudes and values that were entrenched in the schools where students undertook their practicum placements. In this regard teachers colleges maintained the status quo and did not involve themselves in the scholarship of teaching or research into educational change, as this was seen as the role of universities. Fast forward to today, and university-based teacher education now expects beginning teachers to not only engage with research but to become educational researchers or *practitioner enquirers* themselves, since "'research literacy' should be seen as a fundamental element of teaching and therefore of teacher education" (Menter 2016: 3). This has been an important shift in moving on from the initial apprenticeship model of teacher education to one in which beginning teachers are encouraged to explore new and emerging ideas about teaching content, classroom pedagogies, and assessment practices and bring those ideas with them into school settings where *professional learning communities* involve long-serving teachers who can benefit from this ongoing professional development. This is the *lifelong learning approach to teaching the teachers;* fine in theory but often in practice meeting with resistance from teachers who are entrenched in established ways of thinking.

8.3   Content Knowledge Versus Pedagogical Knowledge

In Australia in the 1960s, a teaching credential consisted of a two-year Diploma of Teaching. By the 1970s this had been extended to a three-year award, the equivalent of a bachelor degree, required to qualify as a primary schoolteacher. At the same time, secondary teaching had developed a higher status. As documented in the introduction, I completed a three-year bachelor degree majoring in English and then a one-year Graduate Diploma in Education to qualify as a secondary English teacher. Since teachers' pay scales were linked to credentials, the salaries of secondary teachers were therefore higher than those of primary teachers, creating another two-tiered system. This *credential creep* (see Chap. 3) continued into the 1990s, so that at the time of writing, the minimum primary teaching qualification in Australia is a four-year bachelor degree, while for secondary teaching it requires 'three plus two' years of time served at university—an undergraduate degree in one's subject or discipline area, then a two-year Master of Teaching or equivalent to cover the pedagogical aspects of being able to teach that subject.

The 'three plus two model' was adopted in response to the process established in the Bologna Declaration (European Commission 1999), in which European Ministers of Education agreed to a system of consistent and comparable university qualifications across the European Higher Education Area, at undergraduate, postgraduate, and doctoral levels. While not a member of this area, the fact that Australia followed the Bologna Process in upgrading professional qualifications in higher education demonstrates the impact of globalisation and the movement of knowledge across borders, boundaries, and nations into the twenty-first century.

A significant shift in conceptual thinking also occurred around the *fin de siecle*, and this was a purposeful change in nomenclature from *teacher training* to *teacher education*. The importance of this shift cannot be underestimated, since it represented a recognition of *teaching as a profession* requiring higher order personal and professional development, reflecting the progression from preparing teachers in a 'second-tier' training institution to the level of university, with a symbolic increase in status and creating parity with other similar professions such as psychology and social work. *Educating teachers* rather than simply *training teachers* shifts the focus from 'recipe-based' content and pedagogical knowledge that is predictable and stable to a recognition that educational contexts and content are unpredictable and fluid, evolving and changing, as discussed so far in previous chapters. Training implies a skills-based approach to learning, while the teachers of today and the future require a broader understanding of the educational landscape that covers all domains—cognitive, psychomotor, and affective.

But here we have a conundrum, inviting questions around the separation between *content knowledge* and *pedagogical knowledge*. The acronym 'PCK' represents *pedagogical content knowledge*, a synthesis of the two types of knowledge, or the ability to translate knowledge of a particular subject or learning area in a meaningful way to learners—what 'expert teachers' should be able to understand and deliver in a range of contexts.

A further 'branch of knowledge' has since been added in the twenty-first century with the increased application of ICTs, which is *technological knowledge*, creating the acronym TPACK—shorthand for a teacher's Technological, Pedagogical, and Content Knowledge:

> The expertise embodied in the TPACK of a teacher is different from the knowledge of a discipline expert (say a scientist or a historian), a technologist (a computer scientist), or an expert on learning (a psychologist). Teaching mathematics to Year 5 learners requires different pedagogical uses of ICT than teaching history in secondary school or literacy in the early years. In each case, the expert teacher needs to make creative links between what is being learned (content), how it is taught (pedagogy), and the appropriate tools (technology). (TTF 2017)

For a long time, teacher education was mainly driven by a focus on content knowledge and curriculum studies—the *craft of teaching*—with some academically influenced 'professional studies' in sociology and psychology increasing in more recent times, addressing *theories of education*. As we have seen so far, some of these theories have been with us for a very long time. For example, theoretical frameworks developed in the 1950s and 1960s from the cognitive and behavioural psychological sciences still dominate the professional studies curriculum, with pre-service teachers continuing to study Piaget's stages of development and Vygotsky's views on constructivism. It is interesting to note the suggestion in the quote above that psychologists are 'experts on learning'. If that is the case, why are psychologists not teaching our children? The answer is fairly self-evident: teaching requires a complex range of attributes and a combination of expert knowledge, such that a teacher is not only part psychologist but part social worker, part administrator, part manager, part instructor, part entertainer—to name just a few professions that are wrapped up in this unique role.

The way in which content knowledge can be seen as entirely separate from pedagogical knowledge is entrenched in the 'three plus two' model of teacher education. As an undergraduate studying a degree in science, for example, one learns about scientific facts and concepts which are taught and assessed in the *language of science*. It is well known that many occupations have their own unique jargon, terminology, and acronyms, and teaching is no different; so the shift from studying science as an undergraduate to studying education in a postgraduate program such as a Master of Teaching requires a shift in mindset and coming to terms with a whole new language of concepts and ideas. Terms like *pedagogy, methodology, evaluation, behaviour, objectives*, and so on acquire a whole new meaning in the context of education.

For myself as a Bachelor of Arts graduate majoring in English, then becoming an English teacher, it seemed self-evident that English was my discipline—the learning area and subject content that I had studied and specialised in for three years and was now 'passing on' to high school students. It was not until I had been teaching for ten years and eventually went back to university to study a Master of Education that the penny dropped and I realised that *education was actually my discipline*. This was brought home quite clearly by the recognition that I myself was experiencing continuing further education, that learning did not stop when one finished school, and that a whole new world of adult and lifelong learning had just opened up in front of me. Here I have to acknowledge some very inspiring and influential lecturers who expanded my mind to these ideas. A great teacher can inspire students at all stages of the learning process!

But this raises a question about initial teacher education:

At what point does one transcend being simply a content expert and become an educator?

The realisation that teaching is about more than just subject and specific curriculum areas should come sooner rather than later—and hopefully not ten years later! Of course it is recognised that a beginning teacher will need time and experience in which to develop their professional abilities, according to standards like those developed in Australia which incorporate four distinct career stages (AITSL 2017). However, there is no indication in the AITSL standards framework of how long it might take to progress from the *graduate* career stage to become a *proficient* and eventually *highly accomplished* and even a *lead teacher*. This despite the fact that graduate teachers will remain provisionally registered until such time as they can show progression to proficiency and achieve full registration, linking the standards to professional development as well as performance management requirements. As discussed in Chap. 5, as an accountability mechanism, the AITSL standards framework presents as a clear example of the GERM agenda at work.

As a framework for ongoing teacher education however, the standards are useful but necessarily generalised and generic (e.g. *Standard 3.1—Establish challenging learning goals*) and also very reductionist and instrumental. For example, within the seven AITSL standards there is a total of 37 sub-categories (sub-standards…?!), each described at the four career stage levels, therefore 148 permutations in all to consider—a rather overwhelming matrix of statements for categorising and 'measuring' good teaching. How to make sense of all of this and try to think in a more holistic way about the complexity of the teaching role?

Like any model, the TPACK model is a good place to start at being able to conceptualise and think about teaching as a *synthesis* of various types of knowledge and skill, as exemplified by the higher stages of Bloom's taxonomy of expertise and also reinforced by understanding the combination of *praxis*, *techné*, *episteme*, and *phronesis* that is involved (see Chap. 2).

However, the single word 'context' at the edge of the TPACK model diagram is perhaps the most important consideration in understanding, let alone applying, the model in a holistic way. *Context* should incorporate any number of possible questions such as: How appropriate are ICTs for young children? How accessible are they in the 'village' that is raising the children? How relevant are they to the 'village'? How do they affect a child's emotional life? These questions then lead to meta-questions such as: What actually is the village? What is the teacher's role when the village has 'disappeared' in the face of globalisation and liquid modernity? Is teaching about more than developing expertise in TPACK? If so, what is it and how do we incorporate it into teacher education?

8.4   The Philosophy of Teaching

A two-year qualifying degree (sometimes accelerated into an 18-month program) does not allow much time to cover all the bases that are considered necessary to prepare a graduate to become a qualified teacher. A four-year undergraduate degree should provide an opportunity for more time and space to be inclusive of extended theory and practice. However, much like the teachers colleges before them, university teacher preparation programs are highly regulated and controlled by what the teaching profession itself perceives as important and non-negotiable content. For a primary teaching degree, this includes covering all the learning areas and curriculum content that are delivered by general classroom teachers: science, maths, art, English, humanities and social studies, design and technology, health and physical education, and possibly a second language. In Australia, the professional teacher associations and state registration boards require mandatory subjects in special needs and Aboriginal studies, then there are one or two courses on psychology and child development, and the professional experience practicum components to fit into the program—the 'on-the-job' experience that is still seen as the most important aspect of the learning as strongly influenced by the technocratic and craft-based teachers college model.

In the teacher education programs at my university, there is currently one course on 'managing learning behaviours' and one course which introduces students to educational research—which I teach. While I also believe that research literacy is a fundamental element of teaching and teacher education, every year it is a struggle to get the students to believe this too, as they are so focussed on curriculum content, how to deliver it and how to survive in the classroom. In their feedback about my course they often can't see the connection between research and teaching, don't believe that the course is relevant, and express a desire for "more courses in behaviour management instead". Trying to shift the students' mindsets from seeing teaching as mainly *crowd control* to understanding that as *practitioner inquirers* they can actually develop a bigger picture view of the contexts that lead to behaviour management issues, is based on inculcating an appreciation of existing educational research as well as encouraging involvement in their own action research. Sometimes I can observe this light bulb of understanding switching on by the time the students graduate, but it is really not until they have had time to grow into the role and reflect on their experiences in the context of the complexities of 'the job' that this might really become internalised and fully embraced.

In this process and perspective, each individual student teacher, beginning teacher and even experienced teacher really needs to develop and be able to articulate their own *personal philosophy of teaching*.

I have stated that this is not a book about *how to teach*, it is a book about *why we teach*. In the Introduction I pointed out that the intention of this book is to put educational philosophy back on the agenda of teacher education, educational policy and educational practice. As a distinct topic for consideration and discussion, it seems to have disappeared from the discourse of global reform movements in education driven by technology, marketisation, and managerialism and has certainly dropped off the program in university teacher education courses where the curriculum has become crowded with all the regulatory content required by the profession and the state. It highlights the fact that there is an inherent tension between schools and universities operating as institutions of the state and government, as well as institutions of culture where we as a society would want to develop free-thinking citizens who are not necessarily bound or limited by such regulatory systems. The curriculum of teacher education programs is a case in point—they are regulated and prescribed by tradition, legislation, and formality, yet at the same time we want these programs to produce educators who are creative, reflective, and innovative. With no control over the curriculum they are studying, this seems like a contradiction in purpose. The same could be said of the curriculum that is being offered in our schools and which teachers are expected to maintain and reproduce. Who owns these curricula and decides their structure and content? The next chapter will address this specific question in detail, but it is just one of the deep questions that need to be asked if one is to begin articulating a personal teaching philosophy.

It is unlikely that the 'giant oil tanker' of education that we have constructed will change course quickly or easily, but rather than waiting or hoping for top-down improvements, change can be effected by a grass-roots approach at the local and individual levels, to influence things from the bottom up. However, first we need to ask the big question: *Where is the oil tanker heading?*

It seems self-evident to me now (although I did not understand this at all when I first started teaching) that before one can develop the practical skills, the content knowledge and the appropriate attitudes required to be a good teacher, one first needs to have a clear idea of what one is aiming for in the activity of teaching and for the broader education project. One therefore needs to address a number of questions, some of them rhetorical but still necessary I believe as part of the process of self-talk, self-reflection, and self-development:

1. The big picture first—where are we going?
2. What is the purpose of schools in my village/community/society?
3. What is my philosophy and why am I a teacher?
4. Can I make a difference even when the socio-economic circumstances are massive?
5. What are my values—do they align with the school's values?
6. What are the influences of history, religion and politics, and where do I sit?
7. What should be the outcomes of education and how will we know if we have achieved them?
8. Whose interests are being served in delivering the prescribed curriculum?

Hopefully some of the discourse and discussion around the history, development and critique of educational philosophy in earlier chapters, and in those still to come, provide food for thought in consideration of these questions. There are certainly no straightforward answers as such questions should be addressed individually and in context, and in a process of continual reflection, since contexts—and individuals—will not necessarily remain static over time.

There is nothing new in adopting a questioning attitude towards one's profession, and particularly in the profession of teaching. One of the underlying themes of this book is that we can learn from history, from past mistakes as well as successes, and with the benefit of hindsight all of the questioning, thinking and reflecting on education undertaken by educators and philosophers over the centuries can be useful in considering education today. A more recent contribution to the educational debate has been that of *critical pedagogy*, a philosophy of education and a social movement that grew out of the field of critical theory. Critical theory is a school of thought that arose in 1930s Germany, whose main thesis is a critique of traditional sociological theory which is aimed at *understanding society*, to arrive at a theory aimed at *changing society*. Critical theorists stress that human acts are inherently political and driven by ideology, and that the first consideration of any act or intention is to ask: 'Whose interests are being served by this?', and then go beyond initial and surface impressions to look for underlying influences and assumptions.

One of the originators of critical pedagogy was Paulo Friere (introduced in Chap. 2) who applied critical theory to his analysis of radical, community-based adult education in Brazil. Critical pedagogy applies a critical lens to the field of education, so that its advocates view teaching as an inherently political act, reject the idea that knowledge is neutral, and question whose interests are being served by both the espoused curriculum as well as the hidden curriculum. Friere is probably best known for his concept of *conscientisation* (conscientização), which means realising one's consciousness and becoming aware of one's own assumptions, beliefs, and implicit biases, in order to be able to challenge them (Friere 1996). This process of developing critical awareness of one's social reality involves a cycle of reflection and action for which Freire adopted the term *praxis* to describe and explain. Recalling the definition of praxis, this is a type of knowledge that combines practical action with awareness of the social context and one's agency in influencing and being influenced by social settings.

Critical pedagogy focuses in particular on challenging and even radicalising teachers by asking them to examine "ideological postures" that often unconsciously inform their perceptions and actions, particularly "when working with linguistic-minority and other politically, socially, and economically subordinated students" (Bartolomé 2004). While it is admirable and important to aim for a 'level playing field' in attempting to overcome disadvantage and create equality of educational opportunity for all, the type of praxis for developing a personal teaching philosophy I suggest should look beyond just this minority deficit view to embrace a more holistic picture that takes in the mainstream and majority as well. In other words, taking a stance against discriminatory and hegemonic practices in education is all well and good but it is still operating within the playing field. Pulling back and taking a 'helicopter perspective' of the playing field exposes bigger picture questions to be asked, such as: Which players are included or excluded? What is the purpose of the game? Who has decided the rules of the game? What happens when the rules keep changing? Where is the playing field even located?

8.5   Who Teaches the Teachers?

A further question to be considered in teacher education and in developing a philosophy of teaching is: *Who is responsible for teaching the teachers?* As discussed earlier in the chapter, a traditional apprenticeship model was for many years seen as adequate for passing on teaching skills from master to novice, and even when teacher training institutions were established, the instruction was delivered by practising teachers. There are even recent moves in the United Kingdom to return to this type of apprenticeship model with a policy shift towards allowing "schools to directly recruit their own students and train them to be teachers on the job" (Menter 2016: 2). This model is rather insular and self-referential and, unless the teacher educators themselves are also engaged in reflection on their own beliefs and biases, can produce a self-regulating system that maintains the status quo and never looks outside itself to take that helicopter view.

   Therefore, even in a professional teacher education program of integrated theory and practice such as those now offered at universities, it is incumbent upon the individual themselves to take responsibility for own career and professional development, including a consideration of how, why, and from whom they are being educated. Encouraging pre-service teachers to see themselves as *practitioner enquirers* is based on this notion, but also implies that those of us who are teacher educators should be modelling this professional practice. Enquiring into the practice of those who are passing on the 'received wisdom of experience' should also be part of this model, creating an interactive and collaborative learning experience rather than a one-way transmission of information based on an assumption of authority, wisdom, or position. In other words, if I am going to be any kind of educator, I need to be open to continually being educated myself. I need to act as a role model, much like those teachers who inspired me at school were my role models.

It is interesting to note that the word *mentor*, which has been adopted into the English language to refer to someone who imparts wisdom and shares knowledge with a less experienced colleague, has also been passed down to us from classical Greek mythology and literature. In the tale of *The Odyssey*, most famously told by Homer (2003), when the hero Odysseus leaves for the Trojan War he asks his friend Mentor to look after and advise his son Telemachus until such time as he returns. Odysseus is away for more than ten years and in his absence the relationship between the older and younger man has been characterised as one of passing on wisdom and advice, from the voice of experience to the ears of youth.

The mentoring relationship is an interesting one since it is often unplanned, usually developing spontaneously through circumstance and existing acquaintance or connections, and a person could have many overlapping mentoring relationships over time. Mentoring programs have of course been instigated and contrived in many workplace and educational settings as deliberate programs for inducting, supporting, and educating novices, often with success although some involve measuring and monitoring. These are more formal, highly structured, short-term relationships compared with informal, possibly longer-term relationships, sometimes referred to as 'friendship mentoring'.

The reciprocal nature of the relationship is also interesting, with the word 'mentee' being used to describe the person being mentored, and assumptions often made about the mentor being an older person and usually of the same gender. The fact that the mentor may require some training in the process of mentoring and could also be learning from the mentee makes the traditional top-down master-apprentice idea of mentoring a little redundant. While there is no real term for a mentoring process that might actually be equal and co-dependent, 'reciprocal mentoring' and 'peer-to-peer mentoring' are terms used to describe this type of relationship, which can occur in school settings among colleagues as a result of team teaching, working in faculty groups or project teams.

A 'whole of school' mentoring program has also proved to be successful in encompassing all of the staff in an educational setting, from novice pre-service teachers right through to school leaders (Earp 2017). The importance of mentoring support especially for beginning teachers is highlighted by the fact that:

> Teacher attrition is a current issue in Australia and other economically developed countries, with up to 50 per cent of teachers resigning from teaching within the first five years. (Arnup and Bowles 2016: 229)

In the 'Start Well' study conducted by the Hunter Institute of Mental Health into the mental health of beginning teachers, it was found that 99% of respondents reported the importance of support from peers and mentors in their first years after graduation (Bennett et al. 2016). This reinforces the position already stated that 'teaching the teachers' does not conclude with graduation from a teacher education program but is an ongoing necessity, and introduces the suggestion that those who 'teach the teachers' will range from university lecturers to mentors, colleagues, peers, family, and friends—in fact anyone who is involved either formally or informally in helping teachers develop and maintain not only the skills and knowledge for effective teaching but a clearly articulated philosophy of teaching that underpins them. To be able to look forward to 'a lifetime or preparing young people for their future worlds' and not become an attrition statistic, a philosophy of continual lifelong learning is vital as part of this process, for maintaining resilience and not only keeping up with the current demands of the profession but embracing its unfolding future. Regardless of who, where, and when however, the responsibility to take advantage of all available learning experiences rests with the teacher themselves, since *self-education* is at the heart of it all.

References

AITSL. (2017). *Australian Professional Standards for Teachers*. https://www.aitsl.edu.au/australian-professional-standards-for-teachers/standards/list. Accessed 14 June 2017.

Arnup, J., & Bowles, T. (2016). Should I stay or should I go? Resilience as a protective factor for teachers' intention to leave the teaching profession. *Australian Journal of Education, 60*(3), 229–244.

Aspland, T. (2006). Changing patterns of teacher education in Australia. *Education Research and Perspectives, 33*(2), 140–163.

Barnes, J. (2016). *Working class boy.* Sydney: Harper Collins.

Bartolomé, L. (2004). Critical pedagogy and teacher education: Radicalizing prospective teachers. *Teacher Education Quarterly, 31*, 97–122.

Bennett, G. A., Newman, E., Kay-Lambkin, F., & Hazel, G. (2016). *Start Well: A research project supporting resilience and wellbeing in early career teachers – Summary report.* Newcastle: Hunter Institute of Mental Health.

Dawkins, R. (1988). *Higher education: A policy statement.* Canberra: Australian Government.

Earp, J. (2017, March 9). A whole school mentoring program. *Teacher Magazine.* https://www.teachermagazine.com.au/article/a-whole-school-mentoring-program. Accessed 18 June 2017.

European Commission. (1999). http://ec.europa.eu/education/policy/higher-education/bologna-process_en. Accessed 14 June 2017.

Friere, P. (1996). *Pedagogy of the oppressed.* London: Penguin.

Homer. (2003). *The Odyssey.* London: Penguin.

Menter, I. (2016). *What is a teacher in the 21st century and what does a 21st century teacher need to know?* www.aare.edu.au/blog/?p=1516. Accessed 16 May 2016.

TTF. (2017). *Teaching teachers for the future.* http://www.ttf.edu.au/what-is-tpack/what-is-tpack.html. Accessed 13 June 2017.

9

The Role of the Teacher

The role of the teacher in the bigger picture of education is discussed in this chapter, in which I suggest that teachers need to see themselves as part of a cluster of professional roles providing an integrated and holistic contribution to education that goes beyond the classroom and school to the wider community. Teaching can be seen as one of the 'helping professions' similar to the professions of psychology, social work, and primary health care. Educating and nurturing children and future citizens is a huge responsibility and can put unreal expectations on teachers to do it all alone, and sharing this important task in a joined-up approach with other professions and providers can reduce stress and burnout. In this chapter, some examples of enlivening teaching as an art as well as a science are given via creative and imaginative ways of thinking about pedagogy and curriculum as well as content.

If *pedagogy* is defined as "the art or science of teaching" (dictionary.com), to what extent can we say teaching is a science, and equally what aspects of teaching might define it as an art? How is the practice of art different from the practice of science? We have seen in the previous chapter how teaching has evolved from a craft-based apprenticeship model to a professional occupation requiring tertiary qualifications and knowledge

© The Author(s) 2018
T. Stehlik, *Educational Philosophy for 21st Century Teachers*,
https://doi.org/10.1007/978-3-319-75969-2_9

of theory as well as practice. Yet there are still many myths, assumptions, and questions about the role of the teacher in the education process, about what makes a 'good' teacher, about how teachers should be educated, and to what extent they are able to influence or change the education systems and traditions in which they are defined. This chapter goes deeper into identifying and analysing the role of the individual teacher, suggesting that they are just one part of the bigger picture of the education project, which includes a consideration of the curriculum and who owns it; socio-economic factors that affect the life-worlds of children and their families; other adults and professionals who are involved; educational policies that drive the schools agenda; conditions under which teachers are employed and supported; and the interactions and relationships between all of these various factors that actually determine to a large extent the effectiveness of teaching. We have already identified the importance of the physical environment and its possible positive or negative effects on teaching and learning, and in fact the founder of the Reggio Emilia movement in Early Childhood Education, Loris Malaguzzi (1920–1994), referred to it as the *third teacher*:

> There are three teachers of children: adults, other children, and their physical environment. (Edwards et al. 2012)

9.1   Teaching as Art and Science

Chapter 8 introduced the distinction between content knowledge, pedagogical knowledge, and technological knowledge. Content knowledge is clearly associated with the prescribed curriculum or the specific subjects that are deemed important and form the basis of not only the school timetable but the teacher education programs and the way in which schooling is structured and sequenced. A random glance at any school's weekly timetable will show that the school day is usually divided into lessons or periods in which classes are meant to focus on a particular learning area, or defined content. This reductionist and instrumental approach to knowledge being compartmentalised into separate subject areas, as inherited from modern philosophy and the Enlightenment (see Chap. 2), could be seen as the *science* aspect of teaching and will be unpacked later in this chapter. The pedagogical knowledge required to not only deliver this content but to enliven it, make it interesting and engaging, and motivate students to want to learn it, is the more *artistic* side of the role. It requires creativity, imagination, and thoughtful planning as well as the ability to respond flexibly to the students and the situation. It speaks much more to the *personality of the teacher* and their own temperament, motivation, and interest in the content. Of course, we have also assumed there is a distinction between the arts and the sciences and acknowledge that it is contrived and simplistic, since it is possible, for example, to teach science in an 'artistic way' and to teach art in a 'scientific way'. Even better is to view this as an integrated approach, for example, teaching colour theory with the science of the light spectrum.

However, if Comenius was right, and "the secret of teaching lies in the method" (cited in Dahlin 2006: 16), then the artistic side of pedagogy would seem to be the more important aspect to focus on. Here we raise an interesting point about the art of teaching which has been implied already; that having content knowledge alone is not sufficient to effectively be able to share that knowledge without some requisite pedagogical skills and knowledge. In fact, the converse is also apparent, as it is anecdotally well known that there are some educators who can take any content and make it engaging, interesting, and motivating for students, regardless of their depth of knowledge of the subject. Such people have often been labelled as 'natural born teachers'. Popular culture has often presented teachers who are charismatic, inspiring, and passionate about their work as somehow gifted, special, and above average, for example, in films like *To Sir, with love* (1967), *Stand and Deliver* (1988), and *Dead Poets Society* (1989).

Famous names who have been described as born teachers also include those whose main occupation was something else entirely, such as the composer Leonard Bernstein:

> People often say that Leonard Bernstein was a born teacher, but actually it's more accurate to say that he was a born student who just couldn't wait to share what he learned. In his whole life, he never stopped studying. (jamiebernstein.net)

Here we have further reinforcement of the importance of self-study and lifelong learning in keeping teaching practice vibrant and alive. But the question still remains, are some people 'born teachers' while others are not?

Elizabeth Green (2015) suggests that teaching is a craft which anyone can learn, but that the difference between competence and excellence in teaching is still down to the individual, and that while teaching is not some intangible inherited gift, it does require personal qualities of tenacity and instinct to be able to navigate the complex skills, contexts, and relationships involved.

But is teaching a craft or a vocation? Recall that the definition of vocation included the implication that it is a 'calling'… so that while the ideal of the natural born teacher may be a romantic one, the idea of being called to the profession is perhaps more realistic. As noted, there are many people who aspire to the profession because they love children and always wanted to be a teacher…but if you love aeroplanes and always wanted to be a pilot it is not simply a matter of getting into a cockpit and being able to fly a plane! Neither should the profession of teaching be an assumed skill, but even when educated to the same theoretical and practical level, undoubtedly some people seem to 'naturally' do better than others.

What are the role attributes of the teaching situation? You could find out by taking a quiz to see if you have the natural attributes and inclinations to thrive in the teaching role, including 'reality check' questions like: "Do you really mean it when you say 'I love kids'?" and "Are you inspired to work long hours?" (Kangan Institute 2017).

As discussed so far, in addition to the content, pedagogical and technological knowledge now required in the profession, teachers also require knowledge of the regulatory and legal requirements that are increasingly incumbent upon them, as well as knowledge of the changes occurring in the characteristics of children and their parents and society in general. Dealing on a daily basis with the type of chaos, complexity, unpredictability, paradox, and contradiction apparent in the post-modern world of educational bureaucracy, classroom teaching is just one role among many that are now required in the profession. Teachers also act as administrators, managers, social workers, counsellors, psychologists, nurses, mentors, assessors, advisors as well as learners themselves. In reality, not everyone will be able to fulfil all of these roles, and the *art of teaching* becomes lost in the scientistic world of high-stakes testing, mandated reporting and accountability requirements, curriculum frameworks, and performance standards. One way to cope with this and build teacher resilience and effectiveness is to take an *inclusive* view of the teaching role and emphasise one of the major themes of this book: that teachers should not be alone in carrying out the important job of educating our children.

9.2   You Are Not Alone

98% of respondents to the study said that the teaching profession leaves them feeling inundated by pressure. (Start Well study report, *The World Today*, ABC RN June 2, 2017a)

Loris Malaguzzi rather starkly referred to the 'pitiful isolation' of the teacher in conjuring up the image of the lone adult in a classroom full of children or adolescents, single-handedly delivering a curriculum, managing behaviours, assessing learning, and trying to develop meaningful relationships with up to 30 diverse individuals. No wonder some people are naturally better at this than others! In the development of the Reggio Emilia movement, Malaguzzi believed that the burden of teaching should be shared in the classroom by at least two teachers, but also by children themselves who could teach and learn from each other, as well as from the physical environment (Edwards et al. 2012). However, a move towards an even more holistic view in which the teacher has the support of 'the whole village' in the education process is occurring in many instances, so that teachers are part of a larger group of people and services 'wrapped around' the students.

The teacher as member of a team of professionals and ancillary support workers can be seen as part of a 'joined-up approach' to dealing with 'the problem of education' that initially arose out of working with disadvantaged and at-risk young people, for example, through programs developed as a result of *social inclusion initiatives*. In South Australia, for example, the state Labour government set up a Social Inclusion Unit in the early 2000s after a similar initiative in the United Kingdom by the Blair Labour government in the 1990s. The programs that came out of the South Australian unit targeted youth homelessness, early school leaving, drug and alcohol abuse, and mental health issues among young people. I was involved in evaluating the School Retention Action Plan, which had committed $28 million over four years to a number of strategies and programs addressing the rate of school retention in the state, which was very low in comparison with other states and territories.

Some of the specific social inclusion education programs will be discussed in more detail in Chap. 11, but a number of salient findings which came out of that evaluation report relating to the role of teachers included the following:

- The goodwill of the local community and input from unpaid volunteers are significant factors in many educational programmes, and a whole-of-community approach to education is emerging as a key factor in successfully engaging young people at risk.
- The role of social workers and youth workers is crucial in providing support for students at risk. At the same time, teachers are increasingly taking on counselling and welfare support roles, often without adequate training. However, working in partnership, teachers and social workers can become more aware of social work and educational practice respectively, a process which could be formalised in pre-service and in-service training in both professions. (Stehlik 2006: 3)

While researching the social inclusion programs in education, what became apparent to me was the extent to which teachers and schools relied on the input of the local community as well as other professionals in delivering *education for all*, not only in working with students identified as 'at risk' (at risk from disadvantage, domestic dysfunction, mental health issues, etc.). This really reinforced for me that the aphorism 'it takes a village to raise a child' was not just rhetoric but reality.

Many schools have a 'welfare team' in place that may include counsellors, psychologists, nurses, and social workers, all working together with teachers as a team to provide the kind of individualised support that is 'wrapped around' a particular student identified as at risk. In Finland, for example, the welfare team is a part of the school staffing structure and works with all students to reinforce the concern for wellbeing that is central to their educational ethos (see Chap. 10).

In some of the alternative learning programs that were developed from the South Australian social inclusion initiative, I observed teachers taking on the roles of social worker with young people and social workers actually delivering teaching to school students. Despite both professions having distinct and differing qualification and registration requirements, it was obvious that the roles were increasingly overlapping and becoming blurred. The suggestion in my 2006 report for an integrated approach to training in both professions must have been prescient, since now there are professional preparation programs being offered that combine both social work and teaching, such as the Master of Social Work with a Secondary Education Teaching Certificate at the University of Pittsburgh.

However, such innovative programs are few and far between, and universities, employers, and even professional associations continue to uphold the traditional separation of disciplines, job roles, and careers that maintain the status quo:

> We want to create a nation of critical thinking, creative, flexible and innovative people who understand the importance of collaboration. Yet teachers are not supported to be truly innovative and the system is far from flexible, creating barriers to desired practice, and frustration. (McKinnon 2016)

The importance of collaboration is clearly needed in all the 'helping professions' working together rather than in isolation at the school and community level; however, a joined-up approach is also needed at the policy level. A large part of the social inclusion initiative was to get government departments to work together rather than in isolation, with their conventional approach of focussing on just one or two portfolios producing the effect of a number of unconnected 'silos' beavering away while missing the bigger picture. Examples of 'the left hand not knowing what the right hand is doing' are rife in the public sector and reinforced by having separate departments for education, health and social work when not only experience but research tell us that in practice these portfolios should be interconnected.

For example, programs offering parenting education and support to vulnerable and disadvantaged families are generally provided by social services departments, yet they should be directly linked to schools and the children under compulsion to attend them—although that portfolio belongs to education departments. Similarly, absenteeism and school truancy will necessarily involve social service departments working with families, so it is vital that they adopt a joined-up approach and work with education administrators in addressing such issues. Legislative requirements can make this seemingly simple and obvious task complicated; for example, in some jurisdictions a teacher is allowed to get into a car with a student if they require emergency transport, but social workers are not permitted unless there are two of them, not always a workable proposition.

As Lawson points out, most of the specialised human services professions "also have a specialized organizational home. Educators have schools, social workers have children's service organizations, and nurses have hospitals and health clinics" (2016: 4). However, human needs and wants cannot be reduced to one or more discrete technical problem(s) that conveniently fall within the jurisdiction of a specialised profession and their home organisation, and are not necessarily transferable or transportable to different contexts, places, and cultures. The challenge is to go beyond such traditional structures and develop ways of thinking about human services in a more holistic way.

Since the health and wellbeing of young children has been shown to be a central aspect of the education project, then an integrated or joined-up approach to this at the policy level should also include government agencies that are responsible for these portfolios. This is clearly demonstrated in working with Indigenous communities and schoolchildren, for example, in Australia where the life expectancies and health levels of Aboriginal people are well below those of the general population (ABS), which directly affect and limit educational outcomes. Policy responses to improving school attendance and life opportunities for Aboriginal children therefore require collaboration and cooperation between government departments for health, education, and social services in working together to ensure that basic needs are attended to before any effective education can occur. In remote Aboriginal communities in Australia, for example, poor nutrition can directly disadvantage learning opportunities, and the prevalence of ear infections (*otitis media*) in young Indigenous people can result in hearing loss and difficulty in understanding speech. Add to this the fact that English is a second language for many of these children, and it is apparent that a teacher alone cannot address all of these issues and will need support from other professionals and services, including Aboriginal Education Workers with local language and cultural capability.

As discussed in the previous chapter, the mental health and resilience of teachers—particularly in the first few years in the classroom after graduation—can be fragile, and to avoid feeling 'inundated by pressure', teachers need to know that they are not alone and that their role is one part of a larger community of people who are also involved in raising children. *Resilience*, *relationships*, and *responsibility* could be seen as the 'three Rs' of the role of teacher. Relationships are key in working with students and parents, but also in collaborating with colleagues outside of the classroom and even outside of the school, and the responsibility for developing and maintaining those relationships rests with the teacher as part of their professional practice and hopefully, personal philosophy of education.

9.3   Who Owns the Curriculum?

Although teachers may be responsible for their own practice and for modelling appropriate behaviours, attitudes, and values in the classroom as part of their pedagogical knowledge, they are not always responsible for the actual content that is required to be delivered, and generally must work within the bigger picture of curriculum frameworks and assessment requirements that are laid down, again through the policy interventions of government agencies and many other interested parties. It has been suggested a number of times so far in this book that the curriculum mostly taught in schools today is a product of historical tradition and assumptions around how knowledge should be constructed, understood, and passed on through the generations. One of the questions we need to address in considering the future of education and schooling is: Who owns the curriculum?

[Curriculum: *Latin: action of running, course of action, race, chariot, equivalent to curr(ere) to run* (dictionary.com)]

The dictionary definition and etymology of the word 'curriculum' demonstrate that it really applies to a *course of action*, or a *process*, rather than a fixed set of subjects and content—yet that is how we now think of it when we refer to *the curriculum* of a school, college, qualification, or credential. The link with the verb *to run* is very interesting, and reinforces the idea of a curriculum as a journey with some form of destination. The colloquial usage of the term 'CV' is an abbreviation for Curriculum Vitae, which literally means 'the course of one's life or career'. Here one would refer to formal qualifications but also to life experience and personal skills and qualities, developed and acquired over time. For most people this is a work in progress with a CV being continually brought up to date as the course of one's life and career unfolds, or to refer to the dictionary definition, as the 'race is being run'.

So curriculum is a slippery concept, and we have already mentioned in Chap. 3 that there can be an overt or espoused curriculum as well as a *hidden curriculum*, which can include the beliefs and values of teachers and educational institutions that influence the way in which the stated curriculum is taught. For example, a school motto, just like any organisation's mission statement, will subtly suggest the underlying philosophies and values that students will be expected to respect and internalise. A teacher's own biases and value judgements may be quite unconscious and unwittingly transmitted, reinforcing the need discussed in the previous chapter for a critical self-appraisal of one's own beliefs and assumptions as part of self-education and professional development.

However, the espoused curriculum that teachers work with and that is made publicly available in syllabus statements, school brochures, and education department policy statements is one that I suggest needs critical examination. We have seen with the GERM agenda that there has recently been a shift towards focussing on core subjects at the expense of subjects which become marginalised (see Chap. 5). While literacy and numeracy are capabilities that should be developed through the course of the curriculum, they now tend to be treated as actual subjects and associated with the teaching of the mother tongue (e.g. English) and the teaching of mathematics, rather than being embedded and integrated into all aspects of the curriculum. Furthermore, other *literacies* that are important for successful participation in modern society are assumed to be embedded in the general curriculum, such as computer literacy, technological literacy, social literacy, aesthetic literacy, and so on.

For a first world country with a high standard of living and a robust economy, Australia has a remarkably high level of illiteracy among the adult population, with figures from the Australian Bureau of Statistics showing that 44% of Australian adults don't have the literacy skills they need to cope with the demands of everyday life and work (Better Beginnings 2017). Concerns about the levels of literacy in Australia have therefore driven the focus on language and literacy learning and once again put the spotlight onto teachers and the curriculum as not being effective enough in teaching functional literacy, grammar, and spelling.

Similarly, a secondary school curriculum that provides a range of subject choices has seen less students choosing 'hard science' subjects like chemistry, physics, and mathematics, with a perceived drop in the number of graduates interested in careers in the natural and physical sciences. Young girls are particularly turning away from subject choices in science and maths, prompting a number of programs aimed at encouraging them into considering careers in science with mentoring by female role models sponsored by the scientific community (ABC RN 2017b). Of even more concern to the curriculum policy makers has been the decreasing number of graduates with science degrees going on to become schoolteachers, creating a shortage of qualified science and maths teachers—in particular women—who would be the role models for school students becoming interested in science and maths, hence the recent focus on STEM (science, technology, engineering, and maths) subjects as well as literacy.

'Science' however is not neutral or values-free. Historically, the link between science and religion has been shown in the great paradigm shifts in knowledge of the natural world, such as proving that the earth is round and not flat—a proposition which at the time was seen as complete heresy. Remarkably, at a time when science is making great advances in our understanding of the universe, controversies like this between opposing scientific theorists continue to the present day. For example, *creation science* is on the curriculum in the United Kingdom, the United States, and Australia under the strong influence of fundamentalist Christian groups in promoting the biblical version of human development rather than the evolutionary version, not only in faith-based private schools that receive public funding, but also in some public schools (Ricci 2015). The actual management of Academy schools in the United Kingdom by such doctrinaire organisations, as discussed in Chap. 5, is an example of the way in which the school curriculum as a whole is not neutral or values-free and can be 'owned' by particular interest groups. In working within any curriculum framework therefore, teachers must ask: Whose interests are being served by the curriculum?

The religious influence on our contemporary understanding of curriculum as a course or path of life rather than the original Latin meaning of a chariot race has been attributed to John Calvin (1509–1564), the French theologian who was a major instigator of the Protestant Reformation of Christian theology during the sixteenth century, with a critical pedagogical perspective suggesting that since then "the word and concept of curriculum have been embedded in a Protestant, bourgeois, commercial/capitalist culture" (Doll 2008: 181). Examples of the commercialisation of education have been given in previous chapters, with capitalist interests being reflected in the general view that a major function of schooling is preparing young people for the workforce; but the notion that the modern western curriculum maintains a culture of Protestantism is based on the related idea of the 'Protestant work ethic', which pervades the contemporary practice of schooling as characterised by hard work, discipline, and duty. The German sociologist Max Weber (1864–1920) first proposed this concept and its links with modern capitalist society and economic rationalism in his book *The Protestant Ethic and the Spirit of Capitalism* published in 1905.

The first educational use of the word *curriculum* can also be traced back to the sixteenth century when it was used to describe a systematic study of the Seven Liberal Arts (see Chap. 4) by Petrus Ramus, a French philosopher and Professor of Logic (1515–1572). Ramus was one of the first to propose a structure of sequenced study from the general to the particular that could be represented on a chart, with this 'simple order' having the effect of organising and *methodising* the curriculum. With the aid of the printing press, Ramus was able to widely distribute his ideas which became influential enough for universities to begin structuring their curricula into separate discipline areas and to form the foundation of the subsequent work of Comenius, who as we have seen not only championed the importance of *method* but also proposed the modern education system and curriculum which evolved through Humboldt, Descartes, and others to what we have inherited today (Stanford Encyclopedia of Philosophy 2014).

9.4   Curriculum Responses

Teachers must somehow work within the kind of highly structured and ordered curriculum that has been shaped by such historical and deeply entrenched influences, but also be able to respond to reactive policy shifts such as those coming from the GERM agenda, driven by concerned politicians and policy makers who demand that more attention be given to core subjects and assessment of literacy and numeracy through the use of high-stakes testing. There are ways in which the received curriculum can be creatively manipulated and even subverted however. One way is to take an integrated and more holistic approach to the curriculum rather than viewing it is a matrix of discrete subject areas. A number of examples of this approach are now presented.

At the conceptual level, there have been concerted moves to make the STEM agenda more integrated with Art and Design principles. The STEM to STEAM initiative argues that the high technology economy of the twenty-first century will require innovative thinking that can be enhanced by incorporating 'A for Arts' into what has been seen as a purely technological and scientist domain. In the United States, this extends to encouraging the integration of Art and Design into all levels of school education, placing Art and Design at the centre of STEM research, and influencing organisations to hire artists and designers as innovative thinkers (http://stemtosteam.org/). Arts-based approaches to teaching have long been a feature of creative and integrative ways to make curricula come alive. Research into using performance art and drama with young learners has shown a number of value-added benefits in various areas, such as reading comprehension, writing, motivation, problem-solving, communication strategies, critical thinking skills, empathy, and socioemotional learning as well as artistic skills and creative imagination (Belliveau 2014).

Another variation on the acronym is STEEM which introduces *E for the environment* into the equation, in recognition of the importance of education for sustainability and a global concern for environmental issues that on the one hand are the product of science and technology and on the other are perceived to require scientific and technological solutions for addressing them. Two case studies in the following chapter give more detailed examples of STEAM and STEEM: the central place of the arts in the Steiner/Waldorf curriculum and environmental awareness at the heart of the curriculum of Green School Bali.

At a whole-of-school level, the *middle school movement* was based around the concept of an integrated curriculum and a more holistic approach to teaching the core subjects and major learning areas to children in the 'middle school' years from about Grades 6 to 9, or Grades 7 to 10 in some countries and jurisdictions. These grades straddle the traditional gap between upper primary and lower secondary, and middle schooling approaches and methodologies aim to create a more gradual pathway between junior and senior schooling, since research has shown that young people often fall through this transitional gap. The movement gained momentum in Australia in the 1990s with the National Middle Schooling Project, which defined the middle school curriculum as being learner-centred emphasising self-directed and co-constructed learning, community oriented, flexible and responsive to local needs, and collaboratively organised and ideally delivered with a team teaching approach (ACSA 2017).

Middle schooling is really a pedagogical approach and a philosophy concerned with the appropriate education of children in the age range 10–15 years, which has been discussed in Chap. 6 as representing the stage of development that includes a change from pre-pubescence into adolescence. These years have been identified as 'difficult' and are associated with the beginnings of disengagement from learning, or 'switching off' which can then lead to behavioural problems that may escalate in high school. The middle schooling philosophy is therefore more functional than structural, and generally applied as a distinct approach to teaching the middle years in schools that offer kindergarten to Year 12, although some separate middle school campuses have been created with mixed results (Dinham and Rowe 2008).

A response to the middle school movement in Australia has included influencing the way in which teacher education programs are structured and conceptualised, with some universities introducing specialisations in Primary/Middle teaching in their Bachelor of Education degrees. At the University of South Australia, for example, the Bachelor of Education (Primary/Middle) aims to graduate generalist primary teachers who are also qualified to teach one or two specialist subjects up to Year 10 in secondary school. Generalist teachers are seen as preferred to specialist teachers in the middle years where it is also considered important for students to have fewer teachers in order to be able to develop positive teaching-learning relationships. However, there is some criticism of this approach which argues that depth of subject material cannot be achieved without specialist teachers and with the type of interdisciplinary approach that may not give enough time for students to develop expert knowledge in individual subjects.

This interdisciplinary approach is characterised by integrated curricula which can take various forms, including a *synchronised approach* in which similar content and processes are taught across a number of subjects, a *thematic approach* which links subjects around a particular theme, a *project-based approach* in which subject boundaries are blurred, a *school-specialised approach* with long-term projects such as a school garden or performing arts program, and a *community-focused approach* reaching out beyond the school into the wider community (Dinham and Rowe 2008).

One example of a thematic approach to the integrated curriculum was based around a particular work of art, which was presented to students to stimulate and generate a number of responses that incorporated visual art, language arts, history, geography, and social studies. St Michael's Church of England Primary School in the United Kingdom refers to it as part of their 'Creative Curriculum':

> A unique curriculum designed to meet our children's needs in a changing world and to create above all, lifelong learners who are self-motivated and curious to learn. Each term a new title is introduced and artefacts, non-fiction books, pictures and information provided act as an initial stimulus. Certain skills are planned and taught within each topic, such as chronol-

ogy, timelines, note-taking or map reading, and then the children have the opportunity to develop and pursue the topic into the areas which most interest them. (st-michaels-school.org)

In this example the students viewed the painting *Seaport with the Embarkation of the Queen of Sheba* by Claude Lorrain, painted in 1648 and now in the National Gallery, London: https://www.nationalgallery. org.uk/paintings/claude-seaport-with-the-embarkation-of-the-queen-of-sheba. While contemplating the painting, students also listened to a selection of music from the period. The rich detail of the painting, its historical provenance, and its mythological subject matter provided a range of responses including paintings, drawings, poetry, stories, and maps, both as individual and group efforts. The role of the teacher in this 'creative curriculum' approach is therefore not so much to deliver content as to provide stimulus and a resource-rich and safe environment in which students can respond individually, collectively, and creatively.

Project-based learning has long been a feature of curricula across both primary and secondary schools, and is not limited to a middle school methodology. The curriculum of Steiner/Waldorf schools, as presented in the following chapter, includes a capstone project in Year 12 that is a major part of the assessment contributing to the matriculation result and in some jurisdictions to a university entrance score. My eldest daughter studied black and white portrait photography for her final year project, which included learning to use a camera and a darkroom as well as working with live models and presenting artistic work. It must have constituted a form of deep learning, as she went on to university art school, majored in photography and at the time of writing is completing a PhD in visual art practice.

The International Baccalaureate program is unique in presenting a curriculum that is managed and moderated on a global level in comparison to state-based or national curricula, but delivered locally in IB World Schools across the globe. Since 1968 the IB curriculum in the senior years has also required a capstone project that is a major part of the assessment, and since 1994 there has also been a separate middle school curriculum (http://www.ibo.org/).

The revised South Australian Certificate in Education (SACE) that was developed after a ministerial review of secondary education in 2006 introduced a number of educational reforms for the senior years of high school. Interestingly, one of those reforms included introducing a mandatory research project subject, which at the time of writing is the only subject that all students must take—all other subjects can be elective choices, given various guidelines and university entrance requirements (www.sace.sa.edu.au/). Such project-based learning not only provides the opportunity for deep learning in a particular area of the students' own interests but encourages the improvement of research skills including the development of critical thinking.

However, it has been interesting to observe the response of teachers to the introduction of the SACE research project and reinforces the way in which secondary teachers see themselves as subject/content experts according to their education, training, and self-identity as a specialist. As part of their teaching role, they must supervise students undertaking the research project, which requires a particular set of skills that does not include delivering specialised content as they would do in a traditional subject or classroom. Many teachers have been confronted by their lack of understanding in responding to student-centred projects on a one-to-one basis, and even resent not being able to practice their usual teaching methods based on their subject expertise. For some this has been a steep learning curve in pedagogical practice and suggests that a focus on the teaching-learning relationship may still be seen as secondary to a focus on the prescribed curriculum. In presenting role models to secondary students, I suggest that teachers have a duty of care to not only model a passion or at least an interest in their subject areas but to recognise the importance of modelling lifelong learning through inquiry-based practice and a research orientation. This addresses the key question for this section: *What is my role and purpose as a teacher?*

As discussed earlier in this chapter and the previous one, great teachers can inspire students to follow their dreams and have happy and successful lives, including making career decisions based on the adult role models they admire. However, with regard to the teaching profession, the cycle of 'teachers influencing students who may become teachers and therefore go on to influence more students' can be seen in a number of aspects of schooling, and not just in subject areas like science and maths. For example, Indigenous students often do not complete school without the inspiration and support provided by the role models of Indigenous teachers in their classrooms, who in turn represent a far smaller percentage in the profession than in the general population partly because of this cycle of early school leaving. In Australia the number of Aboriginal people who complete a university degree is growing but still representatively small, and that smaller pool of graduates will often go into professions other than teaching where there are similar needs for role models. So quite often the role of the teacher is subtle and includes many other things than just delivering content and providing appropriate methodologies. A diverse teaching workforce will model and reflect the diversity of the society or 'village' in which the children are being educated and socialised.

In creating the environment for learning, teachers must also model creativity themselves; in developing moral character and appropriate social values with students, teachers have a responsibility to be aware of their own moral character and model the kind of affective behaviours that society would assume to be appropriate. These various roles are examples of the hidden curriculum, and qualities over which teachers have some agency and control if they are aware of them. The stated curriculum, however, is generally presented as a given, and while teachers may be able to contribute to consultations and be part of working groups that develop curriculum materials, they are very often on the receiving end of curriculum frameworks and documents with very little control or input into what they are expected to teach. In this scenario, their role in developing and maintaining social relationships with all stakeholders involved in the education project is more critical than ever.

References

ABC Radio National. (2017a, June 2). *The World Today*. Australian Broadcasting Corporation.

ABC Radio National. (2017b, June 20). *Life Matters*. Australian Broadcasting Corporation.

ACSA. (2017). Australian Curriculum Studies Association. *Principles of middle schooling*. http://www.acsa.edu.au/pages/page28.asp. Accessed 27 June 2017.

Belliveau, G. (2014). *Stepping into drama: A midsummer night's dream in the elementary classroom*. Vancouver: Pacific Educational Press.

Better Beginnings. (2017). https://www.better-beginnings.com.au/research/research-about-literacy-and-reading. Accessed 26 June 2017.

Dahlin, B. (2006). *Education, history and be(com)ing human: Two essays in philosophy and education*. Karlstad: Karlstad University.

Dinham, S., & Rowe, K. (2008, September 3). *Fantasy, fashion and fact: Middle schools, middle schooling and student achievement*. Paper presented to BERA conference, Edinburgh. http://research.acer.edu.au/cgi/viewcontent.cgi?article=1005&context=tll_misc. Accessed 27 June 2017.

Doll, W. (2008). Complexity and the culture of curriculum. Chapter 13. In M. Mark (Ed.), *Complexity theory and the philosophy of education*. Chichester: Wiley-Blackwell.

Edwards, C., Gandini, L., & Forman, G. (Eds.). (2012). *The hundred languages of children* (3rd ed.). Santa Barbara: Praeger.

Green, E. (2015). *Building a better teacher: How teaching works (and how to teach it to everyone)*. New York: W. W. Norton & Company, Inc.

Kangan Institute. (2017). Signs you were born to be a teacher. https://www.kangan.edu.au/students/blog/be-a-teacher. Accessed 21 June 2017.

Lawson, H. (2016). Categories, boundaries and bridges: The social geography of schooling and the need for new institutional designs. *Education Sciences, 6*(32), 1–14.

McKinnon, M. (2016, January 11). Teachers are leaving the profession – Here's how to make them stay. *The Conversation*. http://theconversation.com/teachers-are-leaving-the-profession-heres-how-to-make-them-stay-52697. Accessed 23 June 2017.

Ricci, C. (2015, May 18). Evolution or revolution needed to oust creationism? Creationism may be gone from the curriculum but it still finds its way into some schools. *Sydney Morning Herald*. http://www.smh.com.au/national/education/evolution-or-revolution-needed-to-oust-creationism-20150514-gh1bf3.html. Accessed 27 June 2017.

Stanford Encyclopedia of Philosophy. (2014). *Petrus Ramus*. https://plato.stanford.edu/archives/spr2014/entries/ramus/#Met. Accessed 27 June 2017.

Stehlik, T. (2006). *Levels of engagement: Report of findings prepared for the social inclusion unit on the action research project across school retention initiatives*. Adelaide: UniSA/South Australian Government.

Part V

Case Studies of Educational Philosophies

10

International Comparisons and Case Studies

This section of the book compares education systems, philosophies, and approaches in a number of different countries and cultures and shows that place, space, and ethos do make a difference to educational outcomes. Three case studies are introduced and discussed in this chapter. Firstly, a whole of country case study is made of Finland, its education system and its culture. Secondly, Steiner Education as an example of a holistic educational philosophy and a worldwide network of alternative schools is outlined and analysed. Thirdly, Green School Bali is presented as an example of a school purpose built to develop and deliver education for ecological and social sustainability.

10.1 Finland: Equality Begins at the Blackboard

Ever since Finland quietly emerged as a country which topped the international polls in educational achievement and student outcomes such as PISA (www.oecd.org/pisa/), educators and policy makers around the

© The Author(s) 2018
T. Stehlik, *Educational Philosophy for 21st Century Teachers*,
https://doi.org/10.1007/978-3-319-75969-2_10

world have been turning their gaze on this small Nordic country in the hope of finding out the secret to their success (Tamkin 2014). A number of significant factors have been determined and are well established: teaching is a high-status profession in Finland; all teachers have a master's degree; education is well-funded by the state and free to all; school retention rates are high; and the country whose economic revival was led by companies such as Nokia had become a world leader in high level information technology applications, including in education.

I was as interested as anyone else in Finland's education system, having visited the country in 2006 and 2008 when I had the opportunity to meet and talk to teachers, school principals, and university educators. At the time, the message I received was something like: "Yes, we have achieved good educational success…but we ourselves are not so interested in academic outcomes…we are more concerned that our children are *happy*" (Tonder, 2006, personal communication). This sentiment stayed with me, and in 2013 I applied for an Endeavour Executive Fellowship from the Australian government with the proposal to spend some time in Finland investigating their schools' structure and culture as well as their teacher education programs and processes, to try and find out whether their school students were indeed happy as well as performing well academically.

I spent ten weeks in Finland from July to September 2014, for most of the time being based at the University of Eastern Finland in Savonlinna, at one of its three campuses. Visiting schools, talking to teachers, principals, students, parents, university lecturers, student teachers, and education bureaucrats was an informative experience, and I learned much about not only the Finnish education system but the cultural, societal, and historical factors on which this system is founded. I found that relationships between students, teachers, parents, and even educational administrators are based on trust and that the wellbeing of children is central not only to schooling but to Finnish society and culture. In addition to realising that *equality of educational opportunity* is fundamental to the Finns, the notion of *pedagogical love* emerged as the most salient term and concept which describes and encapsulates the 'secret' to the Finnish approach to education.

Background and History

Finland is a relatively small country (population 5 million) situated in a unique geographic position at the edge of Europe, up against its massive neighbour to the east, Russia. Finns do not really consider themselves to be Scandinavian as the Finnish language shares no common roots with the other Nordic countries of Sweden, Norway, and Denmark. Nevertheless Finland's history is bound up with both Scandinavia and Russia as for 300 years it was under Swedish rule, then for more than 100 years under the control of Russia, to whom it lost some territory after World War II—a fact which is still in living memory and a sore point in Eastern Finland.

Achieving independence in 1918 as a state in its own right was therefore a significant moment in Finnish history and an achievement that Finns still hold on to and fiercely protect. Together with the unique Finnish language, this underpins their particular national character and drives the social democratic welfare state that has since developed, which foregrounds equity and equality of opportunity for all Finns regardless of gender, socio-economic, or regional status. Some important figures responsible for achieving independence and promoting Finnish nationalism included the composer Jean Sibelius and the educator Uno Cygnaeus. These 'movers and shakers' realised early on that education was going to be the key to achieving independence for Finland and creating a civilised state founded on knowledge rather than ignorance, preparing the country for a prosperous future and creating an egalitarian society. Contemporary commentators such as Michael Booth suggest this direct link between education and social welfare is still a salient feature; that in Finland "equality starts at the blackboard" (2014: 279).

The basic right to education is therefore enshrined in the Finnish constitution. Public authorities must secure equal opportunities for every resident in Finland to receive education and be able to develop themselves, irrespective of their financial standing. Legislation provides for compulsory schooling and the right to free pre-primary and basic education, which includes among other things daily meals for students and subsidised transport. The Ministry of Education and Culture is the third largest ministry in Finland and its share of the state budget was 12% (6.6 million Euro) in 2014. There are a very small number of independent schools (e.g. Steiner and Montessori) but even these are fully funded by the state.

Historically teachers were seen as 'Candles of the people' lighting the way to Finnish independence, and this is still a very strong cultural and societal view (Booth 2014). Teaching is seen as a high-status profession in Finland and was described by a number of people I spoke to as a 'favourite occupation'. It is therefore competitive to enter teacher education programs and requires a high standard of entry to university—based on a matriculation score as well as an entrance exam and an interview. The salient feature of the university teacher education programs is their research-based approach, in which student teachers are taught to think critically and must complete a thesis in the three-year bachelor program, then another thesis in the two-year master's program. At the University of Eastern Finland, the students are introduced to the forest—which covers most of their country—as a learning environment and a teaching resource that can be utilised in a variety of cross-curricular research and teaching projects (Fig. 10.1).

How the Finnish Education System Works

The Finnish National Board of Education works with the Ministry to develop educational aims, content, and methods for primary, secondary, and adult education. There is a national curriculum but it is enacted at the municipal level: local administration is the responsibility of the regional municipal authorities, which play a prominent role as education providers. Kindergartens, day-care centres, comprehensive schools, upper secondary schools, vocational, and further education centres are all administered by the local municipality. This includes responsibility for teaching staff salaries, employment conditions, and professional development. The Director of Educational and Cultural Development for the Municipality of Savonlinna, for example, was directly responsible for 24 schools and 900 staff in the region. The school principals reported to him and met regularly as a group, as well as being linked in to centralised policy developments in the capital, Helsinki.

Fig. 10.1   The forest as a teaching resource: trainee teachers on excursion, Eastern Finland

Teachers and schools however are afforded a great amount of independence from bureaucracy and centralised control. There are no school inspectors or quality control processes imposed from above—rather there is a kind of collective compliance based on self-evaluation and self-referential assessment. High-stakes testing such as the Australian

NAPLAN scheme is not mandated and national tests (such as PISA) are voluntary and schools can opt to engage in them for benchmarking against other schools but this does not result in publically available 'leagues tables' such as those associated with the MySchool website information required of Australian Schools (www.myschool.edu.au/).

Higher education is also the responsibility of the Ministry of Education and Culture and all university tuition is free, including for foreign students. Finland has 14 universities, eight of these offer teacher education programs. Every teacher in Finland (apart from kindergarten teachers) has a master's degree as a minimum requirement. Teacher training is organised in a unique way in comparison to the Australian situation: the eight universities offering teacher training all have University Teacher Training Schools which belong to the Faculties of Education. Teachers in these schools are actually employees of the university, while the schools themselves still follow the National Curriculum and enjoy the same independence that other schools do. In Finland they are known as Normaalikoulu (Normal schools); also referred to as Training Schools or Practice Schools.

There are 11 Finnish Teacher Training schools that not only provide an education for students at comprehensive and upper secondary levels but also offer supervision of teaching students undertaking professional experience and act as *demonstration schools* for teaching experiments and educational research, as well as providing and supporting in-service teacher training. The number of students in the Teacher Training Schools totals around 8000, and every year about 3000 teaching students complete their teaching practice there.

Surprisingly, it is interesting to note that despite the high status of teaching in Finland, teacher salaries in general are significantly less in comparison to Australia. On average in 2014, they were 32,400 Euro (AUD$45,600) per annum; by comparison in South Australia, annual salaries ranged between AUD$61,500 for Tier 1 and AUD$89,000 for Tier 9. However, the apparently lower Finnish salaries are offset by the fact that many basic services in Finland—including health, childcare, and education—are heavily subsidised by the state. For example, some early learning centres offer 24-hour childcare—fully subsidised—for working parents.

Finnish children attend kindergarten and pre-school until the age of seven, when they enter comprehensive school which covers Grades 1–9. They are therefore at least a year older than Australian children who currently begin their Reception school year at age five. Senior high schools are separate institutions offering Grades 10, 11, and 12 for students who are usually around 16 when they transition into high school. This transition could involve moving from home to attend high school, particularly for one of the many specialist high schools that offer programs in music, art, or dance. A 16-year-old Finnish high school student could therefore be living independently while studying, supported by a living allowance from the state.

This is not uncommon in Nordic countries, and underpins the approach to senior school in which students are treated and respected as young adults rather than adolescents and given responsibilities which they must honour. For example, Taidelukio School in Savonlinna is a specialist art and music high school with fully equipped music and art studios. On enrolment, all students are given a key to the school by the principal, who trusts them to come and go after school and on weekends to be able to access the facilities. No teachers are required to supervise and there has never been a problem in the ten years that this practice has occurred. Students sign a contract and know that if anything happens, this entitlement will be taken away. Trust is the key to making this work.

In all the schools I visited, behaviour management did not appear to be an issue—teachers were addressed by their first name and the relationship between student and teacher appears to be much closer than the more formal approach adopted in many countries. A significant factor in developing and maintaining this relationship is the daily school lunch, where students and teachers sit and eat together in the school canteen. I observed this in every school, even the kindergartens, since I was always invited to partake in lunch. I firmly believe that the simple fact of eating and socialising together every day has a number of significant educational benefits: the children learn appropriate social manners and rituals related to eating and putting away their dishes; they have a healthy and nutritious meal every day (and I believe this is linked to improved behaviours); they learn to mix freely and socially with each other as well as teaching staff and other adults; teachers can observe social behaviours and peer groupings and whether particular children are eating alone or not mixing with their peers; and parents do not have to worry about packing school lunches!

Of course, once again the free meals are a big expense but the Finnish education budget covers this as well; and despite the cost of introducing a free meal scheme, if there was one thing I would recommend adopting in Australian schools, it would be this, as I believe the benefits would outweigh the costs in the long term. We know that in many parts of the country children come to school hungry and do not eat well, and if they do eat are often consuming unhealthy processed foods containing sugar and preservatives which hype up their behaviour and cause problems for teachers and other students, as well as learning difficulties for the child.

Another feature of the Finnish school is the way the school day is structured, again centred on the wellbeing of the whole child. In the Comprehensive Schools, the first lesson generally starts at 8.30 in the morning and goes for 45 minutes. The children are then given a 15-minute break and inevitably they will go outside into the school yard and play—even in winter when the weather can be snowing and well below 0 °C. This pattern is repeated throughout the day—a lesson, then a break, a lesson, then a break. There is a Finnish word for this 15-minute break time—*välitunti*. The word has more than one meaning, and can be translated as 'the best time' and also 'a lecture between', or in effect a 'gap lesson'. *Välitunti* can therefore be seen as not just random playtime but a key part of the pedagogical approach. The school day itself is not that long, usually finishing by 2 pm, so that 'hothousing' or cramming content through accelerated intensive study and hours of homework is certainly not one of the secrets to Finnish educational success—quite the opposite in fact. It was described to me as 'unhurried working', giving each child time to grow and learn according to their needs, with healthy living, healthy food, sport, culture, art, and creativity being valued more highly than homework.

The Finnish education system therefore can be characterised by trust, freedom, flexibility, and a concern to put the wellbeing of children at the centre of the system, with teachers contributing to a supportive and close relationship with their students balanced with delivering appropriate content and providing a high standard of academic direction. The notion of *pedagogical love* provides an interesting and engaging conceptual term that can be used to capture all of these features in one overarching idea.

Pedagogical Love

Uno Cygnaeus (1810–1888) was one of the founding educators responsible for developing and promoting elementary schooling as well as teacher training in Finland. He was influenced by the work of contemporaries such as Friedrich Froebel and in turn influenced the thinking of others such as John Dewey with his views on the importance of craft and technology studies in schools. In 1910 Cygnaeus described 'good teacherhood' by noting that just delivering content knowledge will not ennoble young people to learn, but that "every teacher has to blaze with the spirit of sacred love" (Cygnaeus 1910: 197). *Pedagogical love* has been defined as a form of love that is distinct from other, perhaps more familiar forms, for example: romantic love, maternal love, love for fellow humans, or love of one's country (Määttä and Uusiautti 2011).

Over a century later we know from research and experience that positive relationships between teachers, students, and parents are central to effective teaching and learning (Stehlik 2011), and the concept of pedagogical love is no different in starting from the premise that human beings are fundamentally *emotional* creatures and that *intellect* and *will* can often be secondary drivers of interest. The German philosopher Max Scheler (1874–1928) strongly promoted this view in his writings on 'the phenomenological attitude', which he regarded as being based on primal impulses such as those characterised by love, further proposing that love can arouse intellectual and logical thinking (Solasaari 2003).

> Max Scheler's philosophy of love emphasizes how important it is for people's development and learning that they learn to direct their interest and love, in addition to temporary pleasures, toward higher mental values and goals. (Määttä and Uusiautti 2011: 33)

Theoretical evidence to support this philosophy of love includes Gardner's multiple intelligence theory, which led to Daniel Goleman and others identifying *emotional intelligence* as a valid concept for guiding thinking and behaviour (Gardner 1983; Goleman 1995). Other contemporary versions of this concept in education settings include the notion of a *strengths-based* approach to learning, which recognises that learners are individuals with particular strengths that can be directly addressed and enhanced in teaching methodologies, harking back full circle to the early theories of Froebel and his first kindergartens, in working with the active power and strength of children (Lopez and Lewis 2009). Here strengths can include emotional intelligence and creative imagination as well as academic ability or physical prowess. Contemporary responses to this in a curriculum sense include play-based learning as discussed in Chap. 6 and individual learning plans and personal development goals as manifest, for example, in senior school Certificates in Education such as the South Australian Certificate in Education (www.sace.sa.edu.au/).

In the same way, "pedagogical love would rather aim at the discovery of pupils' strengths and interests and act based on these to strengthen students' self-esteem and self-image as active learners" (Määttä and Uusiautti 2011: 34).

In Finland however, pedagogical love appears to manifest at a far deeper level than just as curriculum frameworks or individual learning plans. In fact, while all children and young people are valued as individuals, there appears to be a more collective approach to learning in which all children experience the same curriculum, the same opportunities, and the same support from the whole community to achieve collaboratively. The greater good (or the good of the nation, the people) appears to be more highly valued than individual competitiveness and achievement. The Finns are well known for their modest and self-effacing characteristic and this is also deeply embedded in their cultural history, which is founded in part on their hard won independence, but also on their mythology.

A number of teachers spoke to me about the importance of *The Kalevala*—the nineteenth-century epic poem compiled from Finnish oral history and folklore and recognised as one of the most significant works of Finnish literature—in underpinning their whole culture. The stories and characters in The Kalevala promote certain values and morals which are respected and upheld in Finnish culture, and by association in Finnish education. These include the idea that the way to solve problems is by the intellect rather than brute force, that all children are loved and respected, that all Finns strive to be part of a civilised nation (Lönnrot 1835; Synge 1977).

In the schools this can be observed in the level of trust that is apparent at all levels—teachers trusting pupils, parents trusting and respecting teachers, principals trusting teachers to do their job well without formal performance management, municipal directors trusting principals to manage their schools without formal inspectors, and so on. As mentioned earlier, teachers are relatively independent—free to teach in the way they want, but without abrogating their responsibilities for good teacherhood, which relies on establishing reciprocal relationships of trust. Määttä and Uusiautti consider that a teacher who is aware of pedagogical love as a way of teaching will aim for a balance between keeping pupils in constant dependency and allowing complete independence: "Pedagogical love speaks to interdependence – the recognition and acceptance that we need others" (2011: 34).

This two-way relationship between teacher and learner also requires the teacher to recognise that teaching is personal, relational, and dependent on their own personality and the impact of their influence and guidance. The importance of believing in their learners' abilities, with the consequent effect of the learner also coming to believe in their abilities, is an example of another well-known educational conundrum—expectancy theory (Rosenthal and Jacobsen 1968). Pedagogical love therefore is not a form of sentimentalising or watering down of standards and expectations, but an acknowledgement of achieving well and aiming high according to the expectations of self, school, and society—and where these are aligned as in the case of Finland, 'education for all' is not an empty piece of rhetoric.

Finally, the unique Finnish language holds another key to understanding Finnish culture, schooling, and society. No other country or culture speaks or reads this language or any language remotely similar, and it brings the Finns together as a nation in a way that English-speaking countries may not fully be able to understand. The fact that teaching the Finnish language is referred to in the school curriculum as 'the Mother Tongue' demonstrates how deeply embedded it is in the Finnish national psyche and imbued with a personification of unconditional love and care. The word *suomalaisuus* encapsulates this notion; loosely translated as "Finnishness; it should be noted that the word in Finnish has a double meaning, relating both to nation and language" (Klinkmann 2010: 99).

All of the above provides food for thought for educators in other countries, such as Australia. To what extent could we apply the principle of pedagogical love in our schools, given that our country has completely different history, climate, culture, and language as well as educational, teacher training, and school funding systems? Could we become a nation which is child-centred and in which every family respects the child and considers education the foundation to national prosperity as well as personal wellbeing? Many Australian parents have a view of schools that has been coloured by their own experiences—often negative as suggested in the Introduction—and would require a massive cultural shift in mindset. Could we ask Australian teachers to accept a lower salary and invest the funding balance into subsidised school meals instead? If we want to learn from the Finns, these are some of the questions that would need to be addressed at a macro level. At a micro level however, I would like to think that we could still encourage and develop 'good teacherhood' in Australia through practising pedagogical love in the classroom.

10.2   The Worldwide Waldorf School Movement: Education Towards Freedom

> Our task is to educate the human being in such a way that he or she can bring to expression in the right way that which is living in the whole human being, and on the other side that which puts him/her into the world in the right way. (Rudolf Steiner 1968: 35)

Rudolf Steiner (1861–1925) was an Austrian philosopher and scientist who in his lifetime initiated many practical applications of his theories on human and social development in fields as diverse as agriculture, medicine, art, architecture, human movement, and education. The essence of Steiner's world view was that a study of the evolution of humanity through various stages of civilisation and consciousness will reveal the true direction for the development of society and the individual person in modern times. He coined the term *Anthroposophy* to explain this, of which various definitions have been given, but according to Shepherd (1983: 73):

> … perhaps no one definition would contain its whole meaning. The word "sophia" always denotes the divine wisdom, and "Anthroposophy" indicates that this wisdom is to be found in the knowledge of the true being of man and of his relation to the universe.

Given Steiner's considered and wide-ranging interests in the renewal of social forms through individual development, he was asked by the German industrialist Emil Molt in 1919 to establish a school for the children of the workers in his Waldorf-Astoria cigarette factory, and the first 'Waldorf Free School' opened in Stuttgart in September of that year. It was to be 'free' in the sense that it would be accessible to all social classes and not limited by bureaucratic constraints, denominational doctrine or dogmatic ideology. The success of this first school went on to inspire one of the fastest growing independent movements in education which has since spread to all corners of the globe, and at the time of writing there are over 1200 Steiner schools worldwide and 2000 Early Years settings in a total of 60 different countries (Steiner Waldorf Schools Fellowship 2017). The fact that Waldorf schools are to be found in places as diverse as Israel, Africa, Moscow, Thailand, the Philippines, Argentina, and India as well as Europe, America, and Australia reinforces the universal application of Steiner Education that seems to transcend language, religion, culture, and place.

It is remarkable therefore that the original curriculum and teaching methodologies which Steiner developed over a period of three months in 1919 still form the basis of the pedagogical approach taken in Waldorf Schools around the world today, despite—and possibly because of—the rapid rise of teaching technologies and educational theories based on cognitive and educational psychology which became popular over the last century, as discussed in previous chapters. Even more notable is the fact that this pedagogical approach is firmly rooted in its basis in Anthroposophy, providing an underpinning educational philosophy that teachers find support from and parents respond to, something that is increasingly absent from secular state schooling systems which strive to be politically correct and values-neutral—yet as a consequence I would argue suffer from a lack of cohesive direction. In this respect, Steiner Education can be firmly placed within the Humanistic/Holistic tradition and resonates strongly with the curriculum work that has been termed *mythopoetic* (MacDonald 1981).

What Is Steiner Education?

This is a question that is frequently directed at Waldorf educators around the globe, and several schools address 'Frequently asked Questions about Waldorf Education' on their websites. The Cape Ann Waldorf School, for example, replies in part: "Waldorf Schools seek to educate the whole child, integrating rigorous academics with emotional and spiritual growth and physical skills" (1999: 1). This whole-child orientation is often referred to in the literature as 'head, heart and hands', meaning that children learn with their body and their feelings as well as their intellect (Barnes 1991: 54; Easton 1997: 87; Koetzsch 1997: 221).

While it is difficult to provide a full answer to the question in a few paragraphs, a concise and useful summary is provided by Easton (1997), who suggests that Waldorf educational theory and practice can be distinguished by the following six key elements:

1. A theory of child development
2. A theory of teacher self-development
3. A core curriculum that integrates artistic and academic work
4. A method of teaching as an art that pays careful attention to synchronising teaching methods with the rhythm of a child's unfolding capacities
5. Integration of teaching and administration
6. Building the school and the greater Waldorf community as networks of support for students, teachers, and parents

Child Development

An important aspect of Steiner Education that is fundamental to a Waldorf Teacher's understanding of child development is the image of the child as a threefold human being—*body*, *soul*, and *spirit*, as briefly discussed in Chap. 6. Allowing the child to develop according to natural and pre-destined rhythms and patterns is fundamental to an educational philosophy which aims to nurture the kingdom of childhood and draw out each child's inner potential in a holistic way. This threefold view of the human being and the changing soul qualities associated with the seven-year cycles also determine the approach to education taken as each phase develops: working with the child's *will* in the first seven years as they learn through imitation and play, with their *feeling life* during the primary school years as they experience a change in consciousness, and developing their *thinking ability* from puberty into adolescence and young adulthood. As stated in Chap. 6, the task for educators (and parents) is to nourish the seed that each child bears within itself and allow it to grow naturally, in order to lay the foundation for effective learning throughout life—another fundamental aim of Waldorf Schools.

> The strength to do this [learn through life] lies within the core of the individual, the "father to the man" who can never be an object of education but who must rather be enabled to take on the process of self-education from within. (Maier 1994: 13)

In this regard Steiner was also an early champion of the concept of lifelong learning and self-education:

> Consider for a moment that, as adults, you are still learning from life. Life is our great teacher. (Steiner, cited in Murphy 1991: 58)

Teacher Self-Development

This process of self-education also applies to teachers. It would seem apparent that anyone seeking to become a Waldorf teacher would need to develop a clear understanding of the view of child development, a small part of which has been outlined above. They would also need to become familiar with ways of understanding and working with children and their behaviour, such as Steiner's interpretation of the Greek doctrine of the four temperaments—*choleric, sanguine, phlegmatic,* and *melancholic.* Recognising dominant temperaments in children can be useful in relating to them and managing their relations with each other, but the teacher must also recognise that their *own temperament* can dominate the dynamic of a class and should be prepared to work with it in a positive way. A significant aspect of the pedagogical approach in a Waldorf School is the fact that during the primary years, *the teacher stays with the same group of children from Class 1 to Class 7,* corresponding to the second seven-year cycle from age seven to fourteen. They therefore begin with young children who are just experiencing the change of teeth and end with young adolescents who are experiencing puberty.

> This demanding and challenging commitment by the main lesson teacher requires that the teacher follow a path of self-development that makes it possible to keep pace with the changing needs of students. (Easton 1997: 89)

Core Curriculum

In the primary years especially, the Waldorf curriculum is based on rhythm and repetition, so that students become attuned to the rhythm of the day, the week, the seasons, and so on, learning similar content in different ways in subsequent stages that build on a foundation and deepen their learning as new capacities unfold. Throughout the primary and high school years, the main focus of intellectual activity occurs in the morning, with a long main lesson devoted to a specific topic for several weeks. Afternoons involve more artistic, creative, or physical activities.

Whether the main lesson topic is history, science, social studies, or writing, artistic work is incorporated into the learning activities—engaging the head, heart, and hands. For example, a main lesson in botany would involve not only identification of plants in the field, but the students would produce paintings of the plants and write poems about them. This is a classic example of the recognition of the integration of science, art, and nature and goes right back to the influence of Goethe on Steiner's philosophy of education. At the same time, "activities which are often considered frills at mainstream schools are central at Waldorf schools: art, music, handwork and foreign languages" (Cape Ann Waldorf School 1999: 1). In the full 12-year Steiner curriculum, all children learn to play music and to knit, as well as experiencing woodwork, Eurhythmy (a system of expressive body movement), and painting right through from Class 1 to Class 12.

A mythopoetic approach to the universal nature of knowledge is clearly represented in the more fundamental aspect of the Steiner curriculum with its recapitulation of the development of human consciousness over the centuries.

> Curriculum content is shaped, or at least coloured, by what is understood as the consciousness, soul-mood or life principles at work within a given epoch (ontogenesis recapitulates phylogenesis). (Skewes 1996: 7)

[Ontogenesis: The development of an individual organism from the earliest stage to maturity]

[Phylogenesis: The evolutionary development and diversification of a species or group of organisms]

This recapitulation is reflected in the primary school curriculum in the study of great epochs of human civilisation at the corresponding age at which the child's individual consciousness is unfolding. For example, Norse mythology is introduced in Class 4 when the children at around age 9 are able to identify with the moral and ethical issues arising from the great sagas of the Norse gods as they battle with the forces of light and darkness (Leah 1997). In Class 5 the study of Ancient Greece introduces the allegorical and metaphorical nature of the characters of the Greek gods, and by inference the children are made aware of the influence of these archetypes on the collective psyche of modern society and culture. To continue with this epochal chronology, Roman times are dealt with in Class 6, which gives a picture of the origin of the modern-day state and a highly regulated and martial society, at an age when the children are beginning to question authority structures.

The notion of recapitulation is carried through into the high school years when the students would progressively learn about the Middle Ages, Shakespearean times, the Renaissance and Victorian England as well as return to more detailed aspects of ancient cultures through the core subjects of art, English, history, and comparative religion. There are obviously regional variations to this curriculum, as well as a debate in Australia as to whether it should be less Euro-centric and more adapted to a regional and local cultural context (Skewes 1996; Van Kerkhoven 1996); but the principle guiding impulse of basing the curriculum on the evolution of human consciousness through an appreciation of the growing child in its natural environment is universal in Steiner Education.

The use of storytelling is particularly important, and fairy tales, myths, and legends can convey archetypal images and moral messages in a way that speaks to the child's consciousness more deeply than by simply telling as "stories are an age-old means of enlivening the learning process and stimulating students' imaginations" (Easton 1997: 90).

Teaching as an Art

As discussed so far in this book, the prevalence and influence of cognitive and behavioural theories of psychology in teacher education courses have had the effect of turning education into a science, a process that can be reduced to objectives, defined by subject matter and measured by testing. Waldorf schools consider that enabling children to learn in a meaningful and holistic way is an art, requiring creative and aesthetic input, a subjective expressive approach, and attention to intuitive and imaginal processes. The beauty of nature is reflected in the pleasing environment of the classroom, with its warm colours, the nature table with objects typical of the season, and colourful artworks. The cycle of the seasons, the great rhythms of nature, is brought into the classroom and into the curriculum in a living way.

Waldorf teachers make a point of engaging young children by telling stories using the oral tradition, without necessarily reading from printed texts, especially picture books:

One of the key aims of our method of educating is to help the child toward developing the faculty of free imagination. So, for example, we generally tell stories without offering printed pictures. Our words provide the raw materials. The child has to 'clothe' the story with his or her own images. (Mt Barker Waldorf School 2001)

The methods of teaching therefore involve storytelling, poems, songs, and movement, with an intentional use of rhythm in language to engage children in learning—the power of language and the human voice are not only recognised but embraced. A contemporary perspective of a Waldorf classroom would dismiss it as being too teacher-centred, with the focus always on the voice and words of the teacher taking the place of what might otherwise be a text, a video, a worksheet, or some other curriculum resource. However, this approach requires the teacher to continually develop their own aesthetic sensibilities—student-centred, problem-based, and self-directed pedagogies can also be exploited as an end rather than a means to learning.

The overall picture of the Waldorf teaching method can be seen as one of *rhythm*, *respect*, and *reverence*; an appreciation of natural beauty, and an integration of art, music, and movement in all academic work. It therefore becomes important for the child to experience these qualities in the home environment as well, in order to maintain a balance between the values at home and those at school. This can be a challenge for parents as it brings a consideration of what might be appropriate for the young child to be exposed to: for example, natural toys as opposed to plastic ones, dolls without pre-determined facial features, minimising exposure to loud music or mass media, and ideally not exposing young children at all to television or moving images for at least their first seven years.

Steiner was concerned that the modern world, even in 1919, was 'speeding up' the development of children and 'hardening' them to the demands of a fast-paced world when they should be allowed to just enjoy the kingdom of childhood. In a Waldorf kindergarten therefore, the children's play is regarded as their work, and they learn through creative experimentation and cooperation with each other in a safe and supportive environment. In these early years it is considered that the child's consciousness is not wide-awake like that of an adult but still in a dreamy state, and therefore "pictures presented to its imagination in story form should be in the nature of dream-pictures from the world of make-believe" (Childs 1991: 85). As described, the teaching methods reflect this by relying more on the oral than the written tradition, and using art, music, movement, and rhythm to support the absorption of content rather than abstract intellectual methods.

In the primary and high schools, each subject is presented in an artistic and imaginative way whether it is science, maths, or English—art and aesthetic appreciation are integrated into the curriculum and ideally even the children's very exercise books, in which "every page is to be an artistic event" (Skewes 2002). For example, the teaching of the high school science curriculum includes a series of field camps where students experience the natural world in situ and are given the opportunity to gain a more experiential and holistic appreciation of the environment in relation to their own place in the bigger picture of evolution.

Integration of Teaching and Administration

The traditional structure of a Waldorf School, true to the original intent of the very first school, requires leadership and school management to be shared by the entire faculty, which selects members to a steering committee. This committee—referred to as the College of Teachers—acts as the legally constituted management body of the school and carries all of the decision-making responsibilities that would normally fall to one person—a principal. There are many variations on this structure, with some schools having a separate administrator, or a school council whose members include parents. However, in recent times more schools have been moving towards a leadership model that includes a principal or Head of School as a response to increasing bureaucratic demands and accountability requirements as driven by the GERM agenda, as well as changing expectations from parents.

The School as a Learning Community

Easton's statement that "the development of the school as a learning community is one of the major achievements of Waldorf education" (1997: 91) sets Waldorf Schools apart from most other schools, with shared mission, philosophy, educational theories, practices, and rituals seen as key factors in building community. As established in my doctoral research, many parents are drawn to this aspect of the schools which they perceive to be missing from most modern state school systems and feel that being able to participate physically, intellectually, and spiritually in the Waldorf School community can also be strong transformative learning experience. As one parent stated in an interview:

> In that process of seeing what your child goes through, you suddenly start waking up to yourself and understanding your own path as an individual more clearly. (Stehlik 2002: 129)

An Educational Philosophy for the Twenty-First Century?

Despite its apparent successful transition to most countries and cultures for almost 100 years, Steiner Education comes under some criticism for the very fact that the curriculum has been adopted and applied fairly unchanged in most instances and in most situations, since its introduction in 1919. From this perspective it could be argued that Steiner's pedagogy is deterministic and does not allow for individual or regional difference, or is in fact so prescriptive and controlling that each child's own mythologies are ignored and subsumed into an all-consuming 'one size fits all' approach. While there is no doubt that the Steiner curriculum and the associated teaching methodologies are highly structured and prescribed, they are structured around the development of the whole child and adopt processes which focus on their aesthetic and spiritual development in addition to intellectual and physical development. These processes by design require much more subtle and delicate pedagogical approaches which evoke as well as instruct, and actually provide a foundation for the individual child to be able to develop a reflective-imaginal way of viewing the world as well as a logical-rational one.

It could be argued that a laissez-faire approach to education, such as the Summerhill model discussed in Chap. 4, might equally allow children to explore and experience the aesthetic and the numinous through freedom of expression and choice (Neill 1960). Encouraging the natural development of children's emotional, intellectual and social development according to this pedagogical approach also acknowledges that 'the kingdom of childhood' should be nurtured and revered. Yet at the time of writing, the original Summerhill school has an enrolment of less than 80 pupils, while other schools modelled on Neill's 'free' approach to education continue to struggle with small or shrinking enrolments or have even failed. Steiner Education continues to grow worldwide because the schools are founded through grass-roots networks by parents and teachers who are *looking for something new for their children*, adopting an approach that is 'free' in the original sense that Steiner envisaged for the very first 'Free Waldorf School'—accessible to all social classes and free of bureaucratic constraints, denominational doctrine, or dogmatic ideology.

10.3   Green School Bali

The "Green School Way" is to prepare for the real world by being involved in it now; to have impact now; to take responsibility now; and to model and practice the skills and mindsets that we will need later on, now. (https://www.greenschool.org/)

Green School Bali is a very recent experiment in a new form of schooling, established by the Canadian John Hardy and his American wife Cynthia. In 2005 the Hardys had been living on the island of Bali in Indonesia for many years and were looking for a school for their two youngest children. They were interested in Steiner Education but realised that the type of school they really wanted was not available on the island. The result was an initiative to start an entirely new form of school, inspired by the Balinese environment and Hindu culture as well as by a focus on *education for sustainability* and *education as sustainability*. A site of ten hectares in a natural environment near Sibang Kaja with the Ayung River running through was purchased, and construction began in 2006 with a 22 metre bamboo bridge spanning the river. All school buildings have subsequently been constructed from local bamboo, but given the tropical climate, many of the learning spaces are open air, and the grounds, forest, and river also provide spaces for learning.

Green School opened in September 2008 as a new international school ready to 'create a new paradigm for learning' as encapsulated in its original vision:

> Our vision is of a natural, holistic, student-centered learning environment that empowers and inspires our students to be creative, innovative, green leaders. (https://www.greenschool.org/)

Students are enrolled from the early years through to primary, middle, and high school, with an international cohort representing 25 different countries and a conscious policy of achieving 20% enrolment of local Balinese children. From an initial enrolment of 90 the school has grown to 360 students at the time of writing. After being in operation for only four years, the school won the 2012 'Greenest School on Earth' award as assessed by the US Green Building Council (http://www.centerforgreenschools.org/).

The Green School vision or 'new paradigm for learning' is enacted through a pedagogical approach based on three major policy platforms or initiatives: (1) a wall-less learning environment, (2) a purposeful learning program, and (3) a passionate community of learners (https://www.greenschool.org/).

A Wall-Less Learning Environment

Structurally the school is radically very different from the 'factory school' model. The physical environment and architecture of the school features elegant soaring structures built and thatched with bamboo, classrooms without walls with natural lighting and breezes blowing through, desks that are not square, composting toilets and other environmentally sensitive innovations. The centrepiece of the campus with its double-helix spiralling design is the 'Heart of School', possibly the largest freestanding bamboo building in the world. The buildings are consciously designed to be outward-looking and connect with the outdoor environment, rather than enclose the learning spaces within four walls. Located in a tropical jungle, the students are reminded daily of the beauty and also the fragility of nature and the importance of caring for as well as learning from the local environment and community. Permaculture gardens in which the students learn about growing and harvesting their own food are incorporated into the curriculum, agriculture and animal husbandry are included in the daily school life, and as far as possible the school aims to be self-sustaining in terms of waste management, water filtration, renewable energy, and so on.

A Purposeful Learning Program

The pedagogical approach of holistic student-centred practice draws inspiration from a number of different sources including Steiner Education, permaculture practice (Mollison 1988), multiple intelligence theories (Gardner 1983), integrated ways of knowing (Wilber 2000), and project-based and experiential learning methodologies. A 'Three Frame Day' approach was developed to acknowledge and incorporate three different learning styles: *auditory, visual,* and *tactile* that align with the threefold classification of learners as 'thinkers, feelers, and doers' (Metcalfe 2017).

> The three frames basically are this, that there is an integrated holistic child-centred frame of the day, that there is an academically rigorous skills-driven frame of the day and that there's a frame which connects children to the greater working world. (McGurgan 2013, cited in Metcalfe 2017: 122)

The three frames of learning are therefore labelled as *integral, instructional,* and *experimental.*

The *integral frame* offers thematic lessons on a particular cross-curricular theme that is explored over some weeks. In the primary school this manifests exactly like the 'main lesson' in a Steiner School program, occupying the first hour and 45 minutes of the school day. In the middle school, "themes with an inquiry-based approach draw on the critical skills of problem solving, collaboration, communication, decision making, leadership, management, organization, critical thinking and creative thinking" (Green School, "Curriculum Overview, Middle School", 2015).

The *instructional frame* concentrates on the core subjects that through 'proficiency lessons' will develop literacy and numeracy as well as language skills (in this case, Bahasa Indonesia), with individual learning plans guiding the progressive development of each child through the year levels to aim for mastery of core skills.

In what has been described as a 'Bespoke Curriculum', the *experiential frame* is designed to provide a context for solving 'real-life' problems using technological tools and entrepreneurial skills in 'real world' situations and contexts.

> The experiential frame includes 'practical lessons' in the performing, visual and tactile arts; environmental education; health and physical education; social skills; and enterprise education. As the children move through the years this manifests through bringing experts into the classroom, experiences of workplaces and participation in real world scenarios and making a contribution. (Metcalfe 2017: 126)

Green School is not a free school like the experimental schools discussed in Chap. 5. The academic rigour is reflected in the curriculum which is still largely centred on the familiar traditional subjects or learning areas. To achieve the accredited High School Diploma, for example, students study English, maths, science, humanities, health and wellbeing, and arts, but also environmental and enterprise studies, and complete a capstone 'Green Stone' project in Year 12.

A Passionate Community of Learners

The multicultural international community of students and teachers integrated with the local Balinese people has created a unique melting pot of languages, traditions, and multicultural diversity, an example of global consciousness enacted at the local level, all focused on education through sustainability, and sustainability through education. Parents are encouraged to be involved in school activities and the local community is included through outreach programs. Volunteer and internship programs attract visitors from around the globe who are interested in learning about the school through hands-on involvement.

> The teachers are as diverse as the student body, and volunteers are popping up …together with the teachers they are deeply committed to creating a new generation of global green leaders. (Hardy 2010)

A boarding school experience is available for students from 13 to 17 years of age which enables immersion in the Balinese way of life. Lunch is cooked every day in the traditional Balinese way using locally grown ingredients and served to the entire school community. Becoming a community and being part of the community is part of the ethos and the curriculum, for example, the students are involved hands-on in the 'rice cycle', the process of planting, irrigating, and harvesting the staple food of the region. The school actively pursues broader outreach to the world through a number of communication channels accessible well beyond the school community, including its website, a weekly school newsletter, and staff and student blogs.

With 64 teachers and 360 students, the staff-student ratio is 1:7, supported by 15 classroom assistants, six learning support staff, and numerous volunteers and interns (as of 19/6/17). This staffing model creates opportunities to work in small groups, with individual students, and to develop positive and meaningful teaching-learning relationships which, despite all the Green Studies and the beautiful environment, are still the key to making the school work.

How to Be Green

Green School Bali would seem to be an example of the type of 'back to nature' initiatives in education that were described at some length in Chap. 7, but going well beyond the idea of taking learning into the forest, by actually *building the school in the forest* and embedding the forest throughout the curriculum. It appears to have taken on the challenge and the dream expressed by Richard Louv and made it a reality:

Imagine a classroom that turns outward, both figuratively and literally. The grounds would become a classroom, buildings would look outward, and gardens would cover the campus. The works of naturalists would be the vehicle by which we would teach reading and writing. Math and science would be taught as a way to understand the intricacies of nature, the potential to meet human needs, and how all things are interlaced. A well-rounded education would mean learning the basics, to become part of a society that cherished nature while at the same time contributing to the well-being of mankind. (Louv 2005: 192–193)

The salient questions are whether the Green School model, like many alternative schooling models, is place-specific and reliant on the energy and charisma of its founders to make it work and to what extent it may be applicable in other places, contexts, and communities—particularly inner-city urban environments. John Hardy is confident:

Is this doable in your community? We believe it is. Green School is a model we built for the world. (Hardy 2010)

Hardy offers three simple rules to follow in establishing a school with a green philosophy: be local, let the environment lead, and envisage how your grandchildren will be affected by your actions.

10.4   Conclusion to This Chapter

The three case studies purposely presented in this chapter are clearly different in educational context, scope, and concept, yet many connections and comparisons can be drawn between them. They all provide examples of educational philosophies that share a common concern for the natural environment and a respect for nature, as well a central focus on the well-being of children and the education of the whole child: head, heart, and hands.

From my personal experience in Finland, a country that is covered in forests, I find that the theme of the *forest as a learning environment* resonates with the rich description of Green School and its use of the Balinese forest as a learning environment. Both are examples of enacting the movement to *reconnect children with nature* as suggested by the US campaign to 'Leave No Child Inside' (Louv 2005).

Green school Bali is also a case study example of parents who *were looking for something new for their children* (and possibly even choosing an education that they would have wanted themselves) founding a school, which clearly resonates with the case study of Steiner Education and the way in which Waldorf Schools continue to be established around the world through grass-roots initiatives by parents.

All three case studies provide food for thought about how education, schooling, teaching, and learning can be conceived, configured, and contextualised in many different ways in order to achieve good outcomes for not only children but the community and society as a whole. They provide examples of *clearly articulated educational philosophies* from which we can learn in the continual search for the best way to educate our children and ourselves for the future.

References

Barnes, H. (1991). Learning that grows with the learner: An introduction to Waldorf Education. *Educational Leadership, 49*, 52–54.

Booth, M. (2014). *The almost nearly perfect people: The truth about the Nordic miracle*. London: Jonathan Cape.

Cape Ann Waldorf School. (1999). *Frequently asked questions about Waldorf Education*. http://www.capeannwaldorf.org/caws-faq.html. Accessed 11 June 17.

Childs, G. (1991). *Steiner education in theory and practice*. Edinburgh: Floris Books.

Cygnaeus, U. (1910). *Uno Cygnaeus' writings about the foundation and organisation of the Finnish elementary school*. Helsinki: Kirjayhtymä.

Easton, F. (1997). Educating the whole child, "Head, heart and hands": Learning from the Waldorf experience. *Theory into Practice, 36*(2), 87–94.

Gardner, H. (1983). *Frames of mind*. New York: Basic Books.

Green School. (2015). *Curriculum overview, Middle School, 2015–2016 academic year*. http://www.greenschool.org/wp-content/uploads/2015/08/Middle-School-Curriculum-Overview_Photo.pdf. Accessed 8 Nov 2015.

Goleman, D. (1995). *Emotional intelligence*. New York: Bantam Books.

Hardy, J. (2010). *My green school dream*. https://www.ted.com/talks/john_hardy_my_green_school_dream. Accessed 14 June 2017.

Klinkmann, S.-E. (2010). Swedish rock in Finland: "The sound which is not?". Chapter 5, In B. Horgby & F. Nilsson (Eds.), *Rockin' the borders: Rock music and social, cultural and political change*. Newcastle upon Tyne: Cambridge Scholars Publishing.

Koetzsch, R. (1997). *The parent's guide to alternatives in education*. Boston: Shambhala.

Leah, D. (1997). The dawning of conscience: Moral education and the Waldorf curriculum in Class Four. *Steiner Education, 31*(2), 20–25.

Lönnrot, E. (1835). *Kalevala*. J. C. Frenckellin ja Poika.

Lopez, S., & Lewis, M. (2009). The principles of strengths-based education. *Journal of College and Character, X*(4), 1–8.

Louv, R. (2005). *Last child in the woods: Saving our children from nature-deficit disorder*. New York: Algonquin Books.

Määttä, K., & Uusiautti, S. (2011). Pedagogical love and good teacherhood. *In Education, 17*(2), 29–41.

Macdonald, J. (1981). Theory, practice and the hermeneutic circle. *Journal of Curriculum Theorizing, 3*(2), 130–138.

Maier, M. (1994). The child is the father to the man. In N. Gobel (Ed.), *Waldorf Education: Exhibition catalogue on occasion of the 44th session of the international conference on education of UNESCO in Geneva*. Geneva: Fruende der Erzeihungskunst Rudolf Steiners.

Metcalfe, J. (2017). *The story of Green School Bali: An integral narrative of sustainable education*. Unpublished PhD thesis, University of South Australia.

Mollison, B. (1988). *Permaculture: A designer's manual*. Tyalgum: Tagari Publications.

Mt. Barker Waldorf School Parent Association. (2001). *Parent handbook*. Mount Barker: Mount Barker Waldorf School.

Murphy, C. (1991). *Emil Molt and the beginnings of the Waldorf School*. Edinburgh: Floris Books.

Neill, A. S. (1960). *Summerhill: A radical approach to childrearing*. Middlesex: Penguin Books.

Rosenthal, R., & Jacobsen, L. (1968, September). Pygmalion in the classroom. *The Urban Review*.

Shepherd, A. P. (1983). *A scientist of the invisible*. Edinburgh: Floris Books.

Skewes, D. (1996). Beyond curriculum. *Musagetes: Education journal for the community of Steiner Schools, 2*(2), 7–11.

Skewes, D. (2002). *Practicum report. Willunga Waldorf School,* School of Education, University of South Australia.

Solasaari, U. (2003). Love and values rear a personality – Max Scheler's philosophy of education. In*Studies of the Department of Education in the University of Helsinki 187.* Helsinki: University of Helsinki.

Stehlik, T. (2002). *Each parent carries the flame: Waldorf Schools as sites for promoting lifelong learning, creating community and educating for social renewal.* Flaxton: Post Pressed.

Stehlik, T. (2011). Relationships, participation and support: Necessary components for inclusive learning environments and (re)engaging learners. Chapter 7, In T. Stehlik & J. Patterson (Eds.), *Changing the paradigm: Education as the key to a socially inclusive future.* Brisbane: Post Pressed.

Steiner, R. (1968). *The roots of education.* London: Rudolf Steiner Press.

Steiner Waldorf Schools Fellowship. (2017). http://www.steinerwaldorf.org/. Accessed 13 June 2017.

Synge, U. (1977). *Kalevala: Heroic tales from Finland.* London: The Bodley Head.

Tamkin, E. (2014). *Will everyone shut up already about how the Nordic countries top every global ranking?* http://www.slate.com/blogs/the_world_/2014/08/29/will_everyone_shut_up_already_about_how_the_nordic_countries_top_every_global.html. Accessed 6 June 2017.

van Kerkhoven, G. (1996). Aspects of Waldorf Education in Australia. *Musagetes: Education Journal for the Community of Steiner Schools, 2*(2), 1–5.

Wilber, K. (2000). *Integral spirituality: A startling new role for religion in the modern and postmodern world.* Boston: Shambhala.

11

Thinking Outside the Classroom

This chapter introduces and discusses alternative learning programs that operate outside of the traditional confines of school, usually applying adult learning methodologies, often employing the creative arts as a point of interest for young people otherwise disengaged from the standard curriculum, and mostly delivered not by schoolteachers but by community educators, parents, and many others. They are a form of education now characterised as part of the 'Not- school' movement, which includes all out-of-school educational experiences such as homeschooling, which itself is part of an emerging trend of 'unschooling'. School leaving age and school retention are all issues related to how long we expect young people to remain in institutionalised learning situations, while pathways to further education and/or careers are no longer simply linear, and gap years are becoming the norm. These trends require us to think outside traditional classroom and school structures.

The well-known phrase of 'thinking outside the box' is a metaphor referring to the process of viewing things differently, from new perspectives, or in an unconventional way. It has become a shorthand way of describing innovation and creativity in finding solutions to problems, and is associated with the corporate management and marketing world

© The Author(s) 2018
T. Stehlik, *Educational Philosophy for 21st Century Teachers*,
https://doi.org/10.1007/978-3-319-75969-2_11

where the phrase supposedly appeared in the 1970s to describe lateral thinking and brainstorming of new ideas. However, the related idea of 'thinking outside the square' is actually much older and originated with a puzzle that can be traced back at least to 1914 with the publication of Sam Loyd's *Cyclopedia of Puzzles*.

> I have always treated and considered puzzles from an educational stand-point, for the reason that they constitute a species of mental gymnastics which sharpen the wits and train the mind to reason along straight lines. (Sam Loyd 1914: 5)

The 'Nine dots puzzle' presents a square comprised of nine dots arranged in three rows. The trick is to connect all dots with only four lines, but trying to connect the dots by staying within the square is not possible and can be very frustrating. The solution as shown in the below figure literally requires going outside the square. Like many puzzles, the solution once seen looks obvious. However, it represents a new way of seeing, and since there are no rules to suggest that you can't go outside the square, this is an example of how we impose rules on ourselves that are not even there, limited by our pre-determined frames of reference (Fig. 11.1).

This kind of lateral thinking that challenges existing frames of reference is often used in approaching and looking for solutions to what have become known as *wicked problems*.

[Wicked problem: A problem that is difficult or impossible to solve because of incomplete, contradictory, and changing requirements that are often hard to recognise]

Wicked problems present the kind of puzzle for which there is no convenient answer at the back of the book; they are complex and unique and attempting to address them may generate more problems (Lawson 2016); and they arise in the context of social policy issues including environmental, political, and economic, in which purely scientific-engineering problem-solving approaches cannot be applied because of the lack of a clear problem definition as well as the differing perspectives of multiple stakeholders (Rittel and Webber 1973).

The point of all this in relation to 'the problem of education' is to apply this same metaphor of thinking outside the square to thinking outside

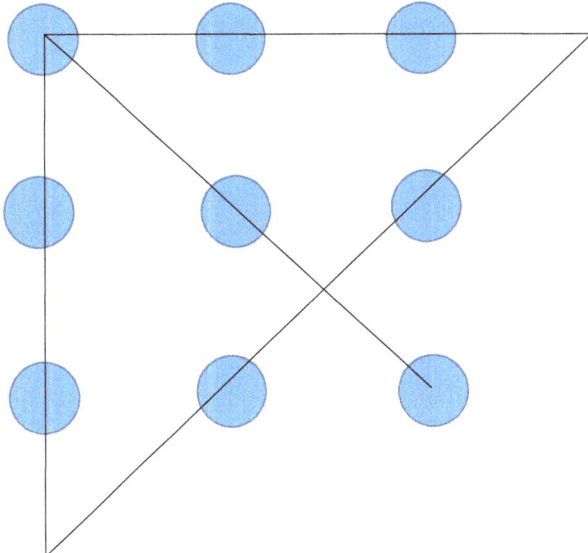

Fig. 11.1 Nine dots puzzle solution

the classroom, and even outside the school. This chapter describes and unpacks examples of educational initiatives and practices that contribute to the schooling of children and young people yet do not occur within the physical boundaries of school, such as the forest school/bush kindy movement already discussed in Chap. 7. *Education outside the classroom* can take many forms, and not always because of political or religious impositions such as the Irish hedge schools, or resource limitations such as outdoor schools in Africa, but for purposeful, pedagogical, and philosophical reasons.

11.1 Deschooling

In 1971 the Austrian philosopher, polymath, and Catholic priest Ivan Illich (1926–2002) published a landmark book entitled *Deschooling Society*, a radical discourse on modern society in which he systematically critiqued formal institutionalised schooling as being responsible for institutionalising society, ineffectual in educating young people, and actually inducing ignorance. At a time when global ecological issues were becoming wicked problems, when the military-industrial complex was overtaking nation states in world politics, and when technological innovations and economic prosperity in the developed world only highlighted the disadvantage and poverty in the third world, Illich believed that schooling was part of the problem:

> School is the advertising agency which makes you believe that you need the society as it is. (Illich 1971: 163)

Disestablishing schools and promoting networks of like-minded people learning, sharing, and caring through *educational webs* would break the nexus of schooling which—through both the overt and the hidden curriculum—simply reproduced the bourgeois capitalist and commercial culture that was responsible for the problems of society as Illich saw them in 1971. As well as being critical however, Illich was actually very prescient in offering innovative suggestions based on the use of computer technology, with his reference to *webs* of learning as the reverse of the *funnels* through which knowledge was transmitted in schools, even predicting social media with his descriptions of computer-based peer-matching networks 30 years before Facebook.

Illich's basic idea of 'deschooling' was centred on a model of self-education, which would replace the need for institutions and bureaucratic structures. Instead, at birth every child would receive entitlements in the form of tuition grants, or 'education credits' which they could expend at 'skill centres' of their own choice. Again Illich was prescient in foreseeing contemporary discussions around the perennial problem of equitable funding of education, which still include debates around the merits of such voucher systems. However, he also flagged the dangers of interest groups stepping into such a free education market and more or less predicted the UK Academy schools, the US Charter schools, and the general McDonaldisation of education which has occurred, even if deschooling has not.

Illich's radical ideas did however spark a lot of interest at the time, and have since led to various other movements away from traditional universal schooling. In his observations that educational activities are also organised around common interest groups and themes found in organisations as diverse as political parties, clubs, neighbourhood centres, unions, and professional societies, Illich reinforced the view taken in this book that much of what we learn occurs outside of and beyond formal schooling. This brings us back to the role of 'the village' in raising children, and also foregrounds the importance of lifelong and adult learning approaches to education which have been seen to be more effective in engaging young people who otherwise have switched off and dropped out of school.

As Illich noted "because school is obligatory it becomes schooling for schooling's sake" (1971: 15). Operating within the rituals and ceremonies of school then becomes self-referential and self-perpetuating and limits thinking to 'inside the box'. Compulsory schooling as discussed earlier is seen as a basic responsibility of civil society, yet for many adolescents it amounts to a sort of prison sentence in which they are required to attend, behave a certain way, dress a certain way, and work in a certain way—all prescribed by circumstances they have little control over. As presented in Chap. 7, the developing adolescent or young adult does not want to be treated like a child, yet this is what compulsion implies. It again raises the question posed in Chap. 4:

> *At what point in our lives are we able to take responsibility for our own education rather than be subjected to what someone else believes we should be learning?*

11.2 Not-school

Programs that have been shown to engage young people and offer educational opportunities in which they are able to contribute agency and learn for their own sake, not just for learning's sake, have been well documented. They comprise an emerging field of educational provision which has been labelled 'Not-school' (Sefton-Green 2013). *Not-school* is a term used to describe learning in educational settings that are generally non-formal or informal, yet contribute to re-engagement, skill development, and increased motivation for young people that can be ends in themselves, but also create pathways into formal learning and/or further education. The salient feature of Not-school programs is that they are literally outside the box—outside the boundaries imposed by traditional compulsory schooling, which include the physical requirements of daily attendance on school grounds as well as more subtle boundaries such as regulations that control dress, behaviour, attitudes, and authority structures.

Programs based outside of school grounds appear to be a preferred option for those young people who genuinely find it difficult to be in a school environment for a range of personal, social, and emotional reasons. During my research for the Social Inclusion Unit in South Australia (see Chap. 9), a number of young people declared that they refused to set foot inside a mainstream school not necessarily for behavioural or learning issues but because of the perceived restrictions of the environment: "they treat us like kids, you have to wear a uniform, they have rules like needing a note just to go to the toilet" (Stehlik 2006: 18). Off-campus alternative learning settings encourage the possibility for young people to be treated as individuals, and for older learners to be treated as adults, usually in class settings where the teacher-student ratio is low (ideally a median of about 1:8), with staff who are generally sympathetic to their needs as well as being understanding of youth culture and the issues facing young people.

Programs operating outside of school restrictions like class timetables and subject lines can also offer a more flexible approach to attendance, which can be negotiated and in some cases includes a weekly afternoon or whole day where attendance is not required. Students may not always attend but keep in touch with teachers via mobile phones and text messaging and often do work 'at home', but in some cases the learning centre is the only constant and regular environment if they are couch-surfing or finding home life dysfunctional, distracting, or even dangerous.

The Education Department in South Australia set up 'Learning Centres' to provide this kind of environment for up to ten weeks for students temporarily excluded from school. Most often these are boys who have been suspended for behavioural issues including violence towards teachers, and they include junior primary students, even students as young as five years old who need some anger management or behaviour modification. Taking them out of the school environment is almost like respite from the situation and acts as a way to offer a program built around each student's needs, including literacy and numeracy, work skills, fitness activities, cooking, and nutrition. The intention is to successfully transition back into mainstream school, but this is problematic for a number of reasons.

Transitioning back into 'mainstream' school settings can be a problem for students who have been involved in entirely off-campus learning, as schools can often make it clear that they are not welcome back, and for students who have experienced a different learning experience, going back into an environment in which nothing has changed is de-motivating and frustrating. For some students, even experiencing off-campus learning for one or two days a week makes school seem more restrictive in comparison.

A further issue for young people in transitioning from an alternative back to a mainstream learning environment relates to the quality of their home life. That is, if a young person is not living in a stable and secure home environment, or receives little or no family support, caring or nurturing, then this situation would also need to change for successful transition to occur.

A number of case studies reinforce the gap between mainstream expectations of compulsory schooling and the realities of life for many young adolescents. One alternative learning environment case study in South Australia was an inner-city state-funded community school, which offered a 'second chance' or in some cases a 'last chance' for around 150 excluded and disengaged young people aged 12–15. The school staff reported that they found themselves dealing more with health and welfare issues rather than educational interventions, and often students were coming to school for respite from dysfunctional domestic situations. However, even this school had an off-campus program of its own, being part of the 'Step Into Learning' program operated in a northern suburban centre by the Service to Youth Council, a non-profit social services organisation that provides case management support for young people. In addition to taking on students excluded for four weeks or more from other schools, this program offered negotiated education plans for students, supported by case workers and with a community focus. Anecdotal evidence suggested that 'the kids behaved brilliantly' and the program was seeing at least 50% achievement by the cohort into various job provider pathways.

The model provided by this type of arrangement was also observed in a 'Youth Pathways Program' supported by a larger southern suburbs high school, in which students were enrolled at the school but attended programs conducted away from the school—through another non-profit service provider Mission Australia, using community facilities as well as those of the local vocational college. The young people enrolled in this program who had disengaged from mainstream schooling included young teenage mothers, a demographic cohort who also feel shunned and judged by teachers and exclude themselves from mainstream schooling. The school received the funding for each student and supplied a staff member who worked exclusively off-campus, supported by case managers. These programs are an example of the emerging model of education provision that involves community, non-government, and charitable organisations as well as government agencies in partnership with schools to provide successful alternative learning pathways.

Another model based on a similar arrangement was set up in a regional centre in South Australia, using the facilities of the local vocational college to bring together students enrolled through the local public and private high schools, offering flexible learning arrangements in a small group environment in which the students were treated as adults, the same as the other tertiary students on campus. In this setting the students felt less restricted by the types of rules and regulations they had experienced in mainstream schools where they found it hard to conform for a range of reasons, and felt like they now had the opportunity to achieve personal goals at their own pace. Interestingly, the college was established initially to offer Year 11 and vocational pathways through work experience for disengaged young people and some who had been out of school for more than a year, but the students themselves identified the desire to achieve Year 12 and the South Australian Certificate in Education (SACE), with the three teaching staff trying to offer as many SACE subject areas as they could. Students who were previously disengaged had gone on to achieve this qualification, and with career guidance and support from the teaching staff had begun to plan for the future and identify further education courses and career options. A key part of the success of this program was using part of the funding to employ a social worker for three days a week to work with the health and welfare issues of the cohort and allow the teaching staff to focus on educational tasks.

11.3   Doing School Differently

The clear advantage of 'doing school differently' (Bills and Howard 2016) through alternative educational programs is to offer more flexibility to young people through a range of indicators including attendance, curriculum choice, learning pathways, and teaching methodologies. Some students simply need more time to cope with studies—for example, completing Year 11 was a major achievement for a student who left school early and later enrolled in an off-campus program because of the flexibility of being able to do two subjects at a time at their own pace. However, schools are generally not flexible enough to accept a student taking three years to complete one year of schooling. Furthermore, some students simply cannot cope with a full day of school every day, so it is also important to be flexible about attendance, and within the bounds of duty of care obligations, being able to negotiate their own timetable empowers students and actually contributes to increased attendance, rather than enforcing attendance at school for a set number of hours each day which does not seem to work for some young people. In fact with the increased use of flexible and online learning methodologies in other education sectors, it is surprising that more alternatives to face-to-face classroom teaching are not being considered in schools. There is also a small but radical movement towards viewing educational provision as a 24-hour-a-day 7-day-a-week concept in order to offer real choice and flexibility, with teachers in alternative settings already reporting the importance of being on call and available after hours by students. While this has all sorts of industrial and resource implications, it is an idea worth expanding upon.

If the benefits of flexible and alternative learning environments are accepted as given, the key question is how to incorporate such programs into mainstream schooling without resulting in the inevitable drift back to a regulated structure and therefore compromising their 'alternative' nature. If it is accepted that one educational size does not fit all students, the challenge is to allow such programs to remain off to one side but still be seen as a necessary and important part of the bigger educational picture. This is a dilemma for policy makers and for planning schooling for the twenty-first century given the funding models, structures, traditions, and legislated limitations that are still entrenched in the way we think about schooling. However, there are examples of flexible alternatives to learning that are clearly demonstrated as operating successfully wholly within a school-based environment, and these demonstration projects can provide a good practice model for other schools to take up within the context of their local community and available resources.

11.4   Youthworx

A case study model of successfully re-engaging disadvantaged and disaffected youth through generating interest and entrepreneurial opportunities in the creative industries is that of *Youthworx*, a program and an enterprise that began in Melbourne in the early 2000s and is now providing a template for arts-based initiatives in other Australian states, giving another example of Not-school that not only aims to educate but to promote alternative and innovative career opportunities in what has been termed the *purpose economy* (Hurst 2014). For millennials, the concept of a conventional career path in the traditional sense as experienced by previous generations is no longer viable, with unemployment and underemployment fuelled by technology and automation leading to disappearing jobs, but at the same time creating new *purposeful* opportunities to launch technology-based start-up enterprises or develop freelance skills and expertise, based in local communities, utilising social media, and operating outside the standard full-time, nine-to-five, job-for-life model that was the norm through most of the twentieth century.

Youthworx has exploited this trend for social enterprise by focussing on a particular niche market—the creative industries, which by definition include the visual arts, the performing arts such as music and dance, and media including radio, film, and television. Beginning as an initiative to re-engage young people who were not learning or earning and often at risk from homelessness and other personal issues, the Youthworx pro-gram initially applied for funding from the Salvation Army to set up a workshop for teaching and learning radio broadcast skills. The success of this eventually progressed to teaching and learning film-making, with more funding to purchase the equipment and technology required. Youthworx Media is now an established enterprise that not only offers workshops and training in film-making but also provides film-making services on a commercial basis, so that the participants can also experi-ence a type of business model that is creative, sustainable, and community-oriented.

Like many such programs, this one has been driven by one inspired person, a former teacher who, despite little previous film-making or social enterprise expertise or experience, had a vision based on a desire to help young people escape the cycle of despair which can escalate through early school leaving, homelessness, and complex social problems. Describing this as "positive youth development theory" based on a strengths-based approach rather than a deficit position, Youthworx Media operates as "a three way relationship between training providers; Industry professionals who provide mentoring and make sure we deliver on a program that leads to job opportunities; and professional youth workers who provide sup-port that goes the full distance" (http://youthworxmedia.org.au/index.html).

Here we have another example of the wrap-around model of educa-tion—providing support as well as learning opportunities for young peo-ple, through a joined-up approach that involves a team effort with educators, social workers, and industry professionals from the local com-munity. The beauty and added value of the Youthworx model is also the creative outlet that is offered through learning and working in media, which enables and empowers the young participants to express them-selves and affirm their identities through film and especially music, which for millennials is usually through the genre of rap. Popular culture, which forms such an essential part of the identity and life-worlds of young peo-ple, can therefore work together with education in a positive way.

11.5   Unschooling, Homeschooling

A more radical response to the 'problem of education' has been the *unschooling* movement, inspired by Ivan Illich's call to 'deschool society' and taken up and promulgated by John Holt in the 1970s and 1980s, which is now manifest in the expanding interest in ways to educate children without sending them to school at all, such as the growing trend of *homeschooling*.

John Holt (1923–1985) was an American teacher who became disillusioned with compulsory schooling and eventually decided that the system was too entrenched and difficult to change, and the only solution was to withdraw from it completely. Holt believed that children did not need to be coerced into learning, that they would do so naturally if given a rich assortment of resources and the freedom to follow their own interests. This line of thought is directly descended from Rousseau, but in the last few decades has developed into an identifiable movement that has come to be called *unschooling*.

Holt believed that one of the main things holding children back from learning in school was fear: fear of getting the wrong answers, fear of being ridiculed by the teacher and classmates, fear of not being good enough; and that this was made worse by children being forced to study things that they were not necessarily interested in. Even without the perceived negative influences of traditional schooling, Holt argued that "home is the proper base for the exploration of the world which we call learning or education. Home would be the best base no matter how good the schools were" (1980).

When challenged about the lack of socialisation opportunities if children were kept at home, Holt was outspoken about the 'dark side' of social interactions that occurred at school, namely, bullying, cliques, competitiveness, acting up, and peer pressure. We have already discussed examples of this, including how girls can 'dumb themselves down' in order not to appear smarter than boys in co-educational school contexts. In fact, the effect of socialisation in compulsory schools is one of the major reasons why many parents are choosing to home school their children. Holt had many other reasons to back his claims for unschooling:

The great advantage is intimacy, control of your time, flexibility of schedule, and the ability to respond to the needs of the child, and to the inclinations. If the child is feeling kind of tired or out of sorts, or a little bit sick, or kind of droopy in spirits, okay, we take it easy, and things go along very calmly and easily. When the child is full of energy and rambunctious, then we tackle big projects, we try tough stuff, we look at hard books. (Holt 1980)

Putting pressure onto children in general can also affect a child's performance in school. Holt pointed out that behavioural problems and disengagement in the classroom often resulted from children reacting to being put under pressure by setting their own limits, tuning out, not paying attention, fooling around, and often just saying that 'they don't get it'. If teachers spend "70% of learning time trying to manage behaviours" (ABC RN 2017), it makes sense to take a long hard look at the causes of this and not just try to deal with the symptoms.

Holt wrote about his own learning experiences as an adult, which influenced his thinking around the way we construct the very ideas of learning and teaching, work and play as either/or constructs rather than integrated contextual activities. For example, learning to play the cello later in life led him to realise that *learning to play the cello and playing the cello are the same thing* (Holt 2004). In other words, while one is learning to play, one is also playing, and most professional musicians will agree that every concert is also learning experience. When a concert pianist goes to work, they go to play—*playing the piano is their work*. The blurring of our entrenched ideas about the concept of work and the concept of play recalls the discussion in Chap. 6 about play being a child's work. In the same way, the concept of *practice* in terms of practising a skill or a profession can refer both to learning the skill or profession and carrying it out on a daily basis, when we may then refer to someone as a *practitioner*. How can we combine these seemingly disparate concepts or even transcend them and come up with a new way of thinking about learning? Doll (2008: 198) suggests that "what is needed is a multi-perspectival view, one that moves beyond an either/or dichotomy to accept a both/and frame".

Blurring the boundaries between school and home could be one approach, and homeschooling takes this approach to its extreme, by keeping children at home and turning everyday activities such as cooking, cleaning, and gardening into opportunities for learning, as well as having dedicated study time and formal lessons which can be mediated by information technology and guided by set curricula. Reasons given by parents who are joining this increasing trend for homeschooling their children include some of the issues mentioned above—bullying, peer pressure, and a competitive environment focussing too closely on academic performance at the expense of wellbeing—as well as a range of other positions such as religious beliefs, personal philosophies, having children with special needs, and a general dissatisfaction with compulsory schooling (ABC TV 2017).

Despite the legislative requirements of compulsory schooling, homeschooling is legal in Australia and parents do not require educational qualifications, although each child must be registered according to the appropriate guidelines and the relevant authorities, which vary between the states and territories. Curriculum guidelines, resources, and support for parents are available through a number of networks and organisations such as *Homeschooling Downunder*, which also provides interesting statistics and information on its website, such as the fact that in countries like Germany and Sweden, homeschooling is illegal (www.homeschooling-downunder.com).

The academic performance of homeschooled students is also claimed to be slightly better than average compared with students who attend school (Smith 2016), but in the main homeschooling parents seem, like the Finns, to be more concerned that their children are happy and experiencing a range of living and learning opportunities in a loving and safe environment, based on the fairly solid argument that parents understand their children more than anyone else.

Homeschooled children go on to university, further education and working lives just like other children. There are some famous examples of successful and influential people who did not go to school at all, like the naturalist, environmentalist, and best-selling author Gerald Durrell, who wrote about his unconventional upbringing surrounded by nature on the Greek Island of Corfu in the 1930s in the book *My Family and Other*

Animals (Durrell 1962). However, not everyone is able to raise their children on a Greek Island, or be able to afford to stay home to teach their children, or have the necessary skills and support needed to take on such a responsibility. So while homeschooling is a growing trend as part of the unschooling movement, it is apparent that it is not necessarily a choice available to all parents, but will depend on domestic and socio-economic circumstances as well as philosophical ideals. In particular, and not only just in families where the father is the main breadwinner, the role of the homeschool teacher appears to fall mostly to mothers.

11.6   Gap Year

The final example of Not-school presented in this chapter can really be seen as an aspect of, or perhaps an adjunct to, traditional schooling. It is included because it raises more questions about the purpose, function, and outcomes of schooling and the types of skills, knowledge, and attitudes that are assumed will be required in the digital, global, and fluid knowledge society of the present and the future, as will be discussed further in the final two chapters.

A *gap year* can be defined as:

> Any period of time between 3 and 24 months which an individual takes "out" of formal education, training or the workplace, and where the time out sits in the context of a longer career trajectory. (Heath 2007)

This definition could include post-university, career, and study breaks as well as pre-university gap years; however, the most salient example and the one to be discussed in this section is that period of time out comprising a break from formal study after completing school, before resuming formal studies at university, or some other further educational institution.

As time out in the context of a longer career or learning trajectory, the gap year phenomenon is interesting for a number of reasons. Firstly, it is on the increase, with more young people choosing to take a break after 12 or 13 years of continuous schooling. Secondly, it has become an institutionalised aspect of career education and spawned an industry in which 'time-off consultants' charge fees for planning gap year experiences for young people. Thirdly, the gap year has been marketed and promoted as a time in which young people will develop what have variously been termed 'life skills', 'soft skills', or 'twenty-first-century skills' through real-world life experiences that typically should involve activities including various combinations of paid and unpaid work, leisure, and travel.

In Australia, data gathered through the Longitudinal Studies of Australian Youth (LSAY) show that in the ten years between 2000 and 2010, the rate of students taking a gap year after school increased from about 10% to nearly 25% (www.lsay.edu.au), commensurate with trends in the United Kingdom and the United States. With one in four young Australians now taking time out from study, the gap year is becoming part of the education landscape and being recognised as offering valuable learning experiences for young people.

The term 'gap' is perhaps unfortunate as it implies a deficit view of something missing, particularly in relation to a study or career path. For example, it is well known that a gap in one's CV is to be avoided, and we have already seen how people are prepared to fabricate something or gild the lily rather than suggest they were not productive for a period of time. This is no doubt viewed differently in different cultures, but:

> In our society [the US], people are suspicious of those who get off the train to success, even for a brief time. (Hoover 2001)

In Australia, there is pressure on young people to be 'learning or earning', with various policies aiming at increasing school retention rates. However, is retention at school always desirable? Most educators would agree that engaging young people in meaningful learning or work is preferable than simply staying at school, especially if the vocational sector might better address their needs. There is also concern about dropping out of the system—a 'disconnect' from formal study that might never be re-connected.

Despite this, the gap year has not only become more popular as outlined above but has also become recognised and commodified to the point where a 'gap year industry' has emerged in response to increasing demand from the large market of young people looking for post-school experiences before 'settling down' to study. There are hundreds of volunteer placement agencies, numerous websites, guide books (e.g. *The Lonely Planet Gap Year Book*), and time-off consultants available to help young people plan their gap year, often at significant cost (Hoover 2001; Simpson 2004). These agencies and sites sell the gap year experience as an important aspect of career development, and claims of benefits for participants include:

- acquiring 'soft skills' needed in the modern world of work (e.g. communication, organisational, team-working skills)
- self-development and personal enrichment
- shaping social values and a sense of community spirit
- adapting better to university life, less likely to drop out
- becoming more attractive to employers, improving 'employability' (Heath 2007)

Although one can find anecdotal evidence and testimonials from gap year participants in the literature to support these claims, they do not appear to be evidence-based or backed by any hard data, and assume inter alia that soft skills are not acquired during schooling or tertiary study and that qualifications alone will not prepare young people for the workplace. Ernst & Young and other large companies hiring graduates seem to confirm this (see Chap. 3). Furthermore, one view of the gap year is based on having the type of experience that has been termed 'Voluntourism' (ABC RN 2008), where young people travel to a developing or third world country and engage in voluntary community work while experiencing the novelty of another country and culture which might 'shape their social values'. This is seen as contributing to citizenship, social capital and development work, and a perceived trend:

> In generations past, twenty-somethings would throw on a backpack and hit the beer and festival trail. Today's gap-year travellers are more socially and environmentally aware. (Hurt 2008: 19)

The need for some sort of 'other' experience is reinforced by this statement from 20-year-old Hannah, who spent five weeks volunteering in Peru:

> I wanted to have a complete culture shock. I wanted to go somewhere very different. You don't get to experience a lot…in Adelaide…I just wanted to travel and see the world and do something meaningful. I'm studying anthropology and it is almost impossible to study cultures when you've never been anywhere. (Hurt 2008: 19)

Regardless of whether there is no culture to study in Adelaide, or whether there is still a distinction between studying 'them' in anthropology compared with studying 'us' in sociology, this kind of brief *voluntourist* experience has been questioned as to whether it is really socially aware development work, or just 'seeing how the other half lives' and realising how lucky you are to live in a developed country (Simpson 2004). It's as though the experience has to occur in an exotic country for it to be valid, as marketed by voluntourist agency *The Leap* on their website:

> Want a different volunteering experience? Why not spend 4 Weeks in Madagascar: Forest Conservation + Island Hopping + Teaching, where you can study weird and wonderful wildlife in the beautiful surroundings of Madagascar. (https://theleap.co.uk/)

The salient questions that arise are: What do volunteer travellers learn about 'the other' that can't be learned at home? Is this cultural imperialism? Does it actually take away from community and social needs in so-called developed countries? In the United Kingdom, a government policy response has been to introduce citizenship education in the National Schools Curriculum as well as financial incentives for young people willing to volunteer locally (Heath 2007), as there are many possibilities in the United Kingdom to have a 'complete culture shock' without going further than some parts of South London. In fact, Heath suggests that if students remain in their home town and work in their gap year, this is "not as highly rated as the experiences of students who can afford to volunteer or travel during their year out" (2008: 98).

This of course highlights another feature of the gap year—it is economically determined and limited to those who can afford it, and generally an experience enjoyed by those from socially advantaged backgrounds. According to the literature, the gap year is associated with privilege—participants are usually white, middle class, and there is a higher proportion of independent school students (Birch and Miller 2007; Cremin 2007; Heath 2007; Hurt 2008).

> Gap years, often promoted by private schools, were more likely to be within reach of wealthier families. (Lane 2008: 23)

As the gap year has been defined as 'time out from formal study', what about any informal learning that might take place during gap year experiences? This seems harder to quantify or even qualify, although as mentioned above, it is claimed that 'soft skills' are better learned outside of formal study programs or beyond school in the 'real world', ideally in another country or culture.

> For many students, a gap year is about crystallising their decision-making, developing self-directed and self-regulation skills, broadening their competencies and self-organisation and perhaps their confidence. (Maslen 2013)

However, it is also clear that in the post-industrial knowledge society, there is not necessarily a seamless pathway in a chronological sequence from School-to-Further Education-to-Work. Working life is not only 'beyond school'—up to 70% of Australian high school students in Years 10–12 are in paid part-time work (www.lsay.edu.au). This trend is reinforced by data from a study of independent school students, which found that 56% of the cohort was working part-time while completing Year 12, and in fact some students were working two or even three jobs, up to 15 hours per week (Stehlik 2010). The fact that all still managed to complete Year 12 means that young people are already learning about managing the work-life balance well before finishing school.

The job areas identified in the study include the predictable ones for teenagers—retail, supermarket, waiting, kitchen hand, farm hand, and other low-skilled jobs in the gig economy. National data from the

Australian LSAY studies suggest there is little correlation between paid part-time work at school and eventual work destinations, yet it is valuable for socialisation into the world of work and for developing employability skills through authentic work experiences. In fact it has been suggested that paid part-time work should be validated as not only vocational preparation but as a recognised aspect of the senior secondary curriculum (Billett and Ovens 2007).

There is also a disconnect in the experiences of senior secondary students who are often in positions of adult responsibility at work such as supervising staff, being responsible for stock, handling money, dealing with customers, and so on, yet still being treated like 'kids' at school. The gap year sits somewhere between being a 'schoolkid' and an 'adult' and may provide a defining marker for this important transition stage of a young person's life.

If the gap year provides a sort of safety valve between school and the serious business of vocational study or work, and a process of 'maturing' and putting things in perspective, should it be officially validated as a recognised part of the post-school transition, or would this only serve to spoil the very spirit of the gap year as 'time-out' from institutional interference?

In the Republic of Ireland, this seems to be happening with the *Transition Year*, an optional year for secondary school students after completing their Junior Certificate, which can extend the senior school cycle from two to three years. Introduced as a pilot in 1974, around 75% of secondary schools in Ireland now offer the Transition Year, and in some schools it is even compulsory (Turnbull 2017). Students undertake non-classroom-based activities, voluntary work placements, and international tours, engage in community-based projects, or attend the Bridge21 program at Trinity College Dublin (see Chap. 12) and experience a whole year free from the stress of examinations and continuing assessment before returning to school for their final year of study.

The Transition Year or gap year experience reminds me of the tradition that evolved before the Industrial Revolution, when, in order to be accepted into a Guild, an apprentice tradesman or artisan needed to complete a final year as a *Journeyman*, which required them to travel to other places offering their skills and expertise pro bono, as a kind of combination finishing school, grand tour, and community service. My grandfather was an apprentice textile printer from Bohemia which in the early 1900s was part of the Austro-Hungarian Empire. We still have his Journeyman's notebook and diary, which lists all the places he visited and is stamped by the various officials from the Textile Guilds who confirmed that he was there offering his services.

It also strikes me that the Journeyman experience could be seen as a *rite of passage* in which a young man makes the transition from apprentice to master, from adolescent to adult, and to full identity as a tradesman or artisan recognised as such by their guild and their community. Rites of passage were important in earlier human societies and associated with sacred—and often secret—rites such as initiation ceremonies in which the lore of the tribe or clan group is passed on to the next generation. In secular society we seem to have lost such formal milestones and *rituals* which mark these important transitions and inductions into adulthood and society, not only for young men but for young women too. Young people are in a unique situation in which they need to feel that they belong and are included, for example, in sports clubs, peer groups, and so on, but also that they are recognised as being in a state of becoming independent and unique individuals. This tension between *being and belonging* can often go unresolved and result in alienation and withdrawal, or joining up to something that may not be appropriate—such as a radical religious organisation or a criminal gang. The gap year then may be an important and necessary transition that also acts as a rite of passage, allowing time to sort out such tensions.

However, what really interests me about the gap year is that it is clearly an example of *Not-school* and *education outside the classroom*, in which young people might experience the kind of real-world learning that they have not learned in school, unencumbered by accreditations, assessments, or evaluations. But it also raises a number of questions: Why is this real-world learning not happening in schools? What is the school curriculum doing if it is not preparing young people for the real world? What are these twenty-first-century skills that can only be developed outside of school, and why don't we all follow Ireland's lead and make the gap year part of the education project? The final chapters will address such questions in the light of all that has been discussed so far, but also pose many other questions, some of which may not even be answerable.

References

ABC Radio National. (2008, April 28). *Life Matters*. Australian Broadcasting Corporation.

ABC Radio National. (2017, June 2). *The World Today*. Australian Broadcasting Corporation.

ABC TV. (2017, June 3). School's out. *Compass*. Australian Broadcasting Corporation.

Billett, S., & Ovens, C. (2007). Learning about work, working life and post school options: Guiding students' reflecting on paid part-time work. *Journal of Education and Work, 20*(2), 75–90.

Bills, A., & Howard, N. (2016). What then must we do? Rethinking social inclusion policy for educational attainment in South Australia. *Journal of Educational Enquiry, 15*(1), 25–43.

Birch, E. R., & Miller, P. (2007). The characteristics of 'gap-year' students and their tertiary academic outcomes. *The Economic Record, 83*(262), 329–344.

Cremin, C. (2007). Living and really living: The gap year and the commodification of the contingent. *Ephemera, 7*(4), 526–542.

Doll, W. (2008). Complexity and the culture of curriculum. Chapter 13. In M. Mark (Ed.), *Complexity theory and the philosophy of education*. Chichester: Wiley-Blackwell.

Durrell, G. (1962). *My family and other animals*. Victoria: Penguin.

Heath, S. (2007). Widening the gap: Pre-university gap years and the economy of experience'. *British Journal of Sociology of Education, 28*(1), 89–103.

Holt, J. (1980). *The natural child project*. https://web.archive.org/web/20110923153702/http://www.naturalchild.org:80/guest/marlene_bumgarner.html. Accessed 7 July 2017.

Holt, J. (2004). *Instead of education: Ways to help people do things better*. Boulder: Sentient Publications.

Hoover, E. (2001). More students decide that college can wait. *Chronicle of Higher Education, 48*(2), A51–A52.

Hurst, A. (2014). *The purpose economy: How your desire for impact, personal growth and community is changing the world*. Boise: Elevate.

Hurt, J. (2008, June 21). Backpackers off to save the world. *The Advertiser*, p. 19.

Illich, I. (1971). *Deschooling society*. New York: Marion Boyars.

Lane, B. (2008, May 7). Gaps show failings of youth allowance. *The Australian*, p. 23.

Lawson, H. (2016). Categories, boundaries and bridges: The social geography of schooling and the need for new institutional designs. *Education Sciences, 6*(32), 1–14.

Loyd, S. (1914). *Cyclopedia of puzzles.* New York: The Lamb publishing Company.

Maslen, G. (2013, November 11). Students find clarity in gap years. *Sydney Morning Herald.* http://www.smh.com.au/national/education/students-find-clarity-in-gap-years-20131110-2x9p3.html. Accessed 9 July 2017.

Rittel, H., & Webber, M. (1973). Dilemmas in a general theory of planning. *Policy Sciences, 4,* 155–169.

Sefton-Green, J. (2013). *Learning at not-school: A review of study, theory and advocacy for education in non-formal settings.* Cambridge, MA: MIT Press.

Simpson, K. (2004). 'Doing development: The gap year, volunteer-tourists and a popular practice of development. *Journal of International Development, 16,* 681–692.

Smith, A. (2016, February 7). Home-schooled kids perform better in NAPLAN: Report. *Sydney Morning Herald.* http://www.smh.com.au/nsw/home-schooled-kids-perform-better-in-naplan-report-20160204-gmlgu9.html. Accessed 8 July 2017.

Stehlik, T. (2006). *Levels of engagement: Report of findings prepared for the social inclusion unit on the action research project across school retention initiatives.* Adelaide: UniSA/South Australian Government.

Stehlik, T. (2010). Mind the gap: School leaver aspirations and delayed pathways to further and higher education. *Journal of Education and Work, 23*(4), 363–376.

Turnbull, C. (2017, April 17). Every student should consider doing transition year. *Western People.*

Part VI

The Future of Education

12

Predicting Unknown Futures

12.1 Twenty-First-Century Skills: What Are They?

'Twenty-first-century skills', otherwise known as 'soft skills' such as communication, collaboration, cooperation, and creativity, are compared with 'hard skills' such as literacy, numeracy, and content knowledge in this chapter, in which I pose a number of questions. What will the classroom of the future look like in delivering these contrasting aspects of the curriculum, given the contemporary demands of the 'fourth industrial revolution'? Can creativity and imagination be taught? How do we turn information into knowledge in a world of information overload? What is the process of the 'getting of wisdom'?

We have seen so far how the rapid pace of change in social, economic, and technological domains has brought about unprecedented differences in the way we live, consume, communicate, and even think; yet developments in education and schooling have been slow to catch up, with traditional models of teaching, teacher education, and assessment of learning still dominating mainstream policies and practices. It is apparent that in economic terms, the developed and developing worlds have largely

© The Author(s) 2018
T. Stehlik, *Educational Philosophy for 21st Century Teachers*,
https://doi.org/10.1007/978-3-319-75969-2_12

moved on from an agrarian and industrial-based model to a more knowledge-based economy, driven by information and communication technologies. Developments in artificial intelligence, automation of jobs, e-commerce, online working, global networking, and the 'internet of things' are increasingly becoming the basis of economies which rely more and more on the transmission, translation, and even trading of knowledge. For example, 20% of young Australians are experiencing their first jobs in roles that will look different or be lost to automation in the next 10–15 years, and 40% of the Australian labour market, or 5 million jobs, could be replaced by computers in the next couple of decades (FYA 2015).

We have moved on from an industrial society defined by the 'constructability of the world' to a situation of post-modernity in which the world we once knew has become deconstructed, chaotic, complex, and dynamic. In the words of Bo Dahlin, "nature is no longer mechanised, it is digitised" (2006: 31). Elsewhere this trend has been labelled as the 'fourth industrial revolution':

> The first industrial revolution used water and steam power to mechanise production. The second used electric power to create mass production. The third used electronics and information technology to automate production. Now a fourth industrial revolution is building on the third, the digital revolution that has been occurring since the middle of the last century. It is characterised by a fusion of technologies that is blurring the lines between the physical, digital and biological spheres. (Sparrow 2017)

Declining employment opportunities in the agricultural and manufacturing sectors are balanced by increases in the service sector and higher skilled jobs, which are in turn driven by more people gaining higher level qualifications. *Ideas* are now a commodity; *entrepreneurship* is now a core skill. So if we now find ourselves in the twenty-first century in a *knowledge economy* and *information society*, how is knowledge packaged, presented, and understood in formal, compulsory education? How do we prepare our children and young people for futures that will be determined by knowledge, and how do we even know what types of knowledge will be useful or necessary? How do we distinguish between information and knowledge?

'What do you want to be when you grow up?' is no longer a realistic or relevant question to ask of a young person when they might be looking forward to possible multiple and simultaneous careers and job roles, in 'pop-up' jobs in the gig economy, as a *flexible worker* in situations and contexts yet to be invented. The idea of a 'dream job' literally could be a non-existent dream now, but a reality in the future.

Therefore, it makes sense to develop the interests and skill sets of young people towards the possibility of *them creating new job opportunities*, rather than just training them to fit the opportunities that exist now, which we can't be sure will exist in the future. A different way of thinking about jobs and occupations and their attendant skill and knowledge requirements is emerging in the idea of *job clusters*.

> Using big data, the Foundation for Young Australians study analysed more than 2.7 million job advertisements to reveal seven new job clusters in the Australian economy where the required skills are more closely related and more portable than we previously understood. The job clusters are the 'Generators', the 'Artisans', the 'Carers', the 'Informers', the 'Technologists', the 'Designers' and the 'Coordinators'. When a person trains or works in one job, they gain skills for around 13 other jobs because employers demand very similar skills in many jobs. (Payton 2017: 5)

What are these 'very similar skills' and are they actually transferrable across jobs within such clusters? Three *skill sets* that have been suggested by the CSIRO (Commonwealth Scientific and Industrial Research Organisation) as increasingly important to future employees are those that include communication skills, technical skills, and STEM (science, technology, engineering, and mathematics) skills. The communication skill set comprises active listening, speaking, writing, coordination, service orientation, instructing, and negotiation; the technical skill set comprises operations analysis, operation and control, equipment maintenance, troubleshooting, management of financial resources, management of personnel resources, and installation; and the STEM skill set includes science, technology design, engineering, mathematics, programming, systems analysis, critical thinking, and computer use (Reeson et al. 2016, passim).

It will be immediately seen that some of these descriptors such as 'active listening' are more specific and could be associated with a particular skill, while others such as 'science' and 'mathematics' could describe a huge range of possibilities and are generally considered as disciplines or subjects, not skills. Being able to use scientific enquiry and/or mathematical applications in say 'troubleshooting' makes more sense, but it also implies that such an activity requires a combination of skills but also an underlying foundation of *domain-specific knowledge* (Hirsch 2009).

Critics of the 'twenty-first-century skills movement' suggest that while being able to think critically, communicate effectively, work in teams, solve problems, innovate, adapt and use computers are, more than ever, important skills for uncertain futures, a focus on developing such skills should not lose sight of the fact that they rely on having a solid foundation of knowledge in order to apply them (Christodoulou 2014; Hirsch 2009; Ravitch 2009). Hirsch goes so far as to declare that "knowledge is skill: skill knowledge" (2009: 3) and, furthermore, that such skills are not necessarily transferable because the underpinning knowledge is specific to its domain, context, or application; what will apply in one situation may not apply in another. As Diane Ravitch argues, "people do not think in the abstract; they need knowledge—ideas, facts, concepts—to think about", and furthermore she points out that "critical thinking skills, creativity, problem-solving, and cooperative group skills are not at all '21st Century'", but have been around in various education reform movements throughout the past century (2009).

A 2016 survey of developments in job-specific skill areas undertaken by the World Economic Forum further suggested that *social and communication skills* are experiencing the most significant and growing demand (WEF 2016). These are not highly technical skills that require rocket science responses in order to develop them, but they do require underpinning knowledge in key areas such as language and literacy, and a broad understanding of culture and cultural differences as well as interpersonal awareness and self-esteem in order to be able to interact in varying social and work situations. As we have seen, communication skills can be generic but also highly specific to the jargon of an industry or occupation, reinforcing the limitations of the transferability argument and the strengths of the domain-specific argument. However, while we are currently fixated on assessing communication skills with mandatory literacy testing, it does not necessarily follow that being an effective communicator is a simple matter of being able to read and write. How then do we develop, encourage and assess a key skill like communication? How are social skills defined? Are they generic or context specific?

We have seen that in a normally developing child, these skills evolve naturally with language acquisition, patterns of communication and social interaction being established well before formal schooling even commences. These things are taken for granted and *assumed* by the time a child starts school, but they can then be *subsumed* by a focus on testing for academic achievement and content knowledge. Rarely would we measure success in child development by recognising a child as 'a good communicator' or 'a good socialiser'; we tend to assess their grades instead. Various moves to 're-envision what constitutes success in our schools' include the National Commission on Social, Emotional and Academic Development in the United States, which advocates for the integration of social and emotional learning in school curricula for a more holistic approach to education (The Aspen Institute 2017). As part of its work, the commission has recognised that schools need community partnerships to promote social, emotional, and academic development with students and the adults in their lives. Here we see another example of *the village* being involved in schooling which goes *beyond the classroom*.

Developing social and emotional skills without having to go outside the classroom, however, has been shown to be successful in mixed-grade classes with composite or multi-age groupings of children in primary school settings.

> Putting students into classes based on their age is an administrative convenience … age is not always an accurate predictor of their actual development. (Cornish 2015)

Yet as we have seen, schools are still structured in this way based on assumptions that all children develop at the same pace, when we know from research and experience that this is not the case. The advantages of mixed age groupings in fostering a more holistic approach to learning and development by allowing children to *learn from each other* is just one example of a different level of thinking in addressing the 'problem' of educating for so-called twenty-first-century skills.

The importance of this approach is recognised in the Bridge21 program based at Trinity College in Dublin, which has been developed to offer a new model of learning to secondary schools in Ireland, and is reflected in the key values of their "innovative team based educational model for 21st Century, technology mediated learning" based on the notion that learning to learn is a key goal of education:

- Young people should be trusted to learn from each other
- Building positive relationships is vital to success in education
- Educational practice should follow the best of theory
- Young people benefit from the experience of working in mixed ability teams
- Young people grow through being given responsibility
- Technology is central to 21st teaching and learning (Bridge21 2017)

These ideas will be discussed further in the final chapter. Other responses to the changing work-education interface and landscape include the re-vamping of senior secondary school curricula. In New South Wales, for example, the Higher School Certificate (HSC) will now feature a "cross-curriculum emphasis on work and enterprise to future-proof its HSC students [and] ensure students have a depth of understanding of the topic, which means their skills are transferable" (Balogh 2017: 1). Such curriculum responses have already been discussed, but can we claim that they will 'future-proof' students when we cannot be at all certain about what the future will bring, just in terms of the environment and world politics, let alone in terms of work and enterprise? And claims that their skills will be transferable are also dependent on the same uncertainties and have already been shown to be questionable in terms of domain-specific knowledge. However, regardless of their worth, these approaches, ideas, and reforms do not exist in isolation and rely on many other parts of the bigger picture lining up to make them happen, not least of which is the role of the teacher and their own changing educational needs.

12.2   The Classroom of the Future

> The future of learning is not the same as the future of schooling. (Lawson 2016: 10)

How does all of the above manifest in the classroom, what will the 'classroom of the future' look like, and how will we prepare teachers for this brave new world? If the kinds of skills we have been talking about are better developed in a gap year or transition year, what is the role of schools and teachers in developing them?

The Bridge21 program has some ideas:

> We also think the physical space of learning is important. We configure the learning space to provide for group learning with breakout areas and alcoves, each facilitating information exchange, team collaboration and individual reflection. We also incorporate a presentation area, for group discussion and reflection. In this way both open space learning and private conversation is supported. Within the space, mentors and teachers become guides and facilitators, learning alongside the pupils. (Bridge21 2017)

The role of the teacher as 'the guide on the side' rather than 'the sage on the stage' is not a new concept, deriving as it does from methodologies and teaching-learning relationships influenced by a variety of theoretical and philosophical positions. It is well known in adult education practice, for example, where the role of *facilitator* to ease the learning situation literally derives from the word *facile*: 'easily done'; and in a Montessori school, the label 'teacher' is replaced with the word 'adult'. However, teaching methods in twenty-first-century classrooms need to go beyond just nominative determinism to embrace new ideas and different levels of thinking that go outside the box while still trying to 'work inside the box', regardless of the actual physical space.

Some basic principles which embody twenty-first-century teaching in secondary education have been described as firstly involving more *flexibility*, which aligns with the ideas of liquid modernity introduced in Chap. 5 and the notion of the flexible worker as described above and responds to the increasingly fluid environment which young people are now used to, in being able to access and exchange information 'anywhere, anytime'. An emerging methodology therefore is the *blended learning* approach in which online learning blends with face-to-face teaching so that learning is accessible in multiple formats on a 24/7 basis. Here the teacher adopts more of a facilitation role, moving from a "*sole dispenser of information* to a *highly skilled orchestrator of blended learning*" (SASPA 2015: 5, original italics).

Dylan Wiliam expresses this in another, very simple way:

> Teachers do not create learning, *learners create learning;* teachers create the conditions in which students learn. (2006: 3, original italics)

This stark realisation can be very confronting for teachers who have always operated under the professional assumption that they are the ones controlling the curriculum, the content, the classroom, and therefore creating the learning. Furthermore, we have seen that the *conditions in which students learn* can vary from being under a hedge, in a playground, at home, from each other or by themselves, as well as being in a purpose-built classroom environment full of resources and access to the latest IT facilities. As Aristotle noted, the motivation, the desire, and the will to learn are universal, even when the conditions can vary widely. How much control teachers have over those conditions however is another question.

> Today's classrooms still very much possess the rank-and-file structure familiar from the 19th century and at the same time are expected to be places in which constructivist concepts are put into practice. This is simply contradictory. Historically speaking, the classroom of the present has the shape of the 19th century and the contents of the 20th century. (Schratzenstaller 2010: 35)

While it would be wonderful to combine architectural, technological, and educational considerations into the design of learning spaces in the twenty-first century, the reality is that most students, schools, teachers, and communities have to make do with what they have, which in many cases still looks like illustrations of classrooms from the early 1800s, unless, like

Willunga Waldorf School, for example, the school and the parents are able to build custom-designed structures that reflect the needs of the age group and the appropriate learning space for that cohort (see Figure 6.2, Chap. 6).

However, it is still important for educators as well as educational planners and policy makers to recognise that the classroom is not a "neutral or passive container" (Burke 2005: 490), but will either encourage or constrain ways of teaching and learning that in effect make space and place a key factor in consideration of the hidden curriculum, and that traditional classroom design actually has more to do with maintaining discipline and control than providing the optimum environment for learning. The 'rank and file' idea of desks in rows clearly arises from a military model of organisation and reflects other aspects of school cultures and structures, such as ranking and sorting students by age, achievement, behaviour, and so on.

Regarding the 'classroom of the future' then, it seems that working within these existing structures is going to be the reality for a while yet, and according to Wiliam:

> … the future is further away than you think. I think that for the foreseeable future we will have groups of between 20 and 40 students, with a teacher, and most of the learning is going to be in classrooms that are the size of classrooms we have now, with some IT of course, but the quality of the learning is going to be dictated by what's going on in that classroom. (2006: 2)

While being aware that the learning space is not neutral or passive, the key approach then is to focus *on what's going on in that classroom*. This brings us back to the role of the teacher, their philosophy of teaching, and their understanding of pedagogical and methodological approaches that will provide the kind of flexibility required to address the challenges of twenty-first-century learning. It therefore reinforces the need for a re-think of teacher education, both pre-service and in-service, as highlighted by this reflective quote from an American high school teacher:

> I am entering my third year teaching at a public high school, and at this point have realized that my students' social/emotional/academic skills,

like teamwork, perseverance, problem-solving, creativity, and critical thinking, are much more important than any math I can teach them. But my training and evaluation is based on teaching math. I would love to see a more explicit effort made to teach these skills (and to train teachers in how to do so, as I currently just do my own idiosyncratic best). (Price 2016)

What an interesting observation recalling the discussion in Chap. 8 regarding the way we still focus on content knowledge as the expense of pedagogical knowledge and the distinction made in Chap. 2 between types of knowledge. Just focussing on *episteme*, or facts and truths, without an understanding of *phronesis*, or practical wisdom, will not provide a holistic learning experience for both teacher and learner(s). Phronesis implies being aware of the conditions in which the learning is occurring and adjusting the pedagogical approach according to the situation, the students, the time, the place, as well as the content—an ongoing process of reflection-in-action. As discussed in Chap. 8, this kind of practical wisdom takes time to develop, but I do believe that teachers can *create the conditions in which students learn* by being open to new and different educational ideas, as well as being open to the social/emotional aspects and collaborative learning opportunities afforded by face-to-face, real-time group interactions in classroom situations.

> It seems imperative that teacher education critically expose pre-service teachers to different ways of seeing, understanding and believing, and unpack the philosophical traditions that underpin different worldviews. (Evans et al. 2012: 9)

That is precisely the intent of this book, which can only provide an introductory perspective on unpacking a sample of philosophical traditions and world views, in the hope that the reader will be inspired to seek out more as part of their own lifelong learning interest in education. The final chapter then attempts to bring together all of what has been discussed so far into a summary, a conclusion, and a reflection on what we can learn from the past to inform the present and plan for the future.

References

Balogh, S. (2017, February 21). Classroom focus shifts to life skills. *The Australian*.

Bridge21. (2017). http://bridge21.ie/about-us/missionvisionvalues/. Accessed 15 Sept 2017.

Burke, C. (2005). Containing the school child: Architecture and pedagogies. *Paedagogica Historica, International Journal of the History of Education, 41*(4–5), 489–494.

Christodoulou, D. (2014). *Seven myths about education*. Oxfordshire/New York: Routledge.

Cornish, L. (2015, April 7). Are mixed-grade classes any better or worse for learning? *The Conversation*. http://theconversation.com/are-mixed-grade-classes-any-better-or-worse-for-learning-38856. Accessed 15 July 2017.

Dahlin, B. (2006). *Education, history and be(com)ing human: Two essays in philosophy and education*. Karlstad: Karlstad University.

Evans, N., Whitehouse, H., & Hickey, R. (2012). Pre-service teachers' conceptions of education for sustainability. *Australian Journal of Teacher Education, 37*(7), 1–13.

FYA. (2015). *The new work order*. Melbourne: Foundation for Youth Australia.

Hirsch, E. D. (2009). *The 21st century skills movement*. http://greatminds.net/maps/documents/reports/hirsch.pdf. Accessed 15 July 2017.

Lawson, H. (2016). Categories, boundaries and bridges: The social geography of schooling and the need for new institutional designs. *Education Sciences, 6*(32), 1–14.

Payton, A. (2017). *Skilling for tomorrow*. Adelaide: NCVER.

Price, H. (2016). *How can we help students thrive?* https://www.aspeninstitute.org/blog-posts/can-help-students-thrive/. Accessed 16 July 2017.

Ravitch, D. (2009). What about 21st century skills? *Bridging Differences*. http://blogs.edweek.org/edweek/Bridging-Differences/2009/03/what_about_21st_century_skills.html. Accessed 15 July 2017.

Reeson, A., Mason, C., Sanderson, T., Bratanova, A., & Hajkowicz, S. (2016). *The VET era: Equipping Australia's workforce for the future digital economy*. Canberra: CSIRO.

SASPA. (2015). *Discussion paper: Educating in the 21st century*. Adelaide: South Australian Secondary Principals' Association.

Schratzenstaller, A. (2010). The classroom of the past. Chapter 2, In K. Mäkitalo-Siegl, J. Zottman, F. Kaplan, & F. Fischer (Eds.), *Classroom of the future: Orchestrating collaborative spaces*. Rotterdam: Sense Publishers.

Sparrow, J. (2017, January 11). Can democracy survive the fourth industrial revolution: Should it? *The Guardian*. https://www.theguardian.com/sustainable-business/2017/jan/11/can-democracy-survive-the-fourth-industrial-revolution-should-it. Accessed 15 July 2017.

The Aspen Institute. (2017). https://www.aspeninstitute.org/programs/national-commission-on-socialemotional-and-academic-development/. Accessed 26 Mar 2018.

WEF. (2016). *The future of jobs: Employment, skills and workforce strategy for the fourth industrial revolution*. Geneva: The World Economic Forum.

Wiliam, D. (2006). *Assessment for learning: Why, what and how?* Paper presented to the Cambridge Assessment Network Conference, 15 September 2006, University of Cambridge.

13

A Holistic View of Education

13.1 'Can't Buy Me Love'

The previous chapter noted that the age-old question 'What do you want to be when you grow up?' is rather redundant in the light of the fourth industrial revolution and the constantly changing uncertainty of the modern workforce, and it is also loaded with assumptions about 'being' and 'identity' necessarily associated with a career, job, or occupation. Why not aim for happiness?

The American educator Nel Noddings has long been a champion of happiness as one of the main *aims* of education, in addition to the '3 Rs' and the academic outcomes that generally take precedence in educational policy provision:

> These great aims are meant to guide our instructional decisions. They are meant to broaden our thinking—to remind us to ask *why* we have chosen certain curriculums, pedagogical methods, classroom arrangements, and learning objectives. (Noddings 2005: 10)

© The Author(s) 2018
T. Stehlik, *Educational Philosophy for 21st Century Teachers*,
https://doi.org/10.1007/978-3-319-75969-2_13

Noddings concedes that happiness is not readily defined or measured by behavioural objectives or standardised testing, nor is happiness a commodity that can be easily acquired and transmitted as content knowledge; instead more subtle approaches are required in the teaching-learning relationship in which "we must allow teachers and students to interact as whole persons, and we must develop policies that treat the school as a whole community" (2005: 13).

In fact we have seen from the case study of education in Finland in Chap. 10 that making happiness and wellbeing the primary concerns for children and young people can flow on to successful results not only in social and emotional learning but in academic achievement, as measured by empirical comparative assessment programs such as PISA. In addition to testing for achievement in academic subject areas, since 2015 the PISA has expanded to include an assessment of the cognitive, psychological, social, physical, and material wellbeing of the 15-year-old age group of students in participating OECD countries. Not surprisingly, the overall findings show that:

> Teenagers who feel part of a school community and enjoy good relations with their parents and teachers are more likely to perform better academically and be happier with their lives, according to the first OECD PISA assessment of students' well-being. (www.oecd.org)

This reinforces at least two of the key messages that have been developed throughout this book: the importance of positive relationships for young people and the importance of community in raising children. It also brings us back to the questions raised in earlier chapters in relation to what the overall purpose of education should be in contemporary society, and how schools could or should be configured to achieve that purpose.

Returning to the Ancient Greek world view, the concept of *Eudaimonia* encapsulated a holistic notion of wellbeing, literally meaning having a 'good spirit' (*eu* 'good' and *daimōn* 'spirit'), and related to our modern notion of *welfare*. It was suggested that in order to promote Eudaimonia, a more holistic view of education is required, one that goes beyond just the institution of schooling to recognise the importance and impact of the whole environment in which a child is raised, including the social, political, and economic milieu. A multidimensional view of student well-being will also necessarily take into account the wellbeing of those adults who are influential in the students' life-worlds—parents, caregivers, and, in particular, teachers. If teachers are experiencing stress and burnout, with many leaving the profession early in their careers, then we must also pay attention to the Eudaimonia of the teaching profession.

In addition, we have seen how important it is for a child's experiences of home and school to be in harmony, or at least not in the sort of opposition which can result in a disconnect between the two, leading on the one hand to responses such as *unschooling* where school is taken out of the picture altogether or on the other to a situation where school is the only safe place in a child's world due to family dysfunction, domestic violence, poverty, or just poor parenting. It is recognised that attending to the well-being of young people today will influence the wellbeing of adults tomorrow, and building human capital and social skills for the future should actually address and begin to change the cycle of intergenerational dysfunction and disadvantage (Borgonovi and Pál 2016). I believe that a significant aspect of the healthy development and education of our children is that they should experience *love*. A loving home environment should be the entitlement of all children, and should also be reflected in the educational environments that they experience. The notion of *pedagogical love* was introduced in Chap. 10 as a foundational aspect of the development of trust and positive relationships between students and teachers in Finland, and is here re-affirmed as an aspirational goal for teachers and educators, one that goes to the very heart of the teaching-learning relationship:

> The original meaning of pedagogy is grounded in the relational and intentional responsibility of adult to child. The vulnerability of the child calls forth a loving attitude from the adult, as pedagogue, that is directed toward the physical security *and* the social, emotional and educational well-being of the child as student. (Hatt 2005: 671)

We understand the notion of *childcare* in the early years, but it is easy to forget not only that children are the most vulnerable members of society but that they remain vulnerable and therefore entitled to love and care right up until they are deemed adult, which according to the UN Convention on the Rights of the Child is at the age of 18. Article 29 of the convention also highlights the reciprocity involved in the educational relationship, between developing each child's potential, and in turn each child respecting parents, cultures, and other cultures (UNICEF 1989). Pedagogical love is a concept and a term that encompasses this relationship, described in Chap. 10 as *interdependence*, but it involves much more. In Finland, it is manifest in the trust that is apparent at all levels of society and therefore flows through the home and school environments, so that teachers, parents, and most importantly children know where they stand in relation to each other. For the Finns, this *high trust capital* means that schools are open to anyone who wants to visit—in stark contrast to the situation in Australia and many other countries where visitors must report to the school office, volunteers need police clearance checks, and strangers are treated with suspicion due to the unfortunate increase in paedophile behaviours and child abuse.

Love in all its forms is a precious thing and not a commodity that can be easily bought and sold. However, neither would it involve a huge cost in terms of educational resourcing—unlike say new technologies, new classrooms, and higher teacher salaries—to promote the idea of love in our schools. Pedagogical love can be developed, encouraged, and applied without having to make expensive structural changes to the education system that we currently have; it would involve a change in mindset across the board and for many would require thinking outside the box, but it is not rocket science and would make a huge difference to the social and emotional wellbeing, or Eudaimonia of all stakeholders. This should be nothing new. Gidley (2016) offers "practical examples for letting love into your classroom"; Montessori believed that "a love of learning lasts a lifetime" (1912); Aristotle noted the importance of *self-love* (1998), Holt wrote that "it is love, not tricks or techniques of thought that lies at the heart of all true learning" (1983), and Steiner advised us to "receive the children in reverence, educate them in love, and let them go forth in freedom" (1968).

The importance of place, space, architecture, and aesthetics in contributing to Eudaimonia and to holistic learning has been discussed, but this is also an issue related to how as a society we fund education. It is interesting to note that PISA actually highlights the correlation between education funding and school performance. For example, PISA results for 2015 showed Australian students "in absolute decline" despite record spending on education, with even the Federal Education Minister arguing that "the debate has concentrated too heavily on the amount of money spent rather than how best to spend it" (Balogh and Hutchinson 2017: 2).

As a society, how do we make these decisions about how best to spend the education dollar? Even in the 1970s, commentators like Ivan Illich and John Holt were calling into question the fact that state education budgets were inequitable, with the majority of funding mostly spent on the education of children between the ages of five to 18 in publicly funded schools, ignoring the very young, the adult, and the elderly as well as alternative options. Not much has changed in the twenty-first century, except for the fact that international comparisons are now highlighting the ineffectiveness of this funding model:

> Educational investment alone is not sufficient to boost educational performance as well as global competitiveness…the way we actually run the school seems to have a massive effect on how the students perform. (Balogh and Hutchinson 2017: 2)

This seems to be stating the glaringly obvious, with *the way we actually run the school* surely something we should have been looking at well before now. The case study examples in Chaps. 10 and 11 suggest that there are already ways in which we can think differently about running our schools. I have often thought it a shame how wasted to the community are the resources and facilities of the local school. Every weekday afternoon after school finishes and for the entire weekend, the school remains lifeless with its buildings empty and playgrounds under-utilised. Schools should be the central focus of a community, school libraries could be buzzing at weekends, many schools should have comprehensive kitchens, workshops, studios, and other facilities where families could gather and interact and get to know each other in a true learning exchange, where children could experience school as something integrated with their family and community life. Some sort of voluntary system of supervision would be required of course, but this is precisely how adventure playgrounds and community organisations have always operated. It seems incredible that instead, public school facilities are kept locked up and inaccessible to the community, in particular those who are actually paying for them through the taxation system. Is this really 'public education'?

Initiatives in the United States have recognised that schools "are viewed as place-based assets for community development", and that both community-based "outside-in" strategies and school-based "inside-out" strategies are required to enable local involvement in developing the school as a community asset rather than a state-owned facility (Lawson 2016: 8). Once again, this would require a joined-up approach at the policy level to make such 'Collective Impact Initiatives' happen, since many communities already have partnerships for things like economic development, crime prevention, and health; but usually these are structured separately, often working at cross-purposes and even competing for the same limited resources and funding sources. As a type of 'wicked problem', any change to the system of funding education therefore needs to take into account a holistic view and will require massive intervention at all levels and aspects of publicly funded services. Just focussing on one service without taking in the bigger picture of a complex and chaotic system is like looking at one tree at a time while ignoring the whole forest.

13.2   Mother Nature's Child

A major theme running through this book has been to investigate the tension between the natural world and the technologised world in relation to child development and educational interventions, respecting the precious nature of childhood while acknowledging the demands of the modern world as well as the possible needs of the future. In Chap. 6 I discussed the unique cases of 'wild children' who were brought up in the forest without being able to develop natural socialisation skills including language and in Chap. 7 made the link with various 'back to nature' initiatives which seem to act as an organic antidote to the digitised and mechanised world. Returning to this theme now, I want to focus on children who have been brought up not only *in the natural world* but *by the natural world*, and in so doing demonstrate the possibility that *children can learn from each other* and may not even need the type of formal institutionalised teacher-centred education programs that we think are important. I am here referring to Indigenous children and, in particular, Indigenous knowledges and ways of seeing and reading the world that, in the case of Australian Aboriginal societies, have been successfully reproducing and educating generations of human beings for at least 65,000 years (Wright 2017).

> If you want to put it visually, if you take the clock face of 60 minutes and give each one of those minutes a thousand years, then you have the recorded time that our people have been on this land. That means Plato was here a minute and a half ago. (Price 2012: 2)

In terms of educational philosophy, we could learn a lot from the longest continual living culture on the planet. Far from being a primitive culture, Australian Aboriginal people prior to European settlement possessed a complex and sophisticated world view and knowledge system based on country, community, and kinship, with hindsight, insight, and foresight combined into a seamless cosmology. The early colonisers and settlers were, to put it mildly, "ignorant of other cultures, languages and societies and were not attuned to different possibilities" (Price 2012: 3). A western-style education system imposed onto traditional Indigenous people ignored their own highly developed system of learning, since from time immemorial the children had learned from inherited guidelines, and for them "the world around us was our 'class room'; the 'five senses' were our means of learning. The grannies were 'examiners', the elders the 'masters' of our educational world" (Lester 1975: 187).

Aboriginal and Torres Strait Islander children and their parents were not familiar with western concepts such as 'failure', 'competition', and 'truancy'. Theirs was a collaborative society in which the children looked out for each other and were reliant on highly developed observational skills from an early age in order to survive in harsh environmental conditions, for example, the Pitjantjatjara children of the Musgrave Ranges in far northern South Australia:

> At three Kalatari was carrying her sister Rosemary, fourteen months, on her back wherever she went, tending her like a small mother. Now almost four she handles fire casually but quite safely, and no-one ever tries to prevent her taking a fire-stick and building her own fire. (Wallace and Wallace 1968: 30)

In our risk-averse modern society, we worry about such things and question how much responsibility a three- or four-year-old child can have for their own learning or for the wellbeing of their peers and siblings. Now we have to develop adventure playgrounds and forest school environments in which children can be re-acquainted with things like building a fire, but still under the guidance of adults. Although it might be confronting and controversial for many parents, the element of risk for young children is important in setting their own boundaries, and the motto of the adventure playground movement associated with 'The Land' in Wales is "better a broken bone than a broken spirit" (Moore 2014a).

Indigenous societies based on such deep knowledge of their physical, social, and spiritual worlds are essentially self-regulating, much like the science of what we now know to be a form of complexity theory which also applies to social groupings as complex adaptive systems. In this holistic perspective, the processes of 'teaching' and 'learning' are not separate from the processes of *living* and *observing*, as shown by a group of young Pitjantjatjara boys:

> When asked who had taught them about the 'spear' bush and how to straighten the wood and make the spears, they laughed and said, 'No-one'. They have watched the men around the campfires from the beginning of conscious thought, and before, as they made the beautiful seven-foot spears that they use for hunting the kangaroo. (Wallace and Wallace 1968: 33)

Fast forward to the twenty-first century and the *unschooling* movement, which is re-visiting the central idea that 'children can be trusted to learn from each other'. Experiments in *self-organised learning environments* have demonstrated that, given the right conditions, children can teach themselves almost anything without the intervention of a teacher. Professor Sugata Mitra from Newcastle University in the United Kingdom is a champion of the 'School in the Cloud', a simple idea that gives groups of children access to computers and the internet and allows their natural curiosity and ability to self-organise themselves to guide their learning. Successful examples of this have been documented in places as diverse as remote parts of India as well as in England, showing that language is no barrier and that children have a universal desire to be curious and find answers to problems if they are genuinely interested.

Mitra's conclusion is that "education is a self-organising system, where learning is an emergent phenomenon" (Future Learning 2012). *Emergence* is a fundamental concept of self-organising systems: that unexpected things which the system was not intentionally planned for can just happen or *emerge*. I find this proposition fascinating, and can see a direct line from the Aboriginal children learning to make spears and light fires through observation, play, and practice, to children learning through observation, play, and practice using technology in what may be the classrooms of the future—without a teacher. Certainly adults are involved (Mitra refers to them as *mediators*) in setting up the learning space and providing some form of guidance and encouragement, and in the 'School in the Cloud' they are often mediating over Skype from another country, maybe even in another language. This is truly global education enacted at the local level.

13.3   The Future Is What We Make It

The key to the success of self-organised learning environments is the *interaction between the children themselves*, showing that human relationships are still important and that the synergy of a group is greater than the sum of its parts. Even with online learning mediated by technology, education remains a relationship activity. There are still some things that cannot be done online—you can't get a haircut on the internet for example! And while many repetitive and low-skilled jobs are becoming automated, the capacity for human creativity and imagination is yet to be replaced by a robot. In terms of cognition, the schooling system we have inherited appears to have been dominated by left-brain thinking: the type of rational, logical approach to knowledge that has been in ascendance since the Enlightenment. What is called for in the present and the future is more right-brain thinking: creative, imaginative, innovative, and aesthetic approaches to learning and problem-solving. 'Playful thinking' with the mind in a more relaxed state is bound to be better for both achievement and wellbeing compared with stressful thinking dominated by high-stakes testing of memorised facts.

Thinking about *the classroom as a playground* where curiosity drives interest, and experimentation can lead to emergence, is a strong metaphor that I believe we can take with us as we look to the future of education. If parents can create a home life that also facilitates learning through play, and if local communities can also provide resource-rich environments for learning through play in all its forms—from nature to technology—then this can only contribute to a holistic learning environment where pedagogical love can flourish. The role of the teacher will continue to be important but needs to become more flexible, to focus more on relationships and to change fundamentally from content expert to blended learning facilitator:

> … assisting students in the formulation of inquiry questions and supporting them to conduct inquiry-based learning in real and online contexts as a means for them to turn information into knowledge (and knowledge into wisdom). (SASPA 2015: 5, original emphasis)

The key skills for students now and in the future, according to Mitra (Future Learning 2012), involve three basic capabilities:

- Reading comprehension
- Information searching and retrieval skills
- Critical thinking skills, or knowing what to believe

Reading comprehension is important because information is still text-based—whether the text is a Shakespeare play or a tweet—and being able to search and retrieve information using whatever technologies are available is also paramount. Then being able to think critically and to make informed judgements about the veracity and provenance of information in order to translate it into knowledge and ultimately wisdom is the most important skill. Interestingly, these are all process skills—none of them are based in content knowledge. My daughter still talks about the single most useful thing that she learned in high school that she makes use of on a daily basis in her life and work, and that is *the ability to think critically*. This was not a separate subject or a tacked-on elective course but was integrated into the whole secondary curriculum, with a whole-of-school approach that gives another example of a more holistic and ultimately more effective approach to education for lifelong learning.

As a teacher, do you have a clearly articulated philosophy of education? As a parent, what is your main concern for your child or children—do you want them to be academic high achievers or do you want them to be happy? As a society, can we agree on the purpose of education and how to manage and fund it at all levels and for all sectors? These are questions that we should be continually asking ourselves as we monitor the progression of the education project now and into the future.

There is hope, however, if these words of wisdom can come from a Year 12 student and millennial teenager in a 2016 graduation speech to the current students of her high school:

> Don't fall into the trap of thinking that Year 12, or a result, defines you. The beautiful thing about being as self-aware as we are, is that we can redefine ourselves at any moment. One thing that helped me was imagining myself in ten years' time. Not so much where I was in life, but what qualities I wanted to possess. Once I had figured out what kind of person I wanted to be in ten years, I began to try to be that person now. So my advice would be: figure out what kind of person you want to be and let Year 12, and the rest of your life as you continually grow, reflect that. (Mather 2017: 10)

I end on this lovely quote because it reinforces a number of important points that I trust have been salient throughout this book—that, given the right conditions, young people can embrace the future now, see themselves as constantly evolving conscious individuals, with human qualities that go beyond just being a number on a credential defined by institutionalised schooling, and that the end of school does not mean the end of education but the beginning of a foundation for lifelong learning.

References

Aristotle's Metaphysics. (1998). Translated with an introduction by H. Lawson-Tancred. London: Penguin

Balogh, S., & Hutchinson, S. (2017, February 21). Discipline beats dollars in driving academic results. *The Australian.*

Borgonovi, F., & Pál, J. (2016). *A framework for the analysis of student well-being in the PISA 2015 study: Being 15 in 2015.* OECD working papers no 140. Paris: OECD Publishing.

Future Learning. (2012). University of Phoenix. https://www.youtube.com/watch?v=qC_T9ePzANg&sns=em. Accessed 26 July 2017.

Gidley, J. (2016). *Postformal education: A philosophy for complex futures.* Switzerland: Springer.

Hatt, B. (2005). Pedagogical love in the transactional curriculum. *Journal of Curriculum Studies, 37*(6), 671–688.

Holt, J. (1983). *How children learn* (Revised ed.). New York: Dell Publishing Company.

Lawson, H. (2016). Categories, boundaries and bridges: The social geography of schooling and the need for new institutional designs. *Education Sciences, 6*(32), 1–14.

Lester, E. (1975). Education by Aborigines for Aborigines. In D. Edgar (Ed.), *Sociology of Australian education: A book of readings.* Sydney: McGraw-Hill.

Mather, A. (2017). *Concordia Community,* Autumn, Issue 64.

Montessori, M. (1912). *The Montessori method.* New York: Frederick Stokes.

Moore, A. (2014a, May 10). Is this the perfect playground, full of junk? *The Guardian.* https://www.theguardian.com/lifeandstyle/2014/may/10/perfect-childrens-playground-the-land-plas-madoc-wales. Accessed 23 July 2017.

Noddings, N. (2005). What does it mean to educate the whole child? *Educational Leadership, 63*(1), 8–13.

Price, K. (2012). *Aboriginal and Torres Strait Islander education: An introduction for the teaching profession.* Cambridge: Cambridge University Press.

SASPA. (2015). *Discussion paper: Educating in the 21st century*. Adelaide: South Australian Secondary Principals' Association.

Steiner, R. (1968). *The roots of education*. London: Rudolf Steiner Press.

UNICEF. (1989). *United Nations convention on the rights of the child*. https://www.unicef.org.au/Upload/UNICEF/Media/Our%20work/childfriendly-crc.pdf. Accessed 30 May 2017.

Wallace, P., & Wallace, N. (1968). *Children of the desert*. Melbourne: Thomas Nelson.

Wright, T. (2017, July 20). Aboriginal archaeological discovery in Kakadu rewrites the history of Australia. *Sydney Morning Herald*.

References

ABC Radio National. (2008, April 28). *Life Matters*. Australian Broadcasting Corporation.

ABC Radio National. (2017a, June 2). *The World Today*. Australian Broadcasting Corporation.

ABC Radio National. (2017b, June 20). *Life Matters*. Australian Broadcasting Corporation.

ABC TV. (2017, June 3). School's out. *Compass*. Australian Broadcasting Corporation.

ABS. (2017). *Australian Bureau of Statistics, Religion in Australia*. www.abs.gov.au. Accessed 17 May 2017.

ACARA. (2017). https://www.acara.edu.au/. Accessed 19 May 2017.

ACSA. (2017). Australian Curriculum Studies Association. *Principles of middle schooling*. http://www.acsa.edu.au/pages/page28.asp. Accessed 27 June 2017.

AITSL. (2017). *Australian Professional Standards for Teachers*. https://www.aitsl.edu.au/australian-professional-standards-for-teachers/standards/list. Accessed 14 June 2017.

Albrecht, N. (2014). Wellness: A conceptual framework for school-based mindfulness programs. *The International Journal of Health, Wellness and Society, 4*(1), 21–36.

Aristotle's Metaphysics. (1998). Translated with an introduction by H. Lawson-Tancred. London: Penguin

© The Author(s) 2018
T. Stehlik, *Educational Philosophy for 21st Century Teachers*,
https://doi.org/10.1007/978-3-319-75969-2

Arnup, J., & Bowles, T. (2016). Should I stay or should I go? Resilience as a protective factor for teachers' intention to leave the teaching profession. *Australian Journal of Education, 60*(3), 229–244.

Aspland, T. (2006). Changing patterns of teacher education in Australia. *Education Research and Perspectives, 33*(2), 140–163.

Atwood, M. (1988). *Cat's eye*. New York: Doubleday.

Baldwin, R. (1989). *You are your child's first teacher*. Berkeley: Celestial Arts.

Baldwin, R. (2016). *The great convergence: Information Technology and the new globalization*. Cambridge, MA: Harvard University Press.

Balogh, S. (2017, February 21). Classroom focus shifts to life skills. *The Australian*.

Balogh, S., & Hutchinson, S. (2017, February 21). Discipline beats dollars in driving academic results. *The Australian*.

Barbour, C., & Barbour, N. (1997). *Families, schools and communities: Building partnerships for educating children*. Upper Saddle River: Prentice-Hall.

Barkham, P. (2014, December 10). Forest schools: Fires, trees and mud pies. *The Guardian*.

Barnes, H. (1991). Learning that grows with the learner: An introduction to Waldorf Education. *Educational Leadership, 49*, 52–54.

Barnes, J. (2016). *Working class boy*. Sydney: Harper Collins.

Bartolomé, L. (2004). Critical pedagogy and teacher education: Radicalizing prospective teachers. *Teacher Education Quarterly, 31*, 97–122.

Bauman, Z. (2012). *Liquid modernity*. Cambridge: Polity Press.

BBC. (2016). What does it mean to be an academy school? http://www.bbc.com/news/education-13274090. Accessed 17 May 2017.

Belliveau, G. (2014). *Stepping into drama: A midsummer night's dream in the elementary classroom*. Vancouver: Pacific Educational Press.

Bennett, R. (2016, September 12). Tiger mums are unhappiest parents. *The Australian*. http://www.theaustralian.com.au/news/world/tiger-mums-are-unhappiest-parents/news-story/b092b9ed68ad1c69b5814ef783cde4ea. Accessed 5 June 2017.

Bennett, G. A., Newman, E., Kay-Lambkin, F., & Hazel, G. (2016). *Start Well: A research project supporting resilience and wellbeing in early career teachers – Summary report*. Newcastle: Hunter Institute of Mental Health.

Bernstein, J. (2017). *Leonard Bernstein: A born teacher*. http://jamiebernstein.net/a_born_teacher.html. Accessed 21 June 2017.

Better Beginnings. (2017). https://www.better-beginnings.com.au/research/research-about-literacy-and-reading. Accessed 26 June 2017.

Biesta, G. (2006). *Beyond learning: Democratic education for a human future.* London: Paradigm Publishers.

Biesta, G. (2012). George Herbert Mead: Formation through communication. In P. Siljander, A. Kivela, & A. Sutinen (Eds.), *Theories of Bildung and growth: Connections and controversies between continental educational thinking and American pragmatism* (pp. 247–260). Rotterdam: Sense Publishers.

Biesta, G., & Tröhler, D. (2008). Introduction: George Herbert Mead and the development of a social conception of education. In G. H. Mead, G. Biesta, & D. Tröhler (Eds.), *The philosophy of education.* London: Paradigm Publishers.

Billett, S., & Ovens, C. (2007). Learning about work, working life and post school options: Guiding students' reflecting on paid part-time work. *Journal of Education and Work, 20*(2), 75–90.

Bills, A., & Howard, N. (2016). What then must we do? Rethinking social inclusion policy for educational attainment in South Australia. *Journal of Educational Enquiry, 15*(1), 25–43.

Birch, E. R., & Miller, P. (2007). The characteristics of 'gap-year' students and their tertiary academic outcomes. *The Economic Record, 83*(262), 329–344.

Blake, W. (1808). *Milton: A poem.*

Bloom, B. S., Engelhart, M. D., Furst, E. J., Hill, W. H., & Krathwohl, D. R. (1956). *Taxonomy of educational objectives: The classification of educational goals.* New York: David McKay Company.

Booth, M. (2014). *The almost nearly perfect people: The truth about the Nordic miracle.* London: Jonathan Cape.

Borgonovi, F., & Pál, J. (2016). *A framework for the analysis of student well-being in the PISA 2015 study: Being 15 in 2015.* OECD working papers no 140. Paris: OECD Publishing.

Bridge21. (2017). http://bridge21.ie/about-us/missionvisionvalues/. Accessed 15 Sept 2017.

Burke, C. (2005). Containing the school child: Architecture and pedagogies. *Paedagogica Historica, International Journal of the History of Education, 41*(4–5), 489–494.

Burrows, L. (2017, May 30). Children benefit from mindful teachers. *The Advertiser.*

Cape Ann Waldorf School. (1999). *Frequently asked questions about Waldorf Education.* http://www.capeannwaldorf.org/caws-faq.html. Accessed 11 June 17.

Childs, G. (1991). *Steiner education in theory and practice.* Edinburgh: Floris Books.

Christodoulou, D. (2014). *Seven myths about education.* Oxfordshire/New York: Routledge.

Chua, A. (2011). *The battle hymn of the tiger mother.* London: Penguin.

Chudacoff, H. (2008). *Children at play: An American history.* New York: New York University Press.

CICA. (2009). Report of the Commission to Inquire into Child Abuse (Ryan Report). http://www.childabusecommission.ie/rpt/pdfs/. Accessed 19 Apr 2017.

Cooper, K., & Stewart, K. (2017). *Does money affect children's outcomes? An update.* London: London School of Economics.

Corderoy, J. (2017). Massive cyber attack creates chaos around the world. http://www.news.com.au/technology/online/hacking/massive-cyber-attack-creates-chaos-around-the-world/news-story/b248da44b753489a3f207dfee2ce78a9. Accessed 2 June 2017.

Cornish, L. (2015, April 7). Are mixed-grade classes any better or worse for learning? *The Conversation.* http://theconversation.com/are-mixed-grade-classes-any-better-or-worse-for-learning-38856. Accessed 15 July 2017.

Creed, B. (2017). *Stray: Human-animal ethics in the anthropocene.* Sydney: Power Publications.

Cremin, C. (2007). Living and really living: The gap year and the commodification of the contingent. *Ephemera, 7*(4), 526–542.

Cygnaeus, U. (1910). *Uno Cygnaeus' writings about the foundation and organisation of the Finnish elementary school.* Helsinki: Kirjayhtymä.

Dahlin, B. (2006). *Education, history and be(com)ing human: Two essays in philosophy and education.* Karlstad: Karlstad University.

Danner, H. (1994). Bildung: A basic term of German education. *Educational Sciences, 9*/1994.

Dawkins, R. (1988). *Higher education: A policy statement.* Canberra: Australian Government.

Demos, J., & Demos, V. (1969). Adolescence in historical perspective. *Journal of Marriage and Family, 31*(4), 632–638.

Dewey, J. (1944). *Democracy and education.* New York: Macmillan.

Dewey, J. (1963). *Experience and education.* New York: Collier Books.

Dinham, S., & Rowe, K. (2008, September 3). *Fantasy, fashion and fact: Middle schools, middle schooling and student achievement.* Paper presented to BERA conference, Edinburgh. http://research.acer.edu.au/cgi/viewcontent.cgi?article=1005&context=tll_misc. Accessed 27 June 2017.

Doll, W. (2008). Complexity and the culture of curriculum. Chapter 13. In M. Mark (Ed.), *Complexity theory and the philosophy of education.* Chichester: Wiley-Blackwell.

Durrell, G. (1962). *My family and other animals*. Victoria: Penguin.

Earp, J. (2017, March 9). A whole school mentoring program. *Teacher Magazine*. https://www.teachermagazine.com.au/article/a-whole-school-mentoring-program. Accessed 18 June 2017.

Easton, F. (1997). Educating the whole child, "Head, heart and hands": Learning from the Waldorf experience. *Theory into Practice, 36*(2), 87–94.

Edwards, R. D. (2006). *Patrick Pearse: The triumph of failure*. Dublin: Irish Academic Press.

Edwards, C., Gandini, L., & Forman, G. (Eds.). (2012). *The hundred languages of children* (3rd ed.). Santa Barbara: Praeger.

European Commission. (1999). http://ec.europa.eu/education/policy/higher-education/bologna-process_en. Accessed 14 June 2017.

Evans, N., Whitehouse, H., & Hickey, R. (2012). Pre-service teachers' conceptions of education for sustainability. *Australian Journal of Teacher Education, 37*(7), 1–13.

Foster, R. F. (1989). *Modern Ireland 1600–1972*. New York: Penguin.

Friere, P. (1996). *Pedagogy of the oppressed*. London: Penguin.

Frohnmayer, J. (2016). *Socrates the rower: How rowing informs philosophy*. Champaign: Common Ground Publishing.

Fuller, B. A. G. (1955). *A history of philosophy* (3rd ed.). New York: Holt, Rinehart and Winston.

Future Learning. (2012). University of Phoenix. https://www.youtube.com/watch?v=qC_T9ePzANg&sns=em. Accessed 26 July 2017.

FYA. (2015). *The new work order*. Melbourne: Foundation for Youth Australia.

Gardner, H. (1983). *Frames of mind*. New York: Basic Books.

George Washington University Milken Institute School of Public Health. (2015, December 8). New report finds 43 percent increase in ADHD diagnosis for US schoolchildren: Girls showed a sharp rise in ADHD diagnosis during eight-year study period. *ScienceDaily*. www.sciencedaily.com/releases/2015/12/151208150630.htm. Accessed 3 June 2017.

Gibran, K. (1923). *The Prophet*. New York: Alfred A Knopf.

Gibson, J. (1917). *Locke's theory of knowledge and its historical relations*. London: Cambridge University Press.

Gidley, J. (2016). *Postformal education: A philosophy for complex futures*. Basel: Springer.

Gleick, J. (1987). *Chaos: Making a new science*. New York: Viking Books.

Goleman, D. (1995). *Emotional intelligence*. New York: Bantam Books.

Green, E. (2015). *Building a better teacher: How teaching works (and how to teach it to everyone)*. New York: W. W. Norton & Company, Inc.

Green School. (2015). *Curriculum overview, Middle School, 2015–2016 academic year*. http://www.greenschool.org/wp-content/uploads/2015/08/Middle-School-Curriculum-Overview_Photo.pdf. Accessed 8 Nov 2015.

Gross, R. (1963). *The teacher and the taught*. New York: Dell Publishing Co.

Hall, B. (2012). Postgraduate numbers double in ten years. *Sydney Morning Herald*. http://www.smh.com.au/national/tertiary-education/postgraduate-numbers-double-in-10-years-20121030-28gz3.html. Accessed 29 Mar 2017.

Hardy, J. (2010). *My green school dream*. https://www.ted.com/talks/john_hardy_my_green_school_dream. Accessed 14 June 2017.

Harford, T. (2014, March 28). Big data: Are we making a big mistake? *Financial Times*. https://www.ft.com/content/21a6e7d8-b479-11e3-a09a-00144feabdc0. Accessed 21 July 2017.

Harford, T. (2017, March 28). Big data: Are we making a mistake? *Financial Times*.

Hargreaves, J., Stanwick, J., & Peta, S. (2017). *The changing nature of apprenticeships: 1996–2016*. Adelaide: NCVER.

Hatt, B. (2005). Pedagogical love in the transactional curriculum. *Journal of Curriculum Studies, 37*(6), 671–688.

Hayes, D., & Wynyard, R. (2002). *The McDonaldization of higher education*. London: Sage.

Heath, S. (2007). Widening the gap: Pre-university gap years and the economy of experience'. *British Journal of Sociology of Education, 28*(1), 89–103.

Hicks, M. (2013, August). Why the increase in ADHD? New research reveals causes for ADHD type behaviors. *Psychology today*. https://www.psychology-today.com/blog/digital-pandemic/201308/why-the-increase-in-adhd. Accessed 3 June 2017.

Hirsch, E. D. (2009). *The 21st century skills movement*. http://greatminds.net/maps/documents/reports/hirsch.pdf. Accessed 15 July 2017.

Hoffmann, H. (1845). *Lustige Geschichten und drollige Bilder mit 15 schön kolorirten Tafeln für Kinder von 3–6 Jahren*. Frankfurt am Main: Literarische Anstalt.

Holt, J. (1980). *The natural child project*. https://web.archive.org/web/20110923153702/http://www.naturalchild.org:80/guest/marlene_bumgarner.html. Accessed 7 July 2017.

Holt, J. (1983). *How children learn* (Revised ed.). New York: Dell Publishing Company.

Holt, J. (2004). *Instead of education: Ways to help people do things better*. Boulder: Sentient Publications.

Homer. (2003). *The Odyssey*. London: Penguin.

Hoover, E. (2001). More students decide that college can wait. *Chronicle of Higher Education, 48*(2), A51–A52.

Hopkins, N. (2017a). Social giant faced with difficult balancing act. *The Guardian Weekly, 26*(05), 17.

Hopkins, N. (2017b). Revealed: Facebook's rules on sex, racism and violence. *The Guardian Weekly, 26*(05), 17.

Hurst, A. (2014). *The purpose economy: How your desire for impact, personal growth and community is changing the world.* Boise: Elevate.

Hurt, J. (2008, June 21). Backpackers off to save the world. *The Advertiser,* p. 19.

Illich, I. (1971). *Deschooling society.* New York: Marion Boyars.

Inskeep, S. (2010). Former 'No Child Left Behind' advocate turns critic. http://www.npr.org/templates/story/story.php?storyId=124209100. Accessed 20 May 2017.

Irish Times. (2017, March 30). Tablets help school cure problem of rote learning. *The Irish Times, Business Technology and Innovation.*

Itard, J. (1802). *An historical account of the discovery and education of a savage man, or of the first developments, physical and moral, of the young savage caught in the woods near Aveyron, in the year 1798.* London: British Museum.

Kangan Institute. (2017). Signs you were born to be a teacher. https://www.kangan.edu.au/students/blog/be-a-teacher. Accessed 21 June 2017.

Kearney, V. (2014). Bush kindy as a childcare centre. Chapter 3, In T. Stehlik & L. Burrows (Eds.), *Teaching with spirit: New perspectives on Steiner Education in Australia.* Murwillumbah: Immortal Books.

Kelly, W., & Tallon, A. (1967). *Readings in the philosophy of man.* New York: McGraw-Hill.

Keyte, J. (2010). Metamorphosis in building design. In F. Hickman, M. Huxholl, & K. Kytka (Eds.), *Weaving threads of community: A patchwork history of Willunga Waldorf School.* Adelaide: Willunga Waldorf School.

Khoshkhesal, V. (1995). Grace before meals. *Education Australia, 32*, 13–15.

Klinkmann, S.-E. (2010). Swedish rock in Finland: "The sound which is not?". Chapter 5, In B. Horgby & F. Nilsson (Eds.), *Rockin' the borders: Rock music and social, cultural and political change.* Newcastle upon Tyne: Cambridge Scholars Publishing.

Knight, S. (2017). *Forest schools in practice.* London: Sage.

Koetzsch, R. (1997). *The parent's guide to alternatives in education.* Boston: Shambhala.

Konrad, F.-M. (2012). Wilhelm von Humboldt's contribution to a theory of Bildung. In P. Siljander, A. Kivela, & A. Sutinen (Eds.), *Theories of Bildung and growth: Connections and controversies between continental educational thinking and American pragmatism* (pp. 107–124). Rotterdam: Sense Publishers.

Kramer, R. (1976). *Maria Montessori: A biography*. Oxford: Basil Blackwell.

Kuhn, T. (1962). *The structure of scientific revolutions*. Chicago: University of Chicago Press.

Lane, H. (1976). *The wild boy of Aveyron*. Cambridge, MA: Harvard university Press.

Lane, B. (2008, May 7). Gaps show failings of youth allowance. *The Australian*, p. 23.

Lawson, H. (2016). Categories, boundaries and bridges: The social geography of schooling and the need for new institutional designs. *Education Sciences, 6*(32), 1–14.

Leah, D. (1997). The dawning of conscience: Moral education and the Waldorf curriculum in Class Four. *Steiner Education, 31*(2), 20–25.

Lester, E. (1975). Education by Aborigines for Aborigines. In D. Edgar (Ed.), *Sociology of Australian education: A book of readings*. Sydney: McGraw-Hill.

Lewis, T. (2014). *Twins separated at birth reveal staggering influence of genetics*. http://www.livescience.com/47288-twin-study-importance-of-genetics.html. Accessed 24 May 2017.

Lievegoed, B. (1991). *Developing communities*. Stroud: Hawthorn Press.

Lievegoed, B. (1993). *Phases: The spiritual rhythms of adult life*. Bristol: Rudolf Steiner Press.

Livingstone, R. (1959). *The rainbow bridge and other essays on education*. London: Pall Mall Press.

Lönnrot, E. (1835). *Kalevala*. J. C. Frenckellin ja Poika.

Lopez, S., & Lewis, M. (2009). The principles of strengths-based education. *Journal of College and Character, X*(4), 1–8.

Lo Shan, Z. (2000). 'Plato's counsel on education', chapter 3. In A. Oksenberg Rorty (Ed.), *Philosophers on education, historical perspectives*. London/New York: Routledge.

Louv, R. (2005). *Last child in the woods: Saving our children from nature-deficit disorder*. New York: Algonquin Books.

Lovelock, J. (1989). *The ages of Gaia*. Oxford: Oxford University Press.

Loyd, S. (1914). *Cyclopedia of puzzles*. New York: The Lamb publishing Company.

Määttä, K., & Uusiautti, S. (2011). Pedagogical love and good teacherhood. *In Education, 17*(2), 29–41.

Macdonald, J. (1981). Theory, practice and the hermeneutic circle. *Journal of Curriculum Theorizing, 3*(2), 130–138.

Maier, M. (1994). The child is the father to the man. In N. Gobel (Ed.), *Waldorf Education: Exhibition catalogue on occasion of the 44th session of the international conference on education of UNESCO in Geneva.* Geneva: Fruende der Erzeihungskunst Rudolf Steiners.

Malson, L. (1972). *Wolf children.* London: NLB.

Maslen, G. (2013, November 11). Students find clarity in gap years. *Sydney Morning Herald.* http://www.smh.com.au/national/education/students-find-clarity-in-gap-years-20131110-2x9p3.html. Accessed 9 July 2017.

Mason, M. (2008). What is complexity theory and what are its implications for educational change? Chapter 13, In M. Mason (Ed.), *Complexity theory and the philosophy of education.* West Sussex: Wiley-Blackwell.

Mather, A. (2017). *Concordia Community*, Autumn, Issue 64.

McCarthy, P. (1988). *McCarthy's bar: A journey of discovery in Ireland.* London: Hodder & Stoughton.

McDonagh, D. (2017, April 16). My PhD is fake. *The Irish Mail on Sunday*, p. 1.

McKinnon, M. (2016, January 11). Teachers are leaving the profession – Here's how to make them stay. *The Conversation.* http://theconversation.com/teachers-are-leaving-the-profession-heres-how-to-make-them-stay-52697. Accessed 23 June 2017.

McMillan, M. (1919). *The nursery school.* London: Dent and Sons.

Mead, G. H. (2008). In G. Biesta & D. Tröhler (Eds.), *The philosophy of education.* London: Paradigm Publishers.

Menter, I. (2016). *What is a teacher in the 21st century and what does a 21st century teacher need to know?* www.aare.edu.au/blog/?p=1516. Accessed 16 May 2016.

Merga, M. K., & Roni, S. M. (2017, March 10). Children prefer to read books on paper rather than screens. *The Conversation.* http://theconversation.com/children-prefer-to-read-books-on-paper-rather-than-screens-74171. Accessed 3 June 2017.

Merriam, S. (2001). Andragogy and self-directed learning: Pillars of adult learning theory. *New Directions for Adult and Continuing Education, 2001*(89), 3–13.

Merz, C., & Furman, G. (1997). *Community and schools: Promise and paradox.* New York: Teachers College Press.

Metcalfe, J. (2017). *The story of Green School Bali: An integral narrative of sustainable education.* Unpublished PhD thesis, University of South Australia.

Miller, A. (1980). *For your own good: Hidden cruelty in child-rearing and the roots of violence.* New York: Farrar, Straus, Giroux.

Miller, R. (1997). *"Partial vision" in alternative education.* http://www.dandu-gan.com/waldorf/articles/partial_vision_in_altern.htm. Accessed 22 June 1999.

Mollison, B. (1988). *Permaculture: A designer's manual.* Tyalgum: Tagari Publications.

Montessori, M. (1912). *The Montessori method.* New York: Frederick Stokes.

Moore, A. (2014a, May 10). Is this the perfect playground, full of junk? *The Guardian.* https://www.theguardian.com/lifeandstyle/2014/may/10/perfect-childrens-playground-the-land-plas-madoc-wales. Accessed 23 July 2017.

Moore, R. (2014b). *Nature play and learning places: Creating and imagining places where children engage with nature.* Raleigh: Natural Learning Initiative and Reston/National Wildlife Federation.

Moore, M. (2015). *Where to invade next.* IMG Films.

Moore, S. (2017, April 13). Shop till you drop belongs to a long-gone decade of boom. *The Guardian*, p. 5.

Morita, E., Fukuda, S., Nagano, J., Hamajima, N., Yamamoto, H., Iwae, Y., Nakashima, T., Ohira, H., & Shirakawa, T. (2007). Psychological effects of forest environments on healthy adults: Shinrin-yoku (forest-air bathing, walking) as a possible method of stress reduction. *Public Health, 121*(1), 54–63.

Mt. Barker Waldorf School Parent Association. (2001). *Parent handbook.* Mount Barker: Mount Barker Waldorf School.

Murphy, C. (1991). *Emil Molt and the beginnings of the Waldorf School.* Edinburgh: Floris Books.

MySchool. http://www.myschool.edu.au/

Neill, A. S. (1960). *Summerhill: A radical approach to childrearing.* Middlesex: Penguin Books.

New World Encyclopedia. *Nikolaj Frederik Severin Grundtvig.* http://www.new-worldencyclopedia.org/entry/Nikolaj_Frederik_Severin_Grundtvig. Accessed 4 July 2017.

Newton, M. (2002). *Savage boys and wild girls: A history of feral children.* New York: Picador.

Noddings, N. (2005). What does it mean to educate the whole child? *Educational Leadership, 63*(1), 8–13.

OECD. http://www.oecd.org/pisa/aboutpisa/. Accessed 17 May 2017.

OECD. http://www.oecd.org/newsroom/most-teenagers-happy-with-their-lives-but-schoolwork-anxiety-and-bullying-an-issue.htm. Accessed 22 July 2017.

Oltermann, P. (2016, July 1). No grades, no timetable: Berlin school turns teaching upside down. *The Guardian*, www.theguardian.com/world/2016/jul/01/no-grades-no-timetable-berlin-school. Accessed 22 Aug 2016.

Oxford Dictionaries. https://en.oxforddictionaries.com/word-of-the-year

Patterson, S. (1971). *Rousseau's Emile and early children's literature*. Metuchen: The Scarecrow Press.

Payton, A. (2017). *Skilling for tomorrow*. Adelaide: NCVER.

Peters, M. (2017). Education in a post-truth world. *Educational Philosophy and Theory, 49*(6), 563–566. Special Section: History Education.

Pidd, H. (2017, March 30). Schoolchildren in northern England falling behind south. *The Guardian*.

Pietzner, C. (1992). Community relations and outreach. In D. Mitchell (Ed.), *The art of administration: Viewpoints on professional management in Waldorf Schools* (pp. 83–97). Boulder: A.W.S.N.A.

Pikkarainen, E. (2012). Signs of reality: The idea of General Bildung by JA Comenius. In P. Siljander, A. Kivela, & A. Sutinen (Eds.), *Theories of Bildung and growth: Connections and controversies between continental educational thinking and American pragmatism* (pp. 19–29). Rotterdam: Sense Publishers.

Plato. (1936). *The Symposium, The Works of Plato* (trans: Jowett, B.). New York: The Dial Press.

Plato. (1955). *Republic* (trans: Lee, H. D. P.). London: Penguin.

Plato. (1961). *Laws* (trans: Taylor, A. E.). New York: Dutton.

Polesel, J., Dulfer, N., & Turnbull, M. (2012). *The experience of education: The impacts of high stakes testing on school students on their families: Literature review*. Sydney: University of Sydney Whitlam Institute.

Postman, N. (1994). *The disappearance of childhood*. New York: Vintage.

Prensky, M. (2001). Digital natives, digital immigrants. *On the Horizon, 9*(5), 1–6.

Price, K. (2012). *Aboriginal and Torres Strait Islander education: An introduction for the teaching profession*. Cambridge: Cambridge University Press.

Price, H. (2016). *How can we help students thrive?* https://www.aspeninstitute.org/blog-posts/can-help-students-thrive/. Accessed 16 July 2017.

Pridham, B. (2014). Bush kindy. Chapter 2, In T. Stehlik & L. Burrows (Eds.), *Teaching with spirit: New perspectives on Steiner education in Australia*. Murwillumbah: Immortal Books.

Pryor, W. (2014). The power of play. Chapter 4, In T. Stehlik & L. Burrows (Eds.), *Teaching with spirit: New perspectives on Steiner education in Australia*. Murwillumbah: Immortal Books.

Pyne, C. (2014, April 17). Australians to have their say on teacher education. *Media Release*, Thursday. https://ministers.education.gov.au/pyne/australians-have-their-say-teacher-education. Accessed 23 Mar 2018.

Ravitch, D. (2009). What about 21st century skills? *Bridging Differences*. http://blogs.edweek.org/edweek/Bridging-Differences/2009/03/what_about_21st_century_skills.html. Accessed 15 July 2017.

Ravitch, D. (2010). *The death and life of the Great American School System: How testing and choice are undermining education*. New York: Basic Books.

Read, H. (1948). *Education through art*. London: Faber and Faber.

Rebanks, J. (2016). *The shepherd's life: A tale of the Lake District*. London: Penguin.

Reed, C. (2017, February). What makes 'Y' tick. *Brand Strategy*.

Reeson, A., Mason, C., Sanderson, T., Bratanova, A., & Hajkowicz, S. (2016). *The VET era: Equipping Australia's workforce for the future digital economy*. Canberra: CSIRO.

Reid, A. (2017). *Public education in South Australia*. Adelaide: SA Department of Education and Child Development.

Reingold, J. (2015). *Everybody hates Pearson*. Fortune. http://fortune.com/2015/01/21/everybody-hates-pearson/. Accessed 16 May 2017.

Ricci, C. (2015, May 18). Evolution or revolution needed to oust creationism? Creationism may be gone from the curriculum but it still finds its way into some schools. *Sydney Morning Herald*. http://www.smh.com.au/national/education/evolution-or-revolution-needed-to-oust-creationism-20150514-gh1bf3.html. Accessed 27 June 2017.

Rittel, H., & Webber, M. (1973). Dilemmas in a general theory of planning. *Policy Sciences, 4*, 155–169.

Ritzer, G. (1998). *The McDonaldization thesis*. London: Sage.

Rizvi, F., & Lingard, B. (2010). *Globalising education policy*. Oxon: Routledge.

Robinson, K. (2006). www.ted.com/talks/ken_robinson_says_schools_kill_Creativity.html. Accessed 14 Apr 2017.

Rosenthal, R., & Jacobsen, L. (1968, September). Pygmalion in the classroom. *The Urban Review*.

Rothman, J. (2017, May 1). The seeker. *The New York Times*, pp. 46–55.

Rousseau, J. J. (1921). *Emile, or on education* (trans: Foxley, B.). London: Dent.

Ruenzel, D. (1995). The Waldorf way. *Teacher Magazine, 7*(2), 22–27.

Ryan, S. M. J. (2009). *Report of the Commission to inquire into child abuse* (Vol. 1). Dublin: CICA.

Sahlberg, P. (2012). https://pasisahlberg.com/. Accessed 17 May 2017.

Salinger, J. D. (1951). *Catcher in the rye*. Boston: Little, Brown and Company.

SASPA. (2015). *Discussion paper: Educating in the 21st century*. Adelaide: South Australian Secondary Principals' Association.

Schratzenstaller, A. (2010). The classroom of the past. Chapter 2, In K. Mäkitalo-Siegl, J. Zottman, F. Kaplan, & F. Fischer (Eds.), *Classroom of the future: Orchestrating collaborative spaces*. Rotterdam: Sense Publishers.

Schwartz, E. (1999). *Millennial child*. Great Barrington: Anthroposophic Press.

Sefton-Green, J. (2013). *Learning at not-school: A review of study, theory and advocacy for education in non-formal settings*. Cambridge, MA: MIT Press.

Seligman, M. (1995). *The optimistic child: A revolutionary approach to raising resilient children*. Sydney: Random House.

Seligman, M., & Csikszentmihalyi, M. (2000). Positive psychology. *American Psychologist, 55*(1), 5–14.

Shepherd, A. P. (1983). *A scientist of the invisible*. Edinburgh: Floris Books.

Sherriff, L. (2015). Ernst & Young removes degree classification from entry criteria as there's 'no evidence' university equals success. http://www.huffingtonpost.co.uk/2016/01/07/ernst-and-young-removes-degree-classification-entry-criteria_n_7932590.html. Accessed 28 Mar 2017.

Siljander, P., Kivelä, A., & Sutinen, A. (2012). *Theories of Bildung and growth: Connections and controversies between continental educational thinking and American pragmatism*. Rotterdam: Sense Publishers.

Simpson, K. (2004). 'Doing development: The gap year, volunteer-tourists and a popular practice of development. *Journal of International Development, 16*, 681–692.

Skewes, D. (1996). Beyond curriculum. *Musagetes: Education journal for the community of Steiner Schools, 2*(2), 7–11.

Skewes, D. (2002). *Practicum report. Willunga Waldorf School,* School of Education, University of South Australia.

Smith, A. (2016, February 7). Home-schooled kids perform better in NAPLAN: Report. *Sydney Morning Herald.* http://www.smh.com.au/nsw/home-schooled-kids-perform-better-in-naplan-report-20160204-gmlgu9.html. Accessed 8 July 2017.

Solasaari, U. (2003). Love and values rear a personality – Max Scheler's philosophy of education. In *Studies of the Department of Education in the University of Helsinki 187*. Helsinki: University of Helsinki.

South Australian Certificate in Education SACE. www.sace.sa.edu.au/. Accessed 13 June 2017.

Sparrow, J. (2017, January 11). Can democracy survive the fourth industrial revolution: Should it? *The Guardian.* https://www.theguardian.com/sustainable-business/2017/jan/11/can-democracy-survive-the-fourth-industrial-revolution-should-it. Accessed 15 July 2017.

Speigel, A. (2008). Old-fashioned play builds serious skills. https://www.npr.org/templates/story/story.php? storyId=19212514. Accessed 23 Mar 2018.

Spooner, R. (2017, May 24). Poor children face higher risk of early puberty, Murdoch Children's Research Institute says. *Sydney Morning Herald*. http://www.smh.com.au/national/health/poor-children-face-higher-risk-of-early-puberty-murdoch-childrens-research-institute-says-20170523-gwb90u. Accessed 25 May 2017.

Stanford Encyclopedia of Philosophy. (2014). *Petrus Ramus.* https://plato.stanford.edu/archives/spr2014/entries/ramus/#Met. Accessed 27 June 2017.

Stehlik, T. (2002). *Each parent carries the flame: Waldorf Schools as sites for promoting lifelong learning, creating community and educating for social renewal.* Flaxton: Post Pressed.

Stehlik, T. (2006). *Levels of engagement: Report of findings prepared for the social inclusion unit on the action research project across school retention initiatives.* Adelaide: UniSA/South Australian Government.

Stehlik, T. (2010). Mind the gap: School leaver aspirations and delayed pathways to further and higher education. *Journal of Education and Work, 23*(4), 363–376.

Stehlik, T. (2011). Relationships, participation and support: Necessary components for inclusive learning environments and (re)engaging learners. Chapter 7, In T. Stehlik & J. Patterson (Eds.), *Changing the paradigm: Education as the key to a socially inclusive future.* Brisbane: Post Pressed.

Stehlik, T. (2015). *Each parent carries the flame: Waldorf Schools as sites for promoting lifelong learning, creating community and educating for social renewal* (2nd ed.). Adelaide: Mylor Press.

Steiner, R. (1927). Reordering of society: The fundamental social law. http://wn.rsarchive.org/Articles/FuSoLa_index.html. Accessed 23 Mar 2018.

Steiner, R. (1968). *The roots of education.* London: Rudolf Steiner Press.

Steiner, R. (1981). *'Greek education and the middle ages', a modern art of education.* London: Rudolf Steiner Press.

Steiner, R. (1982). *The kingdom of childhood.* London: Rudolf Steiner Press.

Steiner Waldorf Schools Fellowship. (2017). http://www.steinerwaldorf.org/. Accessed 13 June 2017.

Strayer, J. (1955). *Western Europe in the Middle Ages: A short history.* New York: Appleton-Century-Crofts Inc.

Sulzer, J. (1748). *Versuch von der Erziehung und Unterweisung der Kinder.*

Sun, Y., Mensah, F., Azzopardi, P., Patton, G., & Wake, M. (2017, May). Childhood social disadvantage and pubertal timing: A national birth cohort from Australia. *Pediatrics*. http://pediatrics.aappublications.org/content/early/2017/05/19/peds.2016-4099. Accessed 25 May 2017.

Synge, U. (1977). *Kalevala: Heroic tales from Finland*. London: The Bodley Head.

Tamkin, E. (2014). *Will everyone shut up already about how the Nordic countries top every global ranking?* http://www.slate.com/blogs/the_world_/2014/08/29/will_everyone_shut_up_already_about_how_the_nordic_countries_top_every_global.html. Accessed 6 June 2017.

Tennant, M. (1997). *Psychology and adult learning*. London: Routledge.

Tennant, M., & Pogson, P. (1995). *Learning and change in the adult years: A developmental perspective*. San Francisco: Jossey Bass.

The Aspen Institute. (2017). https://www.aspeninstitute.org/programs/national-commission-on-socialemotional-and-academic-development/. Accessed 26 Mar 2018.

The Leap. https://theleap.co.uk/. Accessed 9 July 2017.

TTF. (2017). *Teaching teachers for the future*. http://www.ttf.edu.au/what-is-tpack/what-is-tpack.html. Accessed 13 June 2017.

Turnbull, C. (2017, April 17). Every student should consider doing transition year. *Western People*.

UNESCO. (2015). *Education for all 2000–2015: Achievements and challenges*. Paris: UNESCO.

UNICEF. (1989). *United Nations convention on the rights of the child*. https://www.unicef.org.au/Upload/UNICEF/Media/Our%20work/childfriendly-crc.pdf. Accessed 30 May 2017.

University of Chicago Lab Schools. https://www.ucls.uchicago.edu/. Accessed 19 Apr 2017.

US Census Bureau. (2017). *The Changing Economics and Demographics of Young Adulthood: 1975–2016*. https://www.census.gov/library/publications/2017/demo/p20-579.html. Accessed 22 March 2018.

Van Hoorn, J., Scales, B., Nourot, P., & Alward, K. (Eds.). (2011). *Play at the centre of the curriculum*. Upper Saddle River, New Jersey: Prentice-Hall.

van Kerkhoven, G. (1996). Aspects of Waldorf Education in Australia. *Musagetes: Education Journal for the Community of Steiner Schools, 2*(2), 1–5.

Veen, W. (2006). *Homo Zappiens and the need for new education systems*. https://www.oecd.org/edu/ceri/38360892.pdf. Accessed 30 May 2017.

Von Eschenbach, W. (1980). *Parzival*. London: Penguin.

Walker, S., & Danby, S. (2017). Electronic games: How much is too much for kids? *The Conversation*. https://theconversation.com/electronic-games-how-much-is-too-much-for-kids-80396. Accessed 15 July 2017.

Wallace, P., & Wallace, N. (1968). *Children of the desert*. Melbourne: Thomas Nelson.

Warnock, M. (1996). *Women philosophers*. London: Everyman.

Weber, M. (1905). *The protestant ethic and the spirit of capitalism* (trans: Parsons, T. in 1930). London: Allen and Unwin.

WEF. (2016). *The future of jobs: Employment, skills and workforce strategy for the fourth industrial revolution*. Geneva: The World Economic Forum.

Whitbourne, S. K. (2013, June 2). The joys of generativity in midlife. *The Huffington Post*. http://www.huffingtonpost.com/susan-krauss-whitbourne/generativity_b_2575916.html. Accessed 16 Sept 2017.

Whitehead, A. (1922). *The aims of education*. New York: Free Press.

Wilber, K. (2000). *Integral spirituality: A startling new role for religion in the modern and postmodern world*. Boston: Shambhala.

Wiliam, D. (2006). *Assessment for learning: Why, what and how?* Paper presented to the Cambridge Assessment Network Conference, 15 September 2006, University of Cambridge.

Wlodkowski, R. (1999). *Enhancing adult motivation to learn*. San Francisco: Jossey Bass.

Wollstonecraft, M. (1792). *Vindication of the rights of woman*. London: J. Johnson.

Wright, T. (2017, July 20). Aboriginal archaeological discovery in Kakadu rewrites the history of Australia. *Sydney Morning Herald*.

Wullschlager, J. (1995). *Inventing wonderland: The lives and fantasies of Lewis Carroll, Edward Lear, J. M. Barrie, Kenneth Grahame and A. A. Milne*. London: Free Press.

Young, J. (2017, January 25). The effects of "helicopter parenting". *Psychology Today*. https://www.psychologytoday.com/blog/when-your-adult-child-breaks-your-heart/201701/the-effects-helicopter-parenting. Accessed 5 June 2017.

Youthworx Media. http://youthworxmedia.org.au/index.html. Accessed 6 July 2017.

Zajonc, A. (2016). Contemplation in education. In K. A. Schonert-Reichl & R. W. Roeser (Eds.), *The handbook of mindfulness in education*. New York: Springer.

Zeichner, K. M. (1993). Action research: Personal renewal and social construction. *Eduational Action Research, 1*, 199–219.

Index

A

Academy, 1, 3, 20–22, 28, 40, 42,
      43, 45, 46, 54, 76–78, 90, 95,
      97, 99, 135, 140, 142, 153,
      154, 167, 204, 210, 212, 216,
      221, 227, 246, 263, 267, 271,
      272, 281
Action research, 22, 34, 174
Adolescents, 6, 13, 62, 80, 110, 114,
      115, 121, 130–133, 140, 163,
      185, 194, 209, 217, 218, 237,
      239, 253
Adventure playground, 124, 146,
      276, 278
Aesthetics, 21, 23, 24, 28, 32, 34,
      101, 191, 220–223, 274, 280
Affective, 41, 115, 169, 198
Alternative, 4, 8, 11, 69, 73, 74, 78,
      83, 91, 93, 187, 203, 229,
      233, 238–242, 275

Anthroposophy, 215
Aquinas, Thomas, 23, 24
Aristotle, 7, 17, 19, 21, 22, 33, 101,
      266, 274
Assessment, 1–3, 49–51, 92, 93,
      143, 168, 189, 193, 196, 207,
      252, 253, 259, 272
Attention deficit hyperactivity
      disorder (ADHD), 9, 139, 147
Attitude, 18, 40, 41, 47, 140, 151,
      154, 163, 165, 168, 175, 189,
      211, 238, 247, 273
Augustine, 23–24
Australian Institute for Teaching and
      School Leadership (AITSL),
      96, 97, 165, 171, 172
Australian Qualifications Framework
      (AQF), 50
Autism, 9, 139, 145
Auto-didact, 52

© The Author(s) 2018
T. Stehlik, *Educational Philosophy for 21st Century Teachers*,
https://doi.org/10.1007/978-3-319-75969-2

B

Baby boomer, 133, 134, 140
Bamboo, 224, 225
Behaviour management, 2, 6, 74, 173, 209
Big data, 142–144, 261
Bildung, 61, 76, 77
Bloom, Benjamin, 41
Bloom's taxonomy, 41, 172
Body, soul and spirit, 108, 112, 113, 217
Bush kindy, 146–147, 151, 235

C

Calvin, John, 192
Catholic, 3, 67, 68, 71, 84, 235
Charlemagne, 24
Child development, 9, 27, 31, 68, 86, 107, 109, 114, 173, 216–218, 263, 276
Classroom, 3, 5, 6, 11, 12, 32, 34, 47, 73, 74, 93, 94, 139, 140, 150, 161, 162, 168, 173, 181, 184, 185, 189, 197, 198, 214, 220, 221, 225, 227–229, 233–253, 263, 266–268, 271, 274, 280
Classroom of the future, 259, 265–268, 279
Cognitive, 40, 114–116, 135, 146–148, 169, 170, 215, 220, 272
Comenius, 26, 54, 61, 76, 183, 193
Communication, 12, 33, 87, 122, 134, 136, 137, 141, 164, 204, 226, 228, 249, 259–263
Community, 10–12, 22, 32, 46–49, 51, 53, 62, 66, 67, 79, 80, 87, 95–101, 113, 141, 148, 150, 154, 162, 168, 181, 186–189, 191, 194, 195, 212, 216, 222–223, 225–230, 233, 239, 240, 242, 243, 249, 250, 252, 253, 263, 266, 272, 275–277, 280
Comprehensive school, 206, 209
Contemplative activity, 42–44, 167
Content, 2, 3, 11–13, 21, 50, 53, 90, 96, 116, 133, 141, 143, 163, 164, 167–175, 181–184, 189, 190, 195–198, 206, 210, 211, 218, 219, 222, 259, 263, 266, 268, 272, 280, 281
Credential creep, 45, 168
Critical pedagogy, 176, 192
Critical thinking, 24, 32, 43, 132, 187, 193, 197, 227, 261, 262, 268, 280
Curriculum, 1–4, 6, 8, 11–13, 32, 34, 40, 47, 53, 60, 63, 68–70, 72, 83, 92, 93, 95, 122, 144, 150, 152, 167, 170, 171, 173, 174, 176, 181, 182, 185, 189–198, 206, 212, 213, 215, 216, 218–223, 226–228, 233, 236, 241, 246, 252, 253, 259, 263, 264, 266, 267, 271, 281
Cygnaeus, Uno, 205, 211

D

Demonstration schools, 74, 75, 208
Descartes, Rene, 26, 193
Deschooling, 235–237
Dewey, John, 27, 31, 32, 70, 116, 123, 211
Dickens, Charles, 62, 123

Didactic, 27, 52, 118
Digital native, 9, 129, 136, 138
Discipline, 2, 4, 18, 26, 33, 34, 54, 55, 74, 114, 135, 167, 169–171, 187, 192, 193, 262, 267
Dual system, 75–81

E

Education
  compulsory, 79, 260
  continuing, 50, 52, 171
  liberal, 34, 41, 42, 51, 63, 76, 77
  post-compulsory, 80, 81
  public, 27, 45, 61–63, 79, 108, 118
  self, 51, 52, 179, 190, 217, 236
  vocational, 41, 63, 167, 206
Education outside the classroom, 145, 253
Emergence, 24, 33, 126, 132, 279, 280
Emotional quotient (EQ), 40
Empiricism, 22
Enlightenment, 8, 25, 69, 76, 116, 148, 182, 280
Episteme, 29–31, 172, 268
Erziehung, 61, 77
Eudaimonia, 100, 101, 272–274
Experiential frame, 227
Experimental schools, 8, 59, 69, 71, 72, 227

F

Facebook, 87, 130, 141, 236
Facilitator, 265, 280
Feeling, 6, 21, 47, 74, 98, 110, 124, 144–146, 151, 185, 189, 216, 217, 223, 240, 245, 253, 272

Finland, 3, 11, 68, 71, 72, 92, 97, 147, 166, 186, 203–214, 229, 272–274
Forest bathing, 147
Forest school, 145, 146, 235, 278
Freire, Paulo, 27, 32, 45, 176
Froebel, Friedrich, 9, 21, 27, 29, 107, 122, 123, 125, 145, 211, 212

G

Gap year, 12, 233, 247–253, 265
Generation X, 134
Generation Y, 134
Generation Z, 135–137
Gig economy, 134, 251, 261
Global Education Reform Movement (GERM), 8, 83, 90–97, 100, 145, 172, 190, 193, 222
Globalisation, 83, 86, 89, 90, 169, 172
Goethe, J. W., 28, 61, 75, 132, 219
Goodness, 19, 46, 69
Graduate, 2, 45, 63, 88, 140, 168, 171–174, 191, 195, 198, 249
Greece, 7, 17–19, 34, 50, 219
Green School, 11, 146, 194, 203, 224–229
Grundtvig, N. F. S., 51
Gymnasium, 76, 77

H

Happiness, 13, 153, 271, 272
Hellenic culture, 18
Hidden curriculum, 12, 47, 63, 176, 190, 198, 236, 267
Holistic education, 11, 13, 40, 42, 263, 271–282
Holt, John, 244, 245, 274, 275

Homeschooling, 12, 52, 153, 233, 244–247
Homo Zappiens, 136–138
Humanism, 24
Humboldt, Wilhelm, 61, 76, 193

I

Illich, Ivan, 153, 235–237, 244, 275
Incarnation, 108, 109, 112, 149
Individual, 7, 19, 20, 24, 25, 30, 33, 34, 39–42, 45–48, 52, 60, 61, 69, 72, 75, 97, 98, 108, 110–113, 115, 117, 121, 123, 130, 135, 140, 149, 152, 155, 174, 175, 177, 182, 184, 185, 195, 196, 212, 215, 217, 219, 223, 227, 228, 238, 247, 253, 265, 282
Individualism, 98
Industrial revolution, 8, 12, 33, 59, 62, 77, 78, 252, 259, 260, 271
Infancy, 114, 130–133
Information, 9, 12, 25, 27, 29, 30, 33–36, 49, 51, 87, 95, 129, 133, 134, 136–138, 142–144, 177, 195, 204, 208, 246, 259, 260, 265, 266, 280, 281
Instructional frame, 226, 227
Integral frame, 226
Intelligence quotient (IQ), 40
Itard, Jean, 116, 117

J

Joined-up approach, 11, 181, 185, 187, 188, 243, 276

K

Kalevala, 72, 212
Kid, 4, 5, 74, 79, 89, 130, 146, 162, 163, 238, 239, 252
Kindergarten, 9, 21, 26, 27, 118, 122–125, 129, 145, 146, 149–151, 194, 206, 208, 209, 212, 221
Kingdom of childhood, 5, 9–10, 27, 107–116, 126, 133, 142, 154, 217, 221, 224
Knowledge, 3, 8, 12, 13, 18, 20, 22, 23, 25, 26, 29–36, 40, 41, 47, 49–53, 59, 63, 69, 75, 76, 87, 88, 92, 93, 109, 112, 115, 116, 147, 148, 151, 167–172, 175, 176, 178, 179, 181–184, 189, 191, 195, 205, 211, 215, 219, 236, 247, 251, 259–264, 268, 272, 277, 278, 280, 281
Knowles, Malcolm, 80
Kuhn, Thomas, 32

L

Learning
adult, 11, 44, 51, 53, 78, 149, 152, 171, 217, 233, 237, 245
credentialled, 53
early childhood, 21, 29, 119, 122–124, 145
formal, 48, 49, 53, 149, 237
informal, 48, 51, 52, 251
lifelong, 7, 39, 41, 80, 152, 165, 168, 171, 179, 184, 197, 217, 237, 268, 281, 282
non-formal, 48, 50, 88, 149, 237
online, 241, 266, 279

project-based, 196, 197, 226
self-directed, 32, 48, 52, 53, 80,
   152, 194
uncredentialled, 53
Liquid modernity, 87, 88, 172, 265
Literacy, 5, 12, 63, 67, 91–94, 168,
   170, 173, 190, 191, 193, 227,
   239, 259, 262–263
Locke, John, 25, 26, 116
Lutheran, 67, 68

M

McMillan, Margaret, 123, 145
Mainstream, 4, 74, 122, 132, 177,
   219, 238–241, 259
Malaguzzi, Loris, 182, 185
Marketisation, 8, 83, 86–90, 174
Massification, 8, 83, 86–91
Mead, George Herbert, 31
Mentor, 178, 179, 184, 191, 243, 265
Methodology, 3, 11, 22, 68, 72, 78,
   80, 85, 91, 123, 137, 171,
   194, 196, 198, 212, 215, 223,
   226, 233, 241, 265, 266
Mezirow, Jack, 52
Middle school, 194–196, 226
Millennials, 133–138, 141,
   148–155, 242, 243, 281
Mindfulness, 144, 145
Molt, Emil, 44, 62, 215
Montessori, Maria, 28, 66, 68, 117,
   151
Motivation, 29, 44, 52, 53, 80, 93,
   124, 140, 165, 183, 237,
   266
MySchool, 95, 96, 208

N

National Assessment Program–
   Literacy and Numeracy
   (NAPLAN), 94–96, 208
Nature, 9, 18, 26, 27, 32, 33, 41, 51,
   69, 71, 75, 107, 109, 111,
   113, 115–123, 125, 129,
   144–148, 164, 178, 219, 220,
   222, 226, 228–230, 241, 246,
   260, 276–280
Neill, A. S., 69, 224
Neonate, 130
Nomoi, 100, 101
Normaalikoulu, 166, 208
Not-school, 12, 233, 237–242, 247,
   253
Numeracy, 5, 12, 63, 67, 91, 92, 94,
   190, 193, 227, 239, 259
Nurture, 9, 107, 116–121, 217, 224

O

Organisation for Economic
   Co-operation and
   Development (OECD), 45,
   92, 272

P

Paradigm shift, 32, 33, 68, 191
Parenting, 9, 10, 13, 86, 109, 129,
   149–154, 188, 273
Parents, 1–3, 5, 6, 8, 9, 12, 41, 44,
   46, 62, 65, 67, 70, 73, 78, 85,
   89, 90, 95–97, 99, 108, 109,
   114, 117, 119, 120, 122, 124,
   126, 129, 130, 134, 135, 139,

140, 147–155, 163, 184, 189,
204, 208, 210, 211, 213, 214,
216, 217, 221–224, 227, 230,
233, 244, 246, 247, 267,
272–274, 277, 278, 280, 281
Pedagogical content knowledge
(PCK), 169–170
Pedagogical love, 204, 211–214,
273, 274, 280
Pedagogy, 11, 21, 24, 34, 51, 52, 68,
72, 80, 85, 91, 118, 143, 168,
170, 171, 181, 183, 221, 223,
273
Pestalozzi, Johan, 27, 122
Philosophy
ancient, 7, 17–19, 22, 29
educational, 1, 10–12, 27, 31, 32,
36, 54–55, 61, 67, 69, 72, 79,
109, 110, 118, 161, 162, 174,
175, 203, 215, 217, 223–224,
229, 230, 277
medieval, 22–24, 76
metaphysical, 19, 20, 22
modern, 24–29, 182
moral, 19, 20
natural, 19, 20
Phronesis, 30, 31, 172, 268
Plato, 7, 17, 20–22, 40, 46, 54, 60,
121, 130, 277
Plato's Cave, 20, 136
Play, 3, 9, 21, 27, 66, 85, 92, 97,
107, 110, 113, 115, 118,
120–126, 137, 145–148, 151,
176, 177, 206, 210, 217, 219,
221, 245, 279, 280
Politeia, 100
Positive psychology, 144
Postformal, 115

Post-millennial, 135
Practical activity, 42–44, 77, 167
Pragmatism, 2, 26, 31, 32, 70
Praxis, 30–32, 172, 176
Pre-service teacher, 96, 161, 162,
164, 165, 170, 177, 179, 186,
267, 268
Proficient, 172
Program for International Student
Assessment (PISA), 3, 91, 93,
203, 208, 272, 275
Protestant work ethic, 192
Psyche, 20, 69, 108, 115, 214, 219
Psychology, 2, 11, 20, 40, 54, 114,
115, 117, 139, 144, 169, 170,
173, 181, 215, 220
Psychomotor, 41, 169
Purpose economy, 242

Q
Quantified self, 138–144

R
Read, Herbert, 32, 47
Recapitulation, 219, 220
Reciprocity, 7, 39, 42, 45–48, 274
Relationship, 3, 10, 13, 20, 41, 48,
52–54, 65, 68, 79, 83, 99,
110, 123, 132, 143, 152, 155,
164, 165, 178, 182, 184, 185,
189, 195, 197, 198, 204,
209–211, 213, 228, 243, 264,
265, 272–274, 279, 280
Religion, 18, 19, 23, 67, 68, 80,
175, 191, 215, 220
Renaissance, 24, 25, 34, 75, 76, 220

Risk, 121, 124, 145, 186, 243, 278

Rousseau, Jean Jacques, 27, 28, 31, 70, 122, 148, 244

S

Schiller, Friedrich, 28, 61

Scholastic tradition, 24

Schooling, 1–13, 28, 34, 40, 47, 52, 54, 55, 59–61, 63, 65–72, 74, 75, 78, 80, 83, 84, 86, 90, 92, 94, 101, 102, 108, 122, 140, 145, 151–153, 166, 182, 189, 192, 194, 198, 204, 205, 211, 213, 216, 224, 229, 230, 235–242, 244, 246, 247, 249, 259, 263, 265, 272, 280, 282

Schools, 2–6, 20, 40, 59–81, 83–102, 118, 130, 161, 181, 203, 214–224, 229, 233, 241–242, 263, 272

Schoolteacher, 12, 47, 164, 167, 168, 191, 233, 267

Science, Technology, Engineering, and Maths (STEM), 91, 191, 193, 261

Self-organising systems, 251, 279

Serendipity, 52

Seven liberal arts, 76, 192

Skills, 12, 13, 24, 32, 33, 40, 41, 43, 47, 77–79, 91, 93, 94, 117, 137, 149, 151, 153, 172, 175, 177, 179, 183, 184, 190, 191, 193, 195, 197, 216, 224, 226, 227, 236, 237, 239, 242, 243, 245, 247, 251–253, 259–268, 273, 276, 278, 280, 281

Skill sets, 261

Social inclusion, 98, 185–187

Social work, 11, 41, 162, 169, 181, 186, 187

Socratic method, 21, 31, 43

Soft skills, 12, 248, 249, 251, 259

South Australian Certificate in Education (SACE), 197, 212, 240

Standardised testing, 94, 100, 116, 272

STEAM, 193, 194

STEEM, 194

Steiner, Rudolf, 5, 9, 27, 48, 66, 68, 72, 107–110, 214, 215, 217–219, 221, 223, 274

Summerhill, 69, 70, 72, 223, 224

Sustainability, 11, 87, 194, 203, 224, 227

T

Tabula rasa, 25, 116, 148

Techné, 30, 31, 172

Technological, Pedagogical, and Content Knowledge (TPACK), 170, 172

Technology, 9, 25, 30, 31, 33, 36, 42, 46, 76, 87, 89, 129, 134, 136, 141, 142, 144–148, 150, 155, 170, 173, 174, 191, 193, 194, 211, 215, 236, 242, 243, 246, 260, 261, 264, 274, 279–281

Teenagers, 6, 63, 131–133, 152, 251, 272, 281

Thinking, 9, 11, 12, 20, 22, 25, 32–34, 43, 47, 68, 69, 99, 101, 107, 110, 114, 115, 122,

130, 168, 169, 176, 181, 188,
193, 211, 212, 217, 233–253,
261, 264, 265, 271, 274, 280,
281
Toddler, 9, 109, 129, 130, 152
Training, 1, 10, 39–42, 46, 49, 50,
54, 60, 61, 67, 77, 78, 96,
122, 144, 149, 151, 161, 166,
167, 169, 177, 178, 186, 187,
197, 208, 211, 214, 243, 247,
261, 268
Transition Year, 252, 265
Tree of Knowledge, 23, 47, 148
Trust, 85, 90, 136, 204, 209, 210,
213, 264, 273, 274, 278, 281
Tweens, 9, 129, 133
21st century skills, 12, 136, 248,
253, 259–268

U

United Nations Convention on the
Rights of the Child
(UNICEF), 134, 135, 274
Unschooling, 12, 233, 244–247,
273, 278

V

Victor, 116, 117
Välitunti, 210

W

Waldorf schools, 28, 44, 48, 62, 68,
72, 124, 125, 146, 149, 150,
196, 214–224, 230, 267
Welfare team, 186
Wicked problems, 234, 236, 276
Willing, 110, 250
Wisdom, 7, 12, 17, 18, 30, 31, 35,
54, 109, 113, 177, 178, 215,
268, 280, 281
Wollstonecraft, Mary, 28
Workers Educational Association
(WEA), 50, 51

Y

Youthworx, 242–243